ANTITRUST POLICY AND INTEREST-GROUP POLITICS

\#

Recent Titles from Quorum Books

Problem Employee Management: Proactive Strategies for Human Resource Managers
Willa M. Bruce

Electronic Data Interchange in Finance and Accounting
Robert J. Thierauf

Accounting Ethics: A Practical Guide for Professionals
Philip G. Cottell, Jr., and Terry M. Perlin

Privatization and Deregulation in Global Perspective
Dennis J. Gayle and Jonathan N. Goodrich, editors

The Deregulation of the World Financial Markets: Myths, Realities, and Impact
Sarkis J. Khoury

Social Change Philanthropy in America
Alan Rabinowitz

Ethical Decision Making in Everyday Work Situations
Mary E. Guy

Selling to a Segmented Market: The Lifestyle Approach
Chester A. Swenson

Strategies in Global Industries: How U.S. Businesses Compete
Allen J. Morrison

A Cross-Industry Analysis of Financial Ratios: Comparabilities and Corporate Performance
J. Edward Ketz, Rajib K. Doogar, and David E. Jensen

Intellectual Properties and the Protection of Fictional Characters: Copyright, Trademark, or Unfair Competition?
Dorothy J. Howell

ANTITRUST POLICY AND INTEREST-GROUP POLITICS

\#

William F. Shughart II

Foreword by James C. Miller III

Q

Quorum Books

New York • Westport, Connecticut • London

Copyright Acknowledgment
The author and publisher are grateful to the following for allowing the use of excerpts, figures, and tables from:

William F. Shughart II, "Don't Revise the Clayton Act, Scrap It!" *Cato Journal* 6 (Winter 1987), pp. 925–32.

Sam Peltzman, "Toward a More General Theory of Regulation," *Journal of Law and Economics* 19 (October 1976), © 1976 by The University of Chicago.

Richard A. Posner, "A Statistical Study of Antitrust Enforcement," *Journal of Law and Economics* 13 (October 1970). © 1970 by The University of Chicago.

Roger L. Faith, Donald R. Leavens, and Robert D. Tollison, "Antitrust Pork Barrel," *Journal of Law and Economics* 15 (October 1982). © 1982 by The University of Chicago.

Library of Congress Cataloging-in-Publication Data
Shughart, William F. II
    Antitrust policy and interest-group politics / William F.
Shughart II.
        p.   cm.
    Includes bibliographical references.
    ISBN 0-89930-517-2 (lib. bdg. : alk. paper)
    1. Antitrust law—United States.   2. Antitrust law—Economic
aspects—United States.   I. Title.
KF1652.S527   1990
343.73'0721—dc20
[347.303721]   89-24336

British Library Cataloguing in Publication Data is available.

Library of Congress Catalog Card Number: 89-24336
ISBN: 0-89930-517-2

First published in 1990

Quorum Books, 88 Post Road West, Westport, CT 06881
An imprint of Greenwood Publishing Group, Inc.

Printed in the United States of America

The paper used in this book complies with the
Permanent Paper Standard issued by the National
Information Standards Organization (Z39.48-1984).

10 9 8 7 6 5 4 3 2 1

To RDT,
colleague and friend

Contents

Figures

Tables

Foreword

It would be comforting to think that government regulators and others who participate in the regulatory process were led as if by an invisible hand to maximize the social weal—comforting, but mistaken. Recognition of the fact that government regulators—including antitrust officials—are conditioned by their institutional environments and respond to incentives is crucial to appraising the effects of government intervention. So is a recognition that the regulatory process can be and is used by firms and other interests to secure special advantage.

Within a somewhat narrow perspective, the history of economics can be divided into three phases. First, triggered by Adam Smith's extraordinary insights, the profession began the long process of understanding how freely functioning markets operate and how they optimize the allocation of resources. A second phase, commencing roughly during the 1930s, began to question the ability of the market to allocate resources efficiently. In particular, there developed an extensive literature on "market imperfections." The unstated, and unchallenged, assumption in almost all of this literature was that such imperfections could be eliminated by government intervention.

A third phase, which to some extent overlapped the second, was initiated by those who questioned the efficacy of government intervention to cure the market's imperfections. These scholars came from a broad variety of economic and philosophical perspectives. Marxists, who perceived that government regulation was orchestrated by business interests, condemned regulation as something of a "capitalist tool." Microeconomic theorists and econometricians teamed up and found that, despite good intentions, resource allocation was not particularly efficient in markets that were highly regulated. Finally, and most importantly, the public choice theorists, who were addressing the much broader question of how collective choices were made and how efficient they were (in the sense of meshing public-good demands with available supplies) shed considerable light on the regulatory process and how its performance might be improved.

Until recently, most public policy on regulation—indeed the teachings in some universities—was driven by thinking that had not passed the second phase. That this should be so may be difficult to understand from today's perspective. After all, Smith, Marshall, and others had developed a coherent theory to explain why private interests, through the institution of competition, would lead to efficient resource allocation, whereas no one had really developed a theory to explain why government regulators and others who affected regulatory outcomes would be led to make the "right" choices.

The past decade has witnessed considerable regulatory reform based primarily on the dissemination of research concluding that the imperfections created by government intervention outweigh the imperfections of the marketplace. Examples include airlines, trucking, telecommunications, and banking. There also have been changes in antitrust policy, but they have tended to be not nearly so broad in scope or depth. Moreover, they have stemmed primarily from two sources. First, there is the "new learning," which holds that industrial structures and patterns of business behavior initially thought to be anticompetitive turn out to be procompetitive upon closer inspection, and thus it would be a mistake to have antitrust officials challenge them or courts hold them in violation of antitrust law. The other source of change has been the Austrian economists, coupled increasingly with industrial planners; both see the antitrust laws generically as counterproductive and seek to have them either abolished or limited severely in their application.

Another perspective on antitrust law and enforcement has begun to emerge, and that is the notion that passage of antitrust legislation and enforcement of it by public officials and the private antitrust bar is frequently for the purpose of serving so-called special interests. A member of Congress seeks to prevent the takeover of a company in his or her district or state. A retailer brings a Robinson-Patman price discrimination case in order to constrain an aggressive rival. Another manufacturer seeks to enjoin a merger because of a fear the surviving firm will be a more efficient competitor.

The explanatory power this interest-group perspective has for practitioners of antitrust law and economics is remarkable. Moreover, only by understanding this perspective can we begin to ascertain the efficacy of the antitrust institution in securing the goal of economic efficiency or whatever other goals might be deemed appropriate. An understanding is also essential if one is to formulate reforms that have any chance of success.

In this exceptional book, Professor William Shughart expounds the interest-group theory of antitrust law and enforcement in a way that is both persuasive and thought-provoking. He is well-equipped for this task, being a scholar in both industrial organization and public choice, as well as being a practitioner in antitrust enforcement while serving on the senior staff of the Federal Trade Commission. He has seen first-hand much of what he describes in the volume.

Shughart's commentary on the origins and development of antitrust is one of the best short compendiums I have seen. I highly recommend it to my successors at the Federal Trade Commission as well as to anyone else with a need to understand how we arrived at the current institutional arrangement. And his chapter on the interest-group theory of government will lift the veil of those still clinging to the notion that the only reason governmental institutions don't perform flawlessly is that the "right" people haven't been chosen to run them.

In the second part of his book, Shughart discusses antitrust from the perspective of the major groups involved—businesses, the antitrust bureaucracy, Congress, the courts, and private litigators. Each chapter is filled not only with provocative insights but with extensive citations to the literature. This is a scholarly book, not an advocacy tract.

Finally, after discussing how these various groups are served and how the outcome of this clash of interests comports (or fails to comport) with what one might term enlightened public policy, Shughart ventures to assess various proposals for reform. It is here that the author is too analytical for his own good. For his major conclusion— that the antitrust laws are not intended to serve the interest of economic efficiency but to be a vehicle for redistributing wealth— makes him unduly pessimistic about the chances for permanent reform. While one would be extraordinarily gullible to believe that a simple exposition of the "real" uses (and abuses) of any institution would result in immediate and permanent reform, there is good reason to believe that substantial and unrelenting exposure of arguably unintended and undesirable effects of any government program do result in change.

And thus, in so carefully analyzing the institution of antitrust from the interest-group perspective, Dr. Shughart may have cracked open the door to permanent reform a little farther.

James C. Miller III
Citizens for a Sound Economy and
John M. Olin Distinguished Fellow
George Mason University

Preface

My interest in antitrust policy grew out of my experience as a staff economist and, later, as special assistant to the director of the Federal Trade Commission's (FTC) Bureau of Economics. The four and a half years I spent at the FTC were eye-opening, especially as they came so soon after graduate school—only a year of teaching intervened between graduation and my introduction to the antitrust bureaucracy. Suffice to say that I soon learned that the economic theory I had been taught as a student bore little or no resemblance to the analysis typically applied in antitrust cases. Economics was valued not for its power to shed light on the behavior of firms and markets, but rather for how it might be twisted in ways that lent support to monopoly "theories" concocted by the FTC attorneys. Staff economists were evaluated not on the basis of their independent judgments concerning the merits of the cases under review, but instead on the basis of how well they "cooperated" with the team of lawyers to whom they were assigned. I did not prosper in this environment.

Fortunately, however, my tenure at the FTC overlapped the heady first years of the Reagan administration. As a result of personnel changes and staff reorganization initiated by James C. Miller III, the first professional economist to serve as chairman of the FTC, I came in contact with a remarkable group of colleagues. These economists, most of whom were trained at the University of Virginia in the early 1960s and had links to my alma mater, Texas A&M, set about under the intellectual leadership of Robert Tollison to apply the insights of the public choice model to the process of antitrust enforcement. The research agenda developed by this group of scholars, which included Miller, Tollison, Richard Higgins, Fred McChesney, Robert Mackay, Bruce Yandle, myself, and others, resulted in a series of academic papers that appeared in leading journals over the ensuing years and were collected in an edited volume published by the Hoover Institute in 1987.

The centennial anniversary of the Sherman Act seemed to me a propitious occasion for attempting to organize the theory and evidence of the public choice approach to antitrust into a coherent whole and make it available to a wider audience. This book grew out of my wish to communicate what we think we have learned by using the tools of positive economic analysis to study the laws and institutions of antitrust policy and, more importantly, to excite a new generation of students to ask some of the questions we have not asked.

Like all authors, I have benefitted greatly from the comments and suggestions of a number of colleagues and critics. In addition to those mentioned above, I am grateful to Don Boudreaux, who read large parts of the manuscript in draft form and helped clarify the exposition at a number of points.

Thanks are also due to Liliane Miller, the acquisitions editor at Quorum, who first planted in my mind the idea of undertaking the project. Finally, I thank Rosanne Schwalenberg for typing the manuscript and my wife, Hilary Shughart, who supported me with her love and patience throughout.

ANTITRUST POLICY AND INTEREST-GROUP POLITICS

\#

Introduction

One of the most remarkable characteristics of antitrust policy is the enduring faith placed in its purposes despite persistent criticisms of its effects. Antitrust is almost universally conceived as an area of public policy in which government seeks to promote the common good. In this conventional view, the basic legislative framework of antitrust in the United States—the Sherman, Clayton, and Federal Trade Commission Acts—as well as the relevant policymakers and practitioners—the Congress, the judiciary, the antitrust bar, and the law enforcement agencies—are all conceived as existing to serve the public interest, where by "public interest" is meant the pursuit of some normative goal, such as maximizing social welfare by promoting a competitive economy. Thus, whenever antitrust fails to live up to its promise, as it does quite often by most accounts, the failures are attributed to a variety of correctable errors. The critics of antitrust policy accordingly preach reform, calling upon the enforcement agencies to do a better job, for antitrust lawyers and judges to become better acquainted with economic theory, or simply for incumbent policymakers to be replaced by individuals who are better qualified and better able to serve the public interest.[1]

This conception of the purposes of antitrust policy contrasts sharply with the implications of the by now widely known interest-group theory of regulation. The interest-group theory stresses that governmental policies of all sorts are driven by private interests, and not the public interest. With its power to tax and to subsidize, to regulate prices and conditions of entry, to set standards for product quality, and to prohibit or restrict the use of certain business practices, the machinery of the state is a valuable resource that can be called upon to benefit some firms and industries selectively at the expense of others. The existence of such authority gives rise to efforts on the part of well organized interest groups to secure favorable treatment at the hands of public policymakers, and the policymakers, in turn, have an incentive to supply these favors so long as the groups that will be harmed are less effective in withdrawing political support than the beneficiaries are in delivering it. This way of characterizing governmental processes goes far beyond the limits of economic policy, narrowly defined; wherever government holds a policy monopoly, there will be strategic use of that policy by private interest groups having a stake in its exercise.

Modern scholarship in law and economics has shown in case after case that when government takes action to correct perceived "failures" in private markets, an important effect of the intervention is to redistribute wealth to organized interests from the less well organized. Thus, the primary beneficiaries of the Interstate Commerce Commission's authority to regulate land and water carriage are not the shippers who use such services, but rather the railroads, trucking firms, and inland water carriers who supply them; in its heyday the Civil Aeronautics Board served to benefit the commercial airlines, not the flying public; the Securities and Exchange Commission provides large benefits to securities dealers, the organized stock exchanges, and brokers, but virtually none to investors; physicians and lawyers, not their patients and clients, benefit from state occupational licensing laws; and so on. Consumer welfare is reduced and deadweight costs are imposed on the economy as a by-product of a process in which the regulated often successfully implore for regulation.

As a result of the outpouring of research that followed George Stigler's lead in articulating the modern economic theory of regulation,[2] few economists remain who take seriously the notion that public policies aimed at specific industries operate in the interest of consumers. Yet while public-interest theories of regulation have increasingly yielded to private-interest theories, antitrust has largely escaped characterization as an interest-group bargain. One reason for the still widely held belief that antitrust lies outside the realm of ordinary politics is that antitrust policy is not based upon a neatly wrapped bundle of laws that serve a single, unifying purpose. Antitrust cuts across the economy, applying not to a specific industry but rather to specific business practices used in many industries. As such, there is no clear-cut set of winners and losers from antitrust, or, to put it another way, the identities of the winners and losers change across the spectrum of business activities made illegal by the antitrust laws.[3] But while no comprehensive explanation for the origins and purposes of antitrust has yet emerged, the public-interest assumption is beginning to lose ground to a variety of private-interest theories that suggest that antitrust policy operates much like regulatory policy in general. Thus, evidence is accumulating showing how the law on mergers works like an antitakeover statute that serves to insulate incumbent management from the competitive forces of the market for corporate control; how the law on vertical contracting protects small, independent retailers and wholesalers against the competitive pressures exerted by more efficient methods of product distribution; how the law on price discrimination helps newly entering firms secure advantages over established enterprises; how the same law benefits high-cost firms at the expense of their more efficient rivals; and so on.

These developments are important for a number of reasons, not the least critical of which is the fact that the public interest hypothesis keeps the debate about antitrust on a normative level. The conventional wisdom about antitrust policy assumes that anticompetitive business practices in the economy arise from the activities of private individuals who are guided by self-interest–seeking motives in the pursuit of personal gain, but that the corrective actions necessary to harness this behavior in socially beneficial ways are the province of public servants who seek only to promote the general welfare. Thus, in one setting individuals are assumed to be selfish; in another they are selfless.

In James Buchanan's terms, this is not a closed behavioral system.[4] Because the individuals who formulate and enforce the antitrust laws are pictured as possessing a superhuman ability to transcend the bounds of their own self-interests when making public policy choices, policy failures are chalked up to human error. As a result, both the supporters and the critics of antitrust have recourse only to assertions about "good" and "bad" law, or "good" and "bad" enforcement. Such an approach is not very helpful in understanding how antitrust actually works: "Policies may of course be adopted in error, and error is an inherent trait of the behavior of men. But errors are not what men live by or on. . . . [A]n explanation of a policy in terms of error or confusion is no explanation at all—anything and everything is compatible with that 'explanation.'"[5]

Closing the behavioral system is a simple matter of recognizing that the same rational, self-interest–seeking behavior normally assumed to motivate human action in ordinary markets applies to decision making in the public sector. This insight, which also implies that public policymakers are subject to the same limitations on knowledge faced by individuals in the private sector, moves the discussion of policy away from normative issues toward a positive analysis of how public antitrust institutions actually function.

Applying positive economic analysis to the study of antitrust as actually practiced by the public law enforcement agencies opens up a whole set of novel questions previously beyond the reach of scientific investigation. For example, one can ask whether external factors, such as Congress, the executive branch, and private interest groups, exert a systematic influence on decisions to prosecute antitrust violations. Factors internal to the policymaking process, such as agency organizational structure and bureaucratic incentives, can also be considered. In short, the "black box" of public policy toward business becomes susceptible to studies that develop and test hypotheses concerning such topics as the origins of the antitrust laws; why certain groups benefit or bear the cost of antitrust policy actions; what particular form policy interventions into the economy are likely to take; and what forces determine agency budgets, enforcement activities, and program choices.

Finding explanations for the actual effects of antitrust, as opposed to the intended effects, is especially critical in that the current state of the antitrust debate has moved beyond proposals for modest changes in law or enforcement philosophy. The whole purpose of an antimonopoly policy has come under heavy attack from the ideological extremes. On one side, the left sees antitrust enforcement as a major roadblock to the development of a broad-based "industrial policy" that would bring representatives of business, labor, and government together in a joint effort to increase the competitiveness of U.S. firms in the global marketplace. Those taking such a position have recommended in part that agreements among firms to pool their research and development resources or mutually to combat the inroads of foreign competitors be granted immunity from the antitrust laws.[6] On the other side, the right equates firm size with economic efficiency and therefore wants government to halt its antitrust assault on big business. Repeal of the Federal Trade Commission Act and some—perhaps all—of the Clayton Act's provisions is supported by the conservative critics of antitrust.

But, reform does not take place in a vacuum. Both sides of the debate would benefit from an increased understanding of the positive issues associated with antitrust policy. Knowledge of how the institutions of antitrust actually function can help guide the process of reform in whatever direction it ultimately takes.

This book presents in detail the case for characterizing antitrust as an interest-group bargain. In contrast to the conventional wisdom, which assumes that antitrust was designed to promote the general welfare and therefore attributes observed policy failures to error or ignorance, the interest-group model assumes that the observed effects—the "failures"—of antitrust *are* the intended effects. As such, the interest-group approach does not entail value judgments about how public policies toward business *should* work. Instead, it involves positive statements about how antitrust *does* work, based upon the application of sound principles of economic theory to the analysis of policy, and then subjecting the theory to hard-nosed empirical tests.

Implausible as it may seem, especially in light of the fact that U.S. antitrust policy will soon celebrate its one-hundredth anniversary, serious attempts to understand the process of antitrust enforcement have only begun to be made within the last decade or so. Even at present, most scholars continue to treat antitrust as being somehow fundamentally different from other public policies by accepting uncritically the assumption that antitrust is innocent of economic motivation. It is perhaps because scholars have for so long failed to ask the right questions that the ongoing debate about the value of an actively enforced antitrust policy has failed to produce meaningful reform. The right question is not, Why has antitrust policy failed to promote the public interest? Rather, the relevant question is, Whose public and whose interests does antitrust serve?

THE PLAN OF THE BOOK

The book is organized into three main parts. Part I consists of two chapters that describe the antitrust paradox in detail and lay out the theoretical foundation for the analysis to follow. Chapter 1 first summarizes the unresolved (and unresolvable) controversy concerning the intentions of Congress in enacting an antitrust policy in 1890. There are two competing hypotheses about the intended purposes of the Sherman Act. One is that Congress sought to promote consumer welfare by prohibiting monopoly; the other is that antitrust was designed to prevent the aggregation of economic power in large units, thereby preserving a role for small business in the U.S. economy. Both sides of the debate will be presented, but it will be concluded that at least from the perspective of an economist, the promotion of consumer welfare is the sole legitimate concern of antitrust policy. (This, of course, is not to say that the promotion of consumer welfare was the intended purpose of antitrust.) Given this standard, the burden of the second part of Chapter 1 is to draw upon evidence from the literature criticizing specific antitrust cases and other scholarly research in order to show the basis for the widely held belief that antitrust has failed to achieve this goal.

Chapter 2 lays out the elements of the interest-group theory of government. It will be shown how policy outcomes in a representative democracy are determined by the interplay between the private interest of identifiable pressure groups within the polity and the private interests of policymakers themselves. The interest-group model has received a great deal of empirical support when applied to the analysis of public policies in the areas of public finance and the regulation of industry. The main point of Chapter 2 is that antitrust can be fruitfully analyzed from the same perspective.

Part II contains five chapters, each of which is devoted to one of the identifiable interest groups having an important stake in the formulation and execution of antitrust policy. The private incentives motivating the observed behavior of these groups are discussed and empirical evidence supporting the interest-group model is presented.

Chapter 3 argues that private firms are the demanders of antitrust enforcement, but not as a monolithic interest group whose members have a common, single-minded objective. Indeed, it is likely that the private business sector as a whole is harmed by the existence of an actively enforced antitrust policy. What is important to recognize, however, is that winners and losers are created whenever government acts to correct a perceived antitrust problem, and the prospective gains to the firms and industries benefitting from antitrust intervention provide incentives for using antitrust processes to their own profit. In this regard, the decision to "invest" in antitrust as a way of securing competitive advantages over rivals is no different from any other capital-budgeting problem confronted by a firm.

Chapter 4 focuses on the private incentives motivating the individuals who enforce the antitrust laws at the federal level of government. The institutional structures of the Federal Trade Commission and the Department of Justice's Antitrust Division are described and brief histories of their enforcement activities are presented. The principal conclusion of the chapter is that the merits of individual antitrust cases play a secondary role in the agencies' decisions to prosecute. Cases are instead selected on other grounds, one of the most important of which is the probability of going to trial. This factor is critical because trial experience benefits government attorneys by allowing them to develop skills that will subsequently be rewarded when they leave public service to take jobs with private law firms specializing in antitrust. Courtroom litigation is also important to upper-level agency managers and political appointees insofar as case output provides a visible measure of bureaucratic performance to the agencies' congressional overseers. Thus, the private incentives of agency employees and policymakers combine in a way that biases them in favor of bringing large numbers of easily prosecuted antitrust cases that generate few, if any, benefits for consumers.

Chapter 5 discusses the incentive structure facing the congressional overseers of antitrust policy. In a representative democracy, elected representatives have a strong interest in supporting policies that confer direct benefits on their constituents, while ignoring any adverse effects these same policies may impose on parties located outside the relevant political jurisdiction. Given that private firms, who have incentives to use antitrust processes to obtain protection from competitive market forces, are also in a position to provide political support (votes, campaign contributions, and so on) to their elected representatives, these representatives have incentives to supply such protection. The individuals sitting on congressional committees having budgetary and oversight responsibilities with respect to the Federal Trade Commission and the Department of Justice are particularly well situated to influence these agencies to adopt law enforcement strategies that selectively benefit the firms and industries located within the boundaries of their own districts and states. Empirical evidence supporting this "antitrust pork barrel" hypothesis is presented.

The role played by the independent judiciary in the interest-group theory of government is described in Chapter 6. Although the private interests of the judges who resolve antitrust complaints are less obvious and, therefore, less well understood than those of the other groups having a stake in antitrust policy, there is reason to believe that self-interest–seeking motives influence judicial decision making in antitrust proceedings. For example, recent contributions to the literature suggest that, other things being the same, judges tend to decide a greater percentage of antitrust complaints in the government's favor when vacancies exist on higher courts and increased opportunities for promotion are perceived. Similarly, antitrust penalties tend to be stiffer the larger the backlog of cases on the court calendar, perhaps because these heavier penalties will induce some of the parties awaiting trial to settle out of court, thereby reducing the judge's workload.

Part II closes with a chapter on private antitrust litigation (Chapter 7). The private antitrust bar clearly stands to gain from an actively enforced antitrust policy. Its members thereby have more clients to defend and can command higher fees for their services. Indeed, because private parties have standing to sue for treble damages under the antitrust laws, private suits account for the bulk of the antitrust litigation taking place in the economy. Basic theory concerning the incentives of firms to "invest" in antitrust litigation and evidence drawn from private antitrust case statistics are marshalled as further support for the argument that antitrust processes often serve as a competitive weapon, allowing firms to win advantages in the courtroom that they are unable to win in the marketplace.

Part III contains two chapters that tie the analytical components of the book together. Chapter 8 puts the interest-group model to work by presenting a number of specific examples from the case law that illustrate how private interests have influenced antitrust enforcement. Particular attention is paid to the law on mergers and to the law on price discrimination, especially as it pertains to so-called predatory pricing.

Chapter 9 stresses that, like the enforcement process itself, antitrust reform does not take place in a political vacuum. The interest-group theory nonetheless has two important implications for the debate about reform. First, it must be recognized that the same incentives and constraints that operate in the enforcement of existing policy will influence decision making about the design of new policies. Second, as long as government holds a monopoly of antitrust policy, there will be strategic use of that policy by private interest groups having a stake in its exercise. Thus, while the "unintended" consequences of antitrust might in principle be mitigated through efforts to change existing incentives by, for example, carefully considering efficient assignments of the right to sue, the optimal payoffs from antitrust suits, and so on, such consequences cannot be wholly eliminated even by the best-intentioned of reformers.

NOTES

1. Robert H. Bork, *The Antitrust Paradox: A Policy at War with Itself* (New York: Basic Books, 1978), is an excellent example of this point of view.

2. George J. Stigler, "The Theory of Economic Regulation," *Bell Journal of Economics* 2 (Spring 1971), pp. 3–21.

3. See Bruce L. Benson, M. L. Greenhut, and Randall G. Holcombe, "Interest Groups and the Antitrust Paradox," *Cato Journal* 6 (Winter 1987), pp. 801–17, who stress vague statutory language and the broad enforcement mandate of the Federal Trade Commission as key factors linking antitrust policy and interest-group politics.

4. James M. Buchanan, "Toward Analysis of Closed Behavioral Systems," in James M. Buchanan and Robert D. Tollison, eds., *Theory of Public Choice* (Ann Arbor: University of Michigan Press, 1972), pp. 11–23.

5. George J. Stigler, "Supplementary Note on Economic Theories of Regulation (1975)," in George J. Stigler, *The Citizen and the State: Essays on Regulation* (Chicago: University of Chicago Press, 1975), p. 140.

6. Indeed, concern that antitrust hinders the competitive position of U.S. business in the world economy has become something of a bipartisan political issue. See Nadine Cohodas, "Reagan Seeks Relaxation of Antitrust Laws," *Congressional Quarterly Weekly Report* 44 (February 1, 1986), pp. 187–92.

Part I

Normative and Positive Theories of Antitrust

1

The Origins and Critique of Antitrust

Lurid descriptions of late-nineteenth-century sweatshops and car-
toons depicting bloated "robber barons" have popularized a conception of the industrial revolution in the United States that is far
removed from the truth. The tens of thousands, and then hundreds of
thousands, of individuals who flocked from the farms to the factories
beginning in the mid-1800s did so on the belief that they would
thereby improve their economic position in life. That these beliefs
were not wholly mistaken is evidenced by the fact that few ever
migrated in the opposite direction. At the same time, the production
of manufactured goods in the industries dominated by the great trusts
was expanding at rates far exceeding the rate of output growth in the
economy as a whole. Prices in most of these industries were declining
steadily, and they were declining faster than was the general level of
prices. In short, while the great trusts stand everywhere condemned
as exploiters of labor and consumers, the available evidence suggests
otherwise.

But it is within the popularized view of history that antitrust policy
emerged in the United States. The rhetoric appearing in the contemporary congressional debates and in subsequent judicial interpretations of the purposes of the Sherman Act suggests that the antitrust
statutes can be explained as a public-spirited effort on the part of their
framers to limit the extent of monopoly power in the economy. Is there
evidence to support this conclusion? What can be said in a positive
economics sense about the origins of U.S. antitrust policy? More
importantly, how well do the actual effects of antitrust comport with
the intended effects?

THE ORIGINS OF ANTITRUST

The most popular explanation for the origins of U.S. antitrust policy
is that pressure for passage of the Sherman Act arose in the agricultural sector of the economy.[1] Farmers, it is said, saw themselves being

squeezed between falling prices for their own produce on the one hand, and rising prices for purchased manufactured articles and ever higher railway rates for shipping agricultural goods to market on the other. These complaints crystalized into the populist Granger and Alliance movements which targeted the great trusts as a major cause of the farmers' economic troubles. The Sherman Act is thus seen as an important agrarian victory over the forces of industrial monopoly.

A recent attempt to document this explanation has found it to be "gravely incomplete," however.[2] Among the several reasons for rejecting the standard account of the origins of antitrust is the simple fact that because of the vast westward expansion of the railroads during the nineteenth century, railway rates were declining steadily during the years preceding passage of the Sherman Act; they continued to trend downward after the law was enacted. As a result of falling transport costs and the continuous creation of new track networks, which provided farmers with more ready access to growing urban markets, the railroads in all likelihood made farm incomes larger and more stable than they otherwise would have been. In addition, railroad profits represented only about one percent of the value of farm output in 1889. Any reduction in railway rates that might have been expected to follow from antitrust action against the railroads could only have had a trivial effect on farm incomes.[3] In short, "for the farmers to combat the railroads—which were major benefactors of western agriculture—was in fact perverse behavior."[4]

If the popular explanation for the origins of the Sherman Act is not consistent with historical fact, what other factors may have played a role in the emergence of antitrust law as an important component of U.S. antimonopoly policy? Economists have not been very successful in providing a general answer to this question. Only a few loose conjectures have been made to date, none of which is completely satisfactory. The speculations fall into three broad categories.[5] First is the idea that the main interest promoted by antitrust is the public interest, a constituency that is served by using the laws to enhance economic efficiency. Second, it has been suggested that the antitrust bar and the public servants who are charged with responsibility for enforcing the laws were intended to be the primary beneficiaries of antimonopoly policy. Third, the Sherman Act and later antitrust statutes have been described as social documents designed to preserve a place for small business in the U.S. economy.

As we shall soon see, the argument that Congress established an antitrust policy to promote economic efficiency is a worthy, but debatable proposition. While Senator Sherman and other supporters of his proposed bill certainly based a large part of their case for antitrust on assertions that the great industrial trusts had harmed consumers by restricting output and raising prices, their contentions are not supported by the facts.[6] Industrial production was expanding rapidly at century's end. Real gross national product (GNP) increased by about 24 percent between 1880 and 1890. By comparison, real output in many of the trust-dominated industries grew at substantially higher rates over the same decade. Steel production rose by 258 percent, zinc by 156 percent, coal by 153 percent, petroleum by 79 percent, and sugar by 75 percent. Prices in the majority of these industries were declining as a result of expanding output, and they were falling faster than the general level of prices in the economy. The consumer price index fell by 7 percent between 1880 and 1890, but the average price of steel rails fell by 53 percent, refined sugar prices declined by 22 percent, and the price of zinc dropped by 20 percent. Bituminous coal prices remained fairly steady during the 1880s, but fell by 29 percent between 1890 and 1900.[7] Consumers apparently had little to fear from the industrial giants, a point that has been conveniently overlooked by those who accept the standard account of the origins of antitrust.

The majority of the economists of the day were in fact opposed to the Sherman Act.[8] Their opposition was based upon the view that the emergence of the large trusts was a natural and mostly unobjectionable response to the rising forces of competition accompanying the industrial revolution in the U.S. economy. The trust movement enabled the new manufacturing giants to exploit the substantial economies of scale that made these large enterprises economical, and any harm to consumers resulting from price-fixing agreements or other abuses, which surely did occur, was small compared to the benefits of increased price stability and the cost advantages of large-scale production. Although no economists were called to testify before Congress on the proposed antitrust law, their published opinions overwhelmingly "seemed to reject the idea that competition was declining, or showed no fear of decline."[9]

Contrary viewpoints were certainly held. Richard T. Ely, a founding member of the American Economic Association, for example, thought that the trusts had brought great distress to the working class. Ely endorsed proposals limiting the use of child labor and restricting the number of hours adults could be required to work each day. He even went so far as to recommend government ownership of industry to cure these ills. But Ely, too, opposed the Sherman Act, stating that "the so-called trusts are not a bad thing, unless business on a large scale is a bad thing. On the contrary, when they come about as the result of free development, they are a good thing, and it is a bad thing to attempt to break them up."[10] At least two economists, Henry Carter Adams and Allyn Young, came out strongly in favor of an antitrust policy that would destroy the great "monopolies." By and large, however, economists of the 1880s saw no need for antitrust legislation.[11]

A second hypothesis concerning the origins of antimonopoly policy in the United States focuses on the benefits of the legislation to the private antitrust bar and to the public servants charged with responsibility for enforcing the antitrust laws. Empirical support for this proposition is exceedingly weak. While it is quite easy, after the fact, to suggest that the lawyers who gain by representing defendants and the bureaucrats who gain power and prestige by prosecuting law violators were the intended beneficiaries of antitrust, there is little reason to believe that the private interests of these two groups were decisive in influencing the creation of antitrust policy. Except for the legislative debate on the 1950 Celler-Kefauver Amendment to the Clayton Act, representatives of the organized bar and of the public law enforcement agencies were conspicuously absent from the lists of witnesses testifying during hearings on the major antitrust statutes.[12] But while it is doubtful that Senator Sherman designed his bill solely to create jobs for lawyers and bureaucrats, evidence to be presented here (in Chapter 4) suggests that private incentives do play a role in explaining the level and mix of antitrust cases brought by the enforcement agencies. If nothing else, these findings cast doubt on the hypothesis that the main interest promoted by antitrust is the public interest.

The third hypothesis concerning the origins of antitrust is that the laws were designed to prevent the aggregation of economic power in the hands of large firms, thereby preserving a place for small business in the U.S. economy in spite of the higher costs and prices this would entail. Support for this idea rests partly on the interpretations of congressional intent given by leading jurists and others who have argued that the Sherman Act was meant to promote goals other than economic efficiency. Certainly smaller, less efficient firms would have suffered most from the competitive pressures created by the rapidly expanding output and falling prices accompanying the growth of the trusts, and it may well be that small business interests were able to mobilize sufficient political pressure to secure passage of legislation that could then be used to handicap their larger rivals.

George Stigler has found "modest support" for the claim that the Sherman Act derived from self-interest–seeking behavior on the part of small business.[13] His conclusion was based upon the results of three empirical tests that attempted to measure the relative political strengths of two groups, small businesses and firms that operated in "potentially monopolizable" industries, that would have had a stake in the defeat or passage of Senator Sherman's bill. First, Stigler calculated the number of workers employed in each group, by state, as a percentage of the state's total nonagricultural labor force. When these percentages were correlated across states, the average correlation coefficient was -0.86, implying that states having a relatively large small business sector had relatively few potential monopolists, and vice versa. Assuming that small business would have had more to gain from an anti-big-business statute and, therefore, more of an interest in securing passage of the Sherman Act where they faced a larger "potential monopoly" sector, this finding of a negative correlation between employment shares tends to cut against the small business hypothesis about the origin of antitrust.[14]

Secondly, Stigler considered the relative importance of would-be monopolists in states that had enacted their own antitrust statutes prior to 1890, compared with states where no such legislation had been adopted. Beginning with Maryland in 1867, 17 states passed an antitrust law of some sort before Senator Sherman's bill was enacted. (The bulk of these state statutes were passed in 1889.)[15] As a percentage of the nonagricultural labor force, employment in the monopolizable industries was below the national average in 14 of these states, and above average in the other three. By comparison, Stigler found no statistically significant difference between the number of states having below- and above-national-average shares of employment in potential monopolies for the jurisdictions where no antitrust law had been enacted before 1890.[16] This result suggests that pre–Sherman Act antitrust statutes tended to be adopted in states where would-be monopolists were politically weak and where the small business sector had more clout, a finding that is consistent with the self-interest hypothesis. Finally, Stigler reported that the percentage of a state's congressional delegation who voted in favor of the Sherman Act was higher the lower the share of the state's nonagricultural labor force employed in monopolizable industries. The relationship was not statistically significant, however.[17] Overall, then, Stigler found support for the small business theory of the Sherman Act in only one of the three tests he conducted. The evidence favoring the hypothesis is indeed modest.

Stigler's analysis of the origins of the Sherman Act is flawed by the fact that he assumes throughout that the statute was intended to promote competition. This presumption leads him to use the term "potential monopoly" as a synonym for "large" and perhaps more efficient enterprises rather than in the proper sense of firms having the power to restrict output and raise price. Nowhere is this confusion more apparent than in Stigler's attempts to test the small business theory of antitrust. If the Sherman Act was in fact a social-welfare–improving piece of legislation, small business should have *opposed* it for the reason that they had more to lose than larger, more efficient firms from a policy that would make markets more competitive and, thereby, reduce prices. On the other hand, small business would be expected to support the creation of an antitrust policy if that policy was designed to be the enemy of productive efficiencies garnered through large size. Thus, Stigler's paper is largely unsuccessful because he set about to identify which groups had it in their interest to support, and which to oppose, a statute assumed to be procompetitive. It is nevertheless true that his finding with respect to pre–Sherman Act antitrust laws, showing that they tended to be adopted in states where employment in "monopolizable"—read "large-scale, efficient"—industries was below the national average, adds to the evidence suggesting that antitrust policy has a self-interest basis grounded in the benefits small business would realize from legislation that could be used to handicap their larger rivals.

To summarize, attempts by economists to pierce the rhetorical veil of antitrust in order to identify private interests that may have benefited from passage of the Sherman Act have thus far been tentative at best. Because the language of the law itself is quite broad, there may in fact be no single constituency whose interests was served by the emergence of an antitrust policy. Moreover, subsequent antitrust statutes like the Clayton and Federal Trade Commission Acts may have had purposes and effects different from those which might eventually be associated with the legislation sponsored by Senator Sherman. But while no definitive conclusions about the origins of antitrust have yet been drawn, the lack of support for the idea that consumers were the winners is telling.

THE INTENTIONS OF THE FRAMERS

An alternative way of discovering the purposes of the Sherman Act is to attempt to determine the intentions of Congress at the time it enacted the law. This is slippery territory, indeed. The statutory language itself is spare, perhaps purposely leaving it open to a variety of interpretations. Supporting evidence can be found in the record of the legislative debates, in testimony before relevant legislative committees, and in the tally of votes when the law was passed. An outside observer of the legislative process can never be certain, however, that "the" meaning of the law has been uncovered.

As we have seen, there are two competing interpretations of the basic purposes of antitrust as laid out in its legislative centerpiece. One is that the intent of Congress was to promote consumer welfare (allocative efficiency) by preserving *competition* in the private marketplace. The other is that Congress intended to prevent larger, more efficient enterprises from driving smaller rivals out of business, that is, to protect *competitors.* These goals are distinct—and antithetical.

The case supporting the maximization of consumer welfare as the only legitimate goal of antitrust has been stated forcefully by Robert Bork.[18] His conclusion was based upon a thorough review of the Sherman Act's legislative history and interpretations of the law's major provisions.

During the legislative debate on the bill that ultimately bore his name, Senator John Sherman consistently expressed concern with "arrangements, contracts, agreements, trusts, or combinations" that were designed to raise the prices paid by consumers. Indeed, the version of the law initially introduced by Senator Sherman explicitly declared illegal those business practices "made with a view, or which tend, to prevent full and free competition" and those "designed, or which tend, to advance the cost to the consumer" of articles of commerce. Does not Congress, Senator Sherman asked, have the power to "protect commerce, nullify contracts that restrain commerce, turn it from its natural courses, increase the price of articles, and thereby diminish the amount of commerce?"[19] Thus, according to Bork, Senator Sherman thought that his bill would strike at business practices that restrict output and raise price, a goal that can only be interpreted as proconsumer.

Bork also argued that the specific business practices that Congress contemplated as being made illegal by the Sherman Act can only be understood in terms of a consumer welfare standard.[20] In particular, Congress intended that the law would serve as a per se rule against price-fixing agreements. That is, any agreement—any contract, combination, or conspiracy—between firms not to compete with one another on the basis of price was, in Bork's view, meant to be made presumptively illegal. Because such agreements represent attempts by firms to restrict output and raise price jointly, a rule of per se illegality, which admits no defense as to the reasonableness of the price charged or the ineffectiveness of the conspiracy, or allows any other justification put forth by the defendants to be considered, strikes at a practice that reduces consumer welfare. Moreover, a per se rule against price-fixing conspiracies is not consistent with the alternative hypothesis that Congress intended the Sherman Act to protect small business interests. This is because the higher prices resulting from collusion among the leading enterprises in an industry would enhance the survival prospects of smaller, inefficient firms that might otherwise be driven out of business with full and vigorous price rivalry.

To reinforce this interpretation, Bork argued that mergers between horizontal competitors were not intended to be made illegal per se by the framers of the Sherman Act. The distinction between price-fixing agreements and mergers is important to Bork because it suggests that Congress was aware of the fact that mergers, which, like price-fixing conspiracies, eliminate a margin of rivalry in the market, may also be sources of economic efficiency to the extent that they lead to reductions in cost. The Congress assembled in 1890 therefore demonstrated its intention to promote consumer welfare by allowing mergers to be considered on a case-by-case basis, permitting the courts to weigh pro- and anticompetitive effects, with an eye toward prohibiting only those mergers which harm consumers on balance.

Bork's final point was that the supporters of the Sherman Act did not think that the statute would penalize internal growth by firms based upon superior efficiency even if such growth led to monopoly. Only monopoly achieved through merger or by use of unfair business practices was to be attacked. In support of this argument, Bork reported a revealing colloquy in the Senate Judiciary Committee. Senator Kenna inquired whether it was intended that "if an individual . . . by his own skill and energy shall pursue his calling in such a way as to monopolize a trade, his action shall be a crime . . . ?" Senator Hoar responded that he supposed "that the courts of the United States would say . . . that a man who merely by superior skill and intelligence . . . got the whole business because nobody could do it as well as he could was not a monopolist." Rather, the Sherman Act was aimed at "the sole engrossing to a man's self by means which prevent other men from engaging in competition with him."[21]

The principal alternative to Bork's contention that antitrust was conceived as an instrument for promoting consumer welfare is the idea that the framers of the Sherman Act wanted to limit the social and economic power of large firms. This second interpretation of congressional intent has been advanced in several influential court decisions, beginning with *Trans-Missouri Freight*, one of the earliest Sherman Act cases to be decided by the Supreme Court.[22] In the majority opinion, Justice Rufus Peckham expressed concern for the "small dealers and worthy men" who might be driven out of business by larger, more efficient enterprises: "Mere reduction in the price of the commodity dealt in might be dearly paid for by the ruin of such a class."[23]

Justice Brandeis reiterated this sentiment in *Chicago Board of Trade*.[24] But the most important spokesman for the position that the antitrust laws were intended to promote values other than economic efficiency was Judge Learned Hand. The opinion he wrote in *Alcoa* is perhaps the strongest statement of this point of view.[25] Judge Hand wrote that in passing the Sherman Act, Congress was not necessarily actuated by economic motives alone. It is possible, because of its indirect or moral effect, to prefer a system of small producers, each dependent for his success upon his own skill and character, to one in which the great mass of those engaged must accept the direction of a few. These considerations, which we have suggested only as possible purposes of the Act, we think the decisions prove to have been in fact its purposes.

He went on to say that

[w]e have been speaking only of the economic reasons which forbid monopoly; but, as we have already implied, there are others, based upon the belief that *great industrial consolidations are inherently undesirable, regardless of their economic results.* In the debates in Congress Senator Sherman himself showed that among the purposes of Congress in 1890 was a desire to put an end to great aggregations of capital because of the helplessness of the individual before them.[26]

Judge Hand then summed up his reading of congressional intent with a ringing conclusion that would subsequently inform judicial opinion in a number of leading antitrust cases, including *Brown Shoe, Von's Grocery*, and *Procter & Gamble*:

Throughout the history of these statutes it has been constantly assumed that one of their purposes was to *perpetuate and preserve, for its own sake and in spite of possible cost, an organization of industry in small units* which can effectively compete with each other.[27]

On Judge Hand's interpretation, then, the Sherman Act was meant to be more a document of social policy than of economic policy.

Weighing the relative merits of the two distinct purposes that have been attributed to antitrust policy involves normative issues that fall outside the range of questions that can be addressed by positive economic analysis. Economics does have something to say on two related points, however. First, if the goal of perpetuating "an organization of industry in small units" is based upon a theory that the degree of competition in a market is a function of the *number* of rival firms, then the theory is incorrect. Under the usual assumptions made in developing the model of perfect competition, the number and size distribution of firms is indeterminant.[28] Competition is not exclusively, or even mainly, a numbers game.

Secondly, the economist can point out that there are costs associated with a policy of protecting small firms against their larger rivals. To the extent that small firms are less efficient (have higher costs) than large enterprises, protectionism results in a misallocation of scarce productive resources and higher prices for consumers. However, the courts cannot be said to have been unaware of the sacrifices necessary if antitrust policy is to be used for achieving social goals other than economic efficiency. In *Brown Shoe*, Chief Justice Earl Warren did not think that Congress was ignorant of the consequences either:

> [W]e cannot fail to recognize Congress' desire to promote competition through the protection of viable, small locally owned businesses. Congress appreciated that occasional higher costs and prices might result from the maintenance of fragmented industries and markets. It resolved these competing considerations in favor of decentralization. We must give effect to that decision.[29]

Concerns other than consumer welfare were certainly expressed in the legislative debate preceding adoption of the Sherman Act. To the economist, however, who takes the individual, not "society," as the basic unit of analysis, allocative efficiency should be the only purpose of antitrust policy. Pursued consistently, such a goal maximizes the total output of goods and services produced by the private economy, thereby generating the highest possible level of consumer well-being. But there are reasons other than the obvious benefits to consumers for treating allocative efficiency as the sole objective of antitrust.[30] Attempts to infuse the Sherman Act and later antitrust laws with social and political values are inconsistent with the nature and scope of these statutes. Noneconomic goals like protecting and promoting small business can be better (more efficiently) served through the use of other policy instruments such as taxes, subsidies, tariffs, and so on. In addition, stretching antitrust policy beyond the consumer welfare standard makes the laws themselves much more difficult to administer. As we have seen, for example, a per se rule against price-fixing agreements is incompatible with the goal of promoting an organization of industry in small units.

Allocative efficiency has not been universally accepted as a guiding principle of antitrust policy, however. Robert Lande, for example, has recently suggested that allocative efficiency is of secondary importance in explaining the origins of antitrust law.[31] In his view, the primary intention of the Fifty-first Congress was that the Sherman Act be used to prevent transfers of wealth from consumers to firms having market power. Such a goal, which seeks to promote the distribution of wealth that would result if all markets were perfectly competitive, implies that antitrust should strike at all firms charging prices in excess of marginal cost. In cases where such pricing practices arise from collusive agreements between firms not to compete with one another, antitrust policy would lead to the same outcome under Lande's interpretation of congressional intent as it would if law enforcement efforts were instead guided by an allocative efficiency standard. On the other hand, a generalized hostility to wealth transfers would operate to the detriment of consumer welfare in cases where firms achieve size through superior economic efficiency.

A second case in point is provided by the merger guidelines proposed by the National Association of Attorneys General and recently adopted by all 50 states.[32] This document explicitly rejects allocative efficiency in favor of a so-called "consumer interest" theory that would prevent all mergers that increase the prices paid by consumers. Applied consistently, such a standard would again work *against* the interests of consumers in the case of mergers generating cost savings that outweigh the welfare loss associated with higher prices.

Despite the fact that it is impossible to resolve the debate about congressional intent regarding the purpose of antitrust and, therefore, to reject the notion that public policy in this area should incorporate social as well as economic values, the laws themselves are widely supported by modern-day economists. In a survey published in 1984, nearly 83 percent of U.S. economists responding agreed with the statement that the "antitrust laws should be used vigorously to reduce monopoly power from its current level."[33] It is apparent that many economists and other commentators like to think that the Sherman, Clayton, and Federal Trade Commission Acts were motivated mainly by a public-spirited concern for improving consumer welfare, and that the role of the institutions of antitrust enforcement is simply to help maintain a competitive economy "by prohibiting private restrictions of it, and by preventing the development of monopoly."[34]

This public interest view of antitrust is not limited to observers of any one political persuasion. Frederic Scherer, for example, considers antitrust policy to be "one of the more important weapons wielded by government in its effort to harmonize the profit-seeking behavior of private enterprises with the public interest." A benevolent, if fallible, government works to achieve this harmony "by inhibiting or prohibiting certain undesirable kinds of *business conduct*, and by channeling and sharpening *market structure* along competitive lines so as to increase the likelihood that desirable conduct and performance will emerge more or less automatically."[35] Similarly, Richard Posner suggests that the importance of economic efficiency as a social value "establishes a *prima facie* case for having an antitrust policy."[36] And, Kenneth Elzinga and William Breit see antitrust as something of a public good designed to correct the "market failure" (allocative inefficiency) associated with monopoly. They, in fact, argue that "the importance of antitrust enforcement is one of those rare issues that cuts across even the most formidable of ideological barriers."[37]

In the main, then, "it is tempting (and common) to regard the antitrust policy simply as a kind of economic engineering project."[38] Competition leads to efficient resource use, and antitrust is the principal means by which competitive conditions are maintained. Private market forces cannot be wholly relied upon to secure this objective in the conventional view. Danger lies in a policy of laissez-faire because of the abuses of monopoly: Unchecked monopoly power forecloses markets, restricts output, and stifles innovation.[39] As such, "a much more widespread pattern of growth by merger, an efflorescence of collusive agreements of all sorts, and the use of various exclusionary and otherwise anticompetitive practices now forbidden would all follow on the abandonment of a procompetitive public policy."[40] In short, the centerpiece of U.S. antitrust policy, the Sherman Act, "remains above partisan controversy as a 'charter of freedom,' a constitution governing the economy of the United States."[41] Even George Stigler seems to treat antitrust as a rare example of benevolent government policy. He has called the Sherman Act "a public interest law . . . in the same sense in which I think having private property, enforcement of contract, and suppression of crime are public-interest phenomena . . . I like the Sherman Act."[42]

Of course, support for the general principles and objectives of antitrust is not the same thing as support for their implementation. But, given the near consensus of opinion among modern day economists and other students of antitrust policy as to the public interest motives of the framers of the Sherman Act, it seems natural to ask whether or not this presumption is justified. That is, does evidence exist to support the assumption that antitrust promotes consumer welfare in practice?

THE NORMATIVE CRITIQUE OF ANTITRUST

Despite widespread support for its objectives, antitrust policy has been subject to devastating critique almost since the beginning. Given that the purposes of antitrust lie outside economic analysis in the conventional view, however, the many failures of antitrust policy are ascribed to a variety of correctable errors. The most often cited of these is the "neglect of economic principles [by] the judges, lawyers, and enforcement personnel who are responsible for giving meaning to the vague language of the antitrust statutes."[43] Accordingly, an extensive literature has developed whose purpose is to instruct the practitioners and policymakers of antitrust in basic economic theory by offering analyses of specific cases. These studies typically examine the evidence before the court, evaluate the economic merits of the charges brought against the defendants, and then confer approval or disapproval on the decision handed down.

It is fair to say that many more "bad" than "good" antitrust cases have been made example of in this literature. In recent memory, only the *Sylvania* decision, which restored a rule of reason standard for the analysis of vertical territorial restraints, and a handful of other cases have received commendation from economists.[44] The more usual case study finds that the evidence presented was "weak and at times bordered on fiction,"[45] that "neither the government nor the Courts seemed able to distinguish competition from monopolizing,"[46] and that at best "nothing was accomplished by bringing this case."[47] Other critics have suggested alternative, procompetitive explanations for the behavior of the defendants,[48] contended that the economic theory of the case was "erroneous,"[49] or pointed to the ineffectiveness of the remedy imposed on the guilty parties.[50] There are a great many more examples in this regard.

Literally hundreds of antitrust decisions have been subjected to scholarly critique, generating a literature that is impossible to summarize adequately. But, in one way or another the bulk of these studies teach the following general lesson: Antitrust is about what might happen to competition as a result of the business practices adopted by one or more firms. Rarely, however, do the prosecutors or the courts inquire into what actually did happen. Three landmark cases, *Addyston Pipe*,[51] *Standard Oil*,[52] and *Brown Shoe*,[53] are particularly good examples of this point.

Addyston Pipe is considered to be important both for establishing the Sherman Act's authority to reach restraints of trade affecting interstate commerce and because of its distinction between "naked" and "ancillary" restraints. This distinction firmly laid down a rule of per se illegality for price-fixing agreements.[54]

The case involved six firms engaged in the manufacture of cast-iron pipe which they sold to municipal water utilities located mainly in the midwest. The defendants, which were located along the Ohio River at Cincinnati and Louisville and clustered near the Alabama-Tennessee border, faced little effective competition from other pipe manufacturers located in the eastern United States because of the relatively high cost of transport. Shipping charges for cast-iron pipe ranged from 13 percent to 20 percent of the mill price.[55]

In 1896, the Department of Justice brought suit against the six firms, charging them with rigging the bids they submitted to certain of their customers. It was revealed at trial that the coconspirators had divided the total territory they jointly served into three categories of market. There was a "free territory" in which, because the firms could not avoid competing with rival pipe suppliers, no cartel rules applied. Secondly, there were "reserved cities" which the six companies had agreed to allocate among themselves as exclusive territories. These cities, like all of the cartel's customers, purchased their pipe requirements by calling for competitive bids and then selecting the supplier offering to sell at the lowest price. To ensure that the "right" firm was successful in this process, the conspirators met beforehand to discuss prices so that the company to whom the city was reserved was certain to submit the lowest bid. Finally, by far the largest part of the total market was a "pay territory" where the winning bid was determined by a competitive auction among the cartel members themselves. The private auction worked by having each firm "bid a bonus" on the pay territory contract, that is, offer to pay the other colluders for the right to submit the low bid to the purchasing city. The company bidding the largest bonus would win this right, the other five firms would agree to submit higher bids to the customer, and the firm actually supplying the pipe would pay the bonus to its fellow colluders out of the contract proceeds.[56]

In his study of the history of the conspiracy, Alamrin Phillips has suggested that while the agreements entered into by the six defendants were clearly intended to increase their joint profits, the collusion had little or no such effect.[57] Phillips based his conclusion on evidence that there was a substantial amount of cast-iron pipe production capacity in the midwestern region owned by firms not party to the conspiracy, and on admittedly incomplete data concerning costs and prices during the conspiracy period. The latter information indicated that the prices bid by the conspirators were frequently below average total production cost, and possibly below average variable cost. Noting that the colluders were operating well below production capacity during the time the bid-rigging agreements were said to have been in effect, Phillips concluded that the "charge that the general level of prices was exorbitant seems unjustified."[58]

The observation of prices below cost is consistent with a more recent contribution by George Bittlingmayer, who offers a theory implying that because the pipe manufacturers faced conditions of sharply declining marginal costs, a competitive equilibrium did not exist for the industry.[59] That is, absent explicit collusion or merger, excess production capacity led to "too much" competition in the sense that attempts on the part of the individual pipe producers to more fully utilize their plants would inevitably have driven price below average cost, forcing all of the firms to operate at a loss. (In essence, Bittlingmayer has resuscitated the old "ruinous-competition" doctrine which, in fact, the conspirators advanced as part of their defense.) The implication of this theory is that the *Addyston Pipe* conspiracy represented an attempt by the parties to stave off the market forces driving the industry toward reduced production capacity and increased concentration. Indeed, following Judge Taft's decision holding the price-fixing conspiracy to constitute a violation of the Sherman Act, four of the defendants merged to form the American Pipe and Foundry Company. The United Pipe and Foundry Company subsequently acquired American Pipe, the remaining two Addyston defendants, and a number of other pipe manufacturers. The ultimate impact of these acquisitions was that 70 to 75 percent of *national* production capacity came to be concentrated in one firm.[60]

Addyston Pipe has been hailed "as one of the greatest, if not the greatest, antitrust opinions in the history of the law."[61] If the evidence adduced by Phillips and Bittlingmayer is to be believed, however, the per se rule on price fixing handed down by Judge Taft completely ignored critical facts indicating that the conspiracy at issue was wholly ineffective in elevating price above cost. Even if there had been such evidence, the decision accomplished little beyond causing the defendants to substitute one form of agreement for another.

Standard Oil, along with another case decided the same year,[62] established a "rule of reason" for the Sherman Act whereby the Court announced its willingness not to condemn every restraint of trade. At issue were charges of unlawful monopolization against John D. Rockefeller's oil trust which, among a variety of other allegedly illegal practices, was accused by the Department of Justice of forcing smaller oil companies to agree to be bought out by Standard Oil, often on terms favorable to Standard, by selectively cutting prices in the specific local markets where these rivals operated while maintaining much higher prices in other geographic areas where no competition existed.

In a now-famous critique, John McGee reported evidence suggesting that predatory pricing played no role in Standard Oil's merger campaign.[63] The bottom line of McGee's analysis is that predation is a foolish strategy because the predator must inevitably suffer larger financial losses than the prey. It therefore follows that no threat to price below cost can be made credible. To illustrate this point, McGee quotes a Mr. Todd, the manager of an independent refinery threatened with a price war by Mr. Moffett, the manager of one of Standard Oil's plants:

Well, I says, "Mr. Moffett, I am very glad you put it that way, because if it is up to you the only way you can get it [the business] is to cut the market, and if you cut the market I will cut you for 200 miles around, and I will make you sell the stuff," and I says, "I don't want a bigger picnic than that; sell it if you want to," and I bid him good day and left.

According to McGee, "the Standard threat never materialized."[64] Indeed, McGee concluded his extensive analysis of the case by observing that

Standard Oil did not use predatory price discrimination to drive out competing refiners, nor did its pricing practices have the effect. . . . I am convinced that Standard Oil did not systematically, if ever, use local price cutting in retailing, or anywhere else, to reduce competition. To do so would have been foolish; and, whatever else has been said about them, the old Standard organization was seldom criticized for making less money when it could readily have made more.[65]

The court nevertheless found Standard guilty of violating the Sherman Act, and ordered the trust dissolved. Like Judge Taft's per se rule on price fixing, the "rule of reason" announced in *Standard Oil* apparently derives from less than overwhelming evidence of injury to competitors, let alone damage to consumer welfare.

Brown Shoe, perhaps the leading precedent of the law on mergers, has been subjected to withering criticism by both economists and legal scholars.[66] The case involved the government's challenge of Brown Shoe Company's acquisition of G.R. Kinney in 1956. Both firms were engaged in the production and distribution of footwear.

In the early 1950s, Brown was primarily a manufacturer and wholesaler of shoes, accounting for just under 5 percent of total national output, excluding slippers and rubber and canvas footwear. Having no retail outlets of its own, Brown marketed the 85 percent of its shoes that carried the Brown brand name either through independent shoe dealers or larger chains. The remainder were sold on a "make-up" basis, that is, manufactured according to the specifications of buyers and usually carrying the buyers' own names, through other wholesalers.

Beginning in 1951, however, Brown embarked on a campaign designed to establish its own retail network. It purchased the Wohl Shoe Company, which was also engaged in shoe wholesaling, but in addition owned 25 retail shoe stores and operated shoe sales concessions in space leased from about 190 different department stores located in 160 cities across the United States. Brown acquired a smaller shoe retailer, the Regal Shoe Company, for a similar purpose in 1954.

All told, the two mergers gave Brown about one percent of retail shoe sales nationwide.

Prior to its acquisition by Brown, G.R. Kinney operated over 350 retail shoe outlets in 315 cities, accounting for about one percent of total national sales. Kinney also owned four shoe manufacturing plants, producing approximately one-half of one percent of U.S. shoe output. It sold roughly 60 percent of these shoes through its own stores, which sales represented about 20 percent of the Kinney retailers' total requirements, and the remainder on a make-up basis to other wholesalers and retailers. Brown did not supply any shoes to Kinney's stores before the merger. Afterwards, Brown became Kinney's largest supplier, even excluding the output produced by the four plants formerly owned by Kinney but now under Brown's control.

As part of an effort to stem "the rising tide of economic concentration" that had so worried Congress in 1950 as it deliberated the Celler-Kefauver Amendment to the Clayton Act, the Justice Department filed a complaint seeking to undo the Brown-Kinney merger. Now, it would have been astounding had anyone argued at the time that a merger involving a combined national market share of 2 percent was a cause for antitrust concern. The government's case was therefore based on the idea that competition in shoe retailing is local in nature. Adverse effects from the merger were thought likely to occur in 270 cities ("submarkets") where both Brown and Kinney operated retail shoe establishments. The government prevailed, and in 1962 the Supreme Court, finding that the merger violated Section 7 of the Clayton Act, ordered divestiture.

The decision in *Brown Shoe* is important because it represented the first clear statement by the Court concerning the standards it would accept for the purpose of defining relevant antitrust markets. On closer inspection, however, it turns out that the facts presented by the government in support of its case were filled with error.[67] Beginning with the 270 cities originally identified in the government's complaint, 129 were excluded when a lower court pointed out that Brown's wholesale shipments to independent retailers were not relevant in determining Brown's share of the retail shoe market. The government itself withdrew from the list an additional 28 cities where the combined market shares of Brown and Kinney fell below 5 percent. (The government made this decision after the District Court held that the merger's impact on competition in shoe *manufacturing*, where the two firms accounted for about 5 percent of total national shoe production, did not constitute a violation of the Clayton Act. The prosecutors concluded that the courts would not find a lessening of competition in shoe *retailing* in cities where the combined market shares were less than 5 percent.) Thus, 113 cities remained in which the Supreme Court found a violation of the Clayton Act.

John Peterman's careful analysis shows that even this number was much too high. In 51 of these 113 cities, Brown in fact operated no retail shoe outlets prior to the merger. Moreover, the government's market share figures in the remaining 62 cities were inflated because wholesale shipments were often counted erroneously as part of Brown's retail sales. When Peterman reexamined the sales data, he discovered that in only 29 of the 62 cities did the combined sales of Brown and Kinney actually account for 5 percent or more of the local retail market. And, the combined market share in these cities averaged only 8 percent. In the final analysis, there were only 15 cities in which the Brown-Kinney share was more than 15 percent of local shoe sales, and only nine cities in which the merger resulted in a combined market share above 20 percent.

Brown Shoe was the first merger case to be decided by the Supreme Court subsequent to Section 7's amendment by the Celler-Kefauver Act of 1950. The Court used the occasion "to convert the statute to a virulently anticompetitive regulation."[68] It did so by relying upon several doubtful premises, including a fear that there was a rising tide of industrial concentration in the U.S. economy which required halting in its incipiency, and that it is desirable both to retain "local control" over industry and to protect small business against the encroachments of larger enterprises.[69]

The first of these propositions was not consistent with the facts at the time of *Brown Shoe* or, indeed, has it ever been: "Any tendency [in aggregate concentration] either way, if it exists, must be at the pace of a glacial drift."[70] The latter two ideas, which infuse antitrust policy with a social purpose, succeeded in reading the concept of economic efficiency out of the merger law for at least 20 years. Justice Douglas would soon state flatly that "possible economies cannot be used as a defense to illegality. Congress was aware that some mergers which lessen competition may also result in economies but it struck that balance in favor of protecting competition."[71] Taken together, these propositions created a "frame of reference" for analyzing mergers that stands rightfully condemned as "a disaster for rational, consumer-oriented merger policy."[72] Indeed, during the remainder of Chief Justice Warren's tenure *no* merger challenged by the government survived the Supreme Court's scrutiny. How could it be otherwise? *Brown Shoe* "bespeak[s] concern only for small companies and for the ideal of marketplace egalitarianism."[73]

Horizontal antitrust issues are, in principle, the most straightforward of the problems with which the enforcement agencies and the courts must deal. Yet, as the normative literature so persistently demonstrates, the failings of antitrust policy in this area have been monumental.

But, despite how valuable they may be, studies of individual antitrust cases cannot refute the hypothesis that public policy in this area follows a public-interest model. Perhaps the cases selected for analysis are not representative of the general direction of antitrust enforcement. Beginning in the early 1970s, however, an important series of attempts was made to compare systematically the actual distribution of antitrust cases across industries with the pattern that would have been expected to emerge if the antitrust agencies selected cases so as to maximize consumer welfare. In the earliest of these studies, William Long, Richard Schramm, and Robert Tollison sought to determine whether the Justice Department's Antitrust Division chose cases on the basis of their potential net benefit to society, that is, prosecuted first those antitrust matters where the value of the potential reduction in allocative inefficiency net of the cost of bringing the case was greatest.[74] Their basic technique was to regress the number of cases instituted against given industries on various industry-specific welfare-loss measures. The empirical model performed best in predicting case-bringing activity when industry size, measured in terms of total sales, was used as a proxy for welfare loss, but overall the evidence failed to support the hypothesis that the Antitrust Division's decisions to prosecute were made on a benefit-cost basis. Specifically, the results suggested that "the composite measures of the potential benefits from antitrust action . . . tested—the welfare-loss triangle or together with excess profits—appear to play a minor role in explaining antitrust activity." The authors concluded that "much of the explanation of antitrust activity clearly lies outside our model."[75]

Subsequently, two other researchers attempted to refine and expand the model used by Long, Schramm, and Tollison. John Siegfried, for example, noted that the high level of aggregation employed in the earlier study blurred possibly important differences between firms in heterogeneous industries.[76] He therefore reran the regressions using a significantly more disaggregated sample. Some of Siegfried's results suggested that, contrary to the predictions of the consumer-interest model, *greater* levels of excess profits and *lower* levels of welfare loss were associated with more antitrust cases. One interpretation of this finding is that antitrust enforcement activities target successful firms whose profits are based on efficient resource use, not monopoly power. However, when Siegfried refined his model further to include improved measures of industry profitability, its explanatory power plummeted and the initial results lost their statistical significance. Coefficient signs on particular independent variables were unstable and, "in fact, none of the coefficients is very robust in this whole analysis. That fact, coupled with the trivial proportion of the linear variation [in case-bringing activities] explained by the independent variables suggests that economic variables have little influence on the Antitrust Division."[77]

Peter Asch pointed out a further difficulty in using industry data for explaining the decision to prosecute, namely that antitrust cases are filed against firms, not industries.[78] In estimating a model similar to the one employed by the other researchers, but adding data on individual firms and running separate regressions for the Antitrust Division and the Federal Trade Commission, Asch was able to explain a greater proportion of the variation in case-bringing activities across the economy. But his findings were not consistent with any particular hypothesis about antitrust enforcement. Asch remarked that the "appropriate interpretation" of his results was "not entirely clear," perhaps even "puzzling." He concluded that "case-bringing activity cannot be characterized as predominantly 'rational' or predominantly 'random'. . . ."[79]

Overall, then, antitrust enforcement does not appear to be predictable on the basis of social welfare criteria. The empirical evidence indicates that the antitrust agencies do not select cases to prosecute on grounds of their potential net benefit to consumers. This basic result receives support from other studies that have investigated the impact of governmental enforcement efforts in cases involving particular types of law violations. Price-fixing complaints, for example, apparently target ineffective collusive agreements rather than successful ones that might cause significant harm to consumers.[80] Likewise, various studies have found that the mergers challenged by government are generally not anticompetitive.[81] And, a recent study of 203 reported private and public antitrust cases alleging unlawful resale price maintenance between 1976 and 1982 found that anticompetitive theories could account for no more than 15 percent of the total, and for an even smaller percentage of the private cases alone.[82]

In short, there is little or no credible evidence suggesting that the actual effects of antitrust comport with the effects implied by the model of the "public interest." Scholars and policymakers have typically responded to such findings in the past by calling for closer adherence to economic principles in the future,[83] but it is time to abandon this tired rhetoric. The absence of systematic support for the idea that consumers are the beneficiaries of antitrust provides firm ground for rejecting the hypothesis that they were the intended beneficiaries. Indeed, because it requires that all failures of policy be explained by error or ignorance, the consumer interest theory of antitrust is no theory at all. A rethinking of antitrust is clearly in order, but not with the conventional tools of welfare economics. Instead, as we shall see, positive economic analysis offers a potentially fruitful approach to understanding the forces that drive public policy in the area of antitrust.

NOTES

1. Frederic M. Scherer, *Industrial Market Structure and Economic Performance*, 2d ed. (Chicago, IL: Rand McNally, 1980), p. 493.

2. George J. Stigler, "The Origin of the Sherman Act," *Journal of Legal Studies* 14 (January 1985), pp. 1–12.

3. Indeed, John Binder has recently produced capital-market evidence showing that the first of the cases brought against the railroads under the Sherman Act, *U.S. v. Trans-Missouri Freight Ass'n*, 166 U.S. 290 (1897), had a negative but statistically insignificant effect on railroad stock prices. This result has two possible interpretations. One is that antitrust enforcement led the railroads to substitute merger and private, secret price-fixing agreements for the open rate-fixing activities they had engaged in prior to *Trans-Missouri*. The other interpretation is that the capital market did not think enforcement of the Sherman Act would adversely affect railroad profits because federal rate regulation by the Interstate Commerce Commission, which began a decade earlier, was expected to protect railroad cartel agreements against the attacks of antitrust. Binder's evidence is not consistent with the hypothesis that railroad interests were major losers from the creation of an antitrust policy. See John J. Binder, "The Sherman Antitrust Act and the Railroad Cartels," *Journal of Law and Economics* 31 (October 1988), pp. 443–68.

4. Stigler, "Origin of the Sherman Act," p. 3. Although aggregate farm incomes in all likelihood became more stable as a result of railroad expansion, Robert McGuire has shown that farmers' protest activity against the trusts was more vocal in states where the variances of agricultural commodity prices and farm incomes were higher. See Robert A. McGuire, "Economic Causes of Late-Nineteenth Century Agrarian Unrest: New Evidence," *Journal of Economic History* 41 (December 1981), pp. 835–52. The railroads were, in fact, a mixed blessing for at least some farmers. As agricultural markets grew from local to regional to national in scope, individual farmers would have faced increased competition at home from the very same markets that the expanding railroads brought newly within reach. To the extent that these heightened competitive pressures tended to reduce the incomes of small, inefficient producers, these individuals may have rationally targeted the railroads as a cause of their economic troubles. For an attempt to rehabilitate the agrarian distress explanation of the origins of antitrust based upon farmers' self-interests in seeking protection against emerging competitive pressures, see Donald J. Boudreaux and David J. Zorn, "The Origin of the Sherman Act Revisited: A Correction of the Historical Record," unpublished manuscript, George Mason University, March 1989.

5. William F. Baxter, "The Political Economy of Antitrust," in Robert D. Tollison, ed., *The Political Economy of Antitrust: Principal Paper by William Baxter* (Lexington, MA: Lexington Books, 1980), pp. 3–49.

6. Thomas J. DiLorenzo, "The Origins of Antitrust: An Interest-Group Perspective," *International Review of Law and Economics* 5 (1985), pp. 73–90.

7. Ibid., p. 80.

8. Sanford D. Gordon, "Attitudes Toward Trusts Prior to the Sherman Act," *Southern Economic Journal* 30 (October 1963), pp. 156–67. Also see Thomas J. DiLorenzo and Jack C. High, "Antitrust and Competition, Historically Considered," *Economic Inquiry* 26 (July 1988), pp. 423–35.

9. Gordon, "Attitudes Toward Trusts," p. 166.

10. Richard T. Ely, "The Future of Corporations," *Harper's* (July 1887), p. 265; and Richard T. Ely, *Monopolies and Trusts* (New York: Macmillan, 1900), p. 162.

11. DiLorenzo and High, "Antitrust and Competition," p. 429.

12. Baxter, "Political Economy of Antitrust," pp. 45–46. Thirty-six (or 53 percent) of the witnesses called to testify on the Celler-Kefauver Act were employees of the Antitrust Division and the Federal Trade Commission. They were unanimous in supporting the bill.

13. Stigler, "Origin of the Sherman Act," p. 7.

14. Ibid., p. 5. Of course, Stigler's test implicitly assumes that the competitive pressures faced by small business were exerted only by the "potential monopolists" located in their own state. The test ignored the impact of interstate commerce.

15. For a detailed analysis of one of these state antitrust statutes that argues that the law was specifically designed to stifle competition to the benefit of small, inefficient farmers and meat packers, see Donald J. Boudreaux and Thomas J. DiLorenzo, "Antitrust Before the Sherman Act: The Political Economy of Missouri State Antitrust Legislation," unpublished manuscript, George Mason University.

16. Stigler, "Origin of the Sherman Act," pp. 6–7.

17. Ibid., p. 7.

18. Robert H. Bork, "Legislative Intent and the Policy of the Sherman Act," *Journal of Law and Economics* 9 (April 1966), pp. 7–48. Also see Robert H. Bork, *The Antitrust Paradox: A Policy at War with Itself* (New York: Basic Books, 1978), pp. 50–89.

19. Bork, *Antitrust Paradox*, p. 62.

20. Ibid., pp. 66–69.

21. Ibid., p. 68.

22. *U.S. v. Trans-Missouri Freight Ass'n*, 166 U.S. 290 (1897).

23. Ibid., p. 323.

24. *Chicago Board of Trade v. U.S.*, 246 U.S. 231 (1918). See Bork, *Antitrust Paradox*, p. 41.

25. *U.S. v. Aluminum Co. of America*, 148 F.2d 416 (2d Cir. 1945).

26. Ibid., p. 428. Emphasis added. There is certainly evidence in the congressional debates to support Judge Hand's interpretation of the purposes of the Sherman Act. For example, Congressman William Mason stated that "trusts have made products cheaper, have reduced prices; but if the price of oil, for instance, were reduced to one cent a barrel, it would not right the wrong done to the people of this country by the 'trusts' which have destroyed legitimate competition and driven honest men from legitimate business enterprises." See *Congressional*

Record, 51st Cong., 1st Sess., U.S. House of Representatives, June 20, 1890, p. 4100. Additional debate extracts, which tend to counter Bork's conclusion concerning the single-mindedness of congressional intent, are reported by DiLorenzo, "Origins of Antitrust," pp. 77–83.

27. Bork, *Antitrust Paradox,* p. 429. Emphasis added. See *Brown Shoe Co. v. U.S.,* 370 U.S. 294 (1962); *U.S. v. Von's Grocery,* 384 U.S. 270 (1966); and *F.T.C. v. Procter & Gamble Co.,* 382 U.S. 568 (1967).

28. "[I]t is easy to show that under uniform constant costs the demand curve for a firm is horizontal even though it produces 99.9 percent of all that is sold." See Paul A. Samuelson, *Foundations of Economic Analysis* (New York: Atheneum, 1970), p. 79.

29. *Brown Shoe Co. v. U.S.,* 370 U.S. 294 (1962), p. 344.

30. Bork, *Antitrust Paradox,* pp. 69–71.

31. Robert H. Lande, "Wealth Transfers as the Original and Primary Concern of Antitrust: The Efficiency Interpretation Challenged," *Hastings Law Journal* 34 (September 1982), pp. 65–151.

32. National Association of Attorneys General, "Horizontal Merger Guidelines," *Antitrust and Trade Regulation Reporter* 52 (1987), p. 476.

33. Bruno S. Frey, Werner W. Pommerehne, Friedrich Schneider, and Guy Gilbert, "Consensus and Dissension Among Economists: An Empirical Inquiry," *American Economic Review* 74 (December 1984), pp. 986–94.

34. Joe S. Bain, *Industrial Organization,* 2d ed. (New York: Wiley, 1968), p. 515.

35. Scherer, *Industrial Market Structure and Economic Performance,* p. 491. Emphasis in original.

36. Richard A. Posner, *Antitrust Law: An Economic Perspective* (Chicago, IL: University of Chicago Press, 1976), p. 4.

37. Kenneth G. Elzinga and William Breit, *The Antitrust Penalties: A Study in Law and Economics* (New Haven, CT: Yale University Press, 1976), p. ix.

38. A. D. Neale and D. G. Goyder, *The Antitrust Laws of the U.S.A.: A Study of Competition Enforced by Law,* 3d ed. (Cambridge, UK: Cambridge University Press, 1980), p. 441.

39. Clair Wilcox, *Public Policies Toward Business,* 3rd ed. (Homewood, IL: Richard D. Irwin, 1966), p. 49.

40. Carl Kaysen and Donald F. Turner, *Antitrust Policy* (Cambridge, MA: Harvard University Press, 1959), p. 5.

41. Neale and Goyder, *Antitrust Laws of the U.S.A.,* p. 440, quoting the 1955 *Report of the Attorney General's National Committee to Study the Antitrust Laws.*

42. Thomas Hazlett, "Interview with George Stigler," *Reason,* January 1984, p. 46.

43. Posner, *Antitrust Law,* p. 236.

44. *Continental T.V. Inc. v. GTE Sylvania,* 433 U.S. 36 (1977). Citing *Sylvania* with approval, the Supreme Court refused to find an unlawful price-fixing conspiracy in the Monsanto Company's use of resale price maintenance in the distribution of agricultural herbicides. The court also recently refused to uphold a lower court's ruling finding a group of Japanese television manufacturers and their U.S. subsidiaries guilty of predatory pricing to the injury of two U.S. firms. Both decisions relied heavily on well-reasoned economic analysis. See *Monsanto Co.*

v. Spray-Rite Service Corp., 465 U.S. 752 (1984) and *Matsushita Electric Industrial Co., Ltd. et al. v. Zenith Radio Corp. et al.*, 475 U.S. 574 (1986).

45. John L. Peterman, "The Brown Shoe Case," *Journal of Law and Economics* 18 (April 1975), p. 143.

46. Ibid.

47. John L. Peterman, "The Federal Trade Commission v. Brown Shoe Company," *Journal of Law and Economics* 18 (October 1975), p. 393.

48. John L. Peterman, "The International Salt Case," *Journal of Law and Economics* 22 (October 1979), pp. 351–64.

49. David Flath, "The American Can Case," *Antitrust Bulletin* 25 (Spring 1980), pp. 169–93.

50. Arnold Zelenitz, "The Attempted Promotion of Competition in Related Goods Markets: The Ford-Autolite Divestiture Case," *Antitrust Bulletin* 25 (Spring 1980), pp. 103–24.

51. *U.S. v. Addyston Pipe & Steel Co.*, 85 F. 271 (6th Cir. 1898).

52. *Standard Oil Co. v. U.S.*, 221 U.S. 1 (1911).

53. *Brown Shoe Co. v. U.S.*, 370 U.S. 294 (1962).

54. In two earlier cases involving railroad rate-fixing agreements, Justice Peckham had first declared every restraint of trade to be illegal. He later modified his position by holding in *Trans-Missouri Freight* that the Sherman Act prohibited only those restraints having "direct and immediate effect . . . upon interstate commerce." The subtleties involved in Judge Taft's clarification of these precedents are detailed by Bork, *Antitrust Paradox*, pp. 26–30.

55. George Bittlingmayer, "Decreasing Average Cost and Competition: A New Look at the Addyston Pipe Case," *Journal of Law and Economics* 25 (October 1982), p. 213.

56. Neale and Goyder, *Antitrust Laws of the U.S.A.*, p. 72. Also see Dominick T. Armentano, *Antitrust and Monopoly: Anatomy of a Policy Failure* (New York: Wiley, 1982), pp. 139–41.

57. Almarin Phillips, *Market Structure, Organization and Performance* (Cambridge, MA: Harvard University Press, 1962).

58. Ibid., p. 112.

59. Bittlingmayer, "Decreasing Average Cost and Competition." The theory of the "empty core," upon which Bittlingmayer's analysis is based, was developed by Lester Telser. For a concise statement of the theory, see Lester G. Telser, "Cooperation, Competition, and Efficiency," *Journal of Law and Economics* 28 (May 1975), pp. 271–95.

60. John S. McGee, *Industrial Organization* (Englewood Cliffs, NJ: Prentice-Hall, 1988), p. 437. By the 1920s, United Pipe's market share had fallen to about 40 percent.

61. Bork, *Antitrust Paradox*, p. 26.

62. *U.S. v. American Tobacco Co.*, 221 U.S. 106 (1911).

63. John S. McGee, "Predatory Price Cutting: The Standard Oil (N.J.) Case," *Journal of Law and Economics* 1 (October 1958), pp. 137–69.

64. Ibid., p. 155.

65. Ibid., p. 168.

66. Peterman, "Brown Shoe Case"; Phillip Areeda and Donald F. Turner, *Antitrust Law*, Vol. iv (Boston, MA: Little, Brown, 1980), pp. 310–14; and Bork, *Antitrust Paradox*, pp. 198–216. Bork's chapter on *Brown Shoe* is entitled "The Crash of Merger Policy."

67. Peterman, "Brown Shoe Case."

68. Bork, *Antitrust Paradox*, p. 198.

69. Ibid., pp. 202–4.

70. Morris A. Adelman, "The Measurement of Aggregate Concentration," *Review of Economics and Statistics* 33 (November 1951), pp. 295–96. Also see Richard Duke, "Trends in Aggregate Concentration," Working Paper No.61, Bureau of Economics, Federal Trade Commission, June 1982.

71. *FTC v. Procter & Gamble Co.*, 386 U.S. 568 (1967), p. 580.

72. Bork, *Antitrust Paradox*, p. 216.

73. Ibid.

74. William F. Long, Richard Schramm, and Robert D. Tollison, "The Economic Determinants of Antitrust Activity," *Journal of Law and Economics* 16 (October 1973), pp. 351–64.

75. Ibid., pp. 361–62.

76. John J. Siegfried, "The Determinants of Antitrust Activity," *Journal of Law and Economics* 18 (October 1975), pp. 559–74.

77. Ibid., p. 573.

78. Peter Asch, "The Determinants and Effects of Antitrust Policy," *Journal of Law and Economics* 18 (October 1975), pp. 575–81.

79. Ibid., pp. 579–81.

80. Peter Asch and Joseph J. Seneca, "Is Collusion Profitable?," *Review of Economics and Statistics* 58 (February 1976), pp. 1–12.

81. B. Espen Eckbo and Peggy Wier, "Antitrust Policy under the Hart-Scott-Rodino Act: A Reexamination of the Market Power Hypothesis," *Journal of Law and Economics* 28 (April 1985), pp. 119–49.

82. Pauline M. Ippolito, *Resale Price Maintenance: Economic Evidence from Litigation* (Washington, DC: Federal Trade Commission, 1988).

83. In the words of one critic, "the time has come to rethink antitrust with the aid of economics." See Posner, *Antitrust Law*, p. 236.

2

The Interest-Group Theory of Government

If "majority rule" were in fact a meaningful way of characterizing political outcomes in a representative democracy, there would be no minimum wage law, no agricultural price supports, no import tariffs and quotas, in short, none of the many and varied government programs and policies that benefit the few at the expense of the many. Yet, such special interest measures exist—indeed flourish—in the United States and elsewhere. This simple observation about political life raises two important questions. If a large number of governmental activities generate no discernible benefits for the majority, why are such policies adopted? Given the very real costs, both direct and indirect, borne by taxpayers in supporting the machinery of wealth redistribution, why do such policies persist?

One approach to answering these questions, which might be termed the "market failure" approach, derives from the work of Arthur Pigou.[1] This way of analyzing government emphasizes the reasons why in many cases the private market economy cannot be wholly relied upon to allocate and distribute resources in a socially optimal way. For example, the existence of positive or negative "externalities"—benefits or costs associated with economic activities not received or borne directly by market participants—causes some goods to be oversupplied and some to be undersupplied. Left alone, private markets would produce too much environmental pollution and not enough education. Similarly, the informational disadvantages of buyers respecting the quality or performance characteristics of certain products and services leaves them vulnerable to exploitation by sellers. The suggestion is that government intervene in policy-specific ways, using taxes, subsidies, price regulation, and the like to correct these market failures: "In the Pigovian approach the state is a productive entity that produces public goods, internalizes social costs and benefits, regulates decreasing cost industries effectively, redistributes income Pareto optimally, and so forth."[2]

The market failure theory of government, assuming as it does that government benignly pursues the objective of maximizing social welfare, implies that failures of policy result only from error or ignorance on the part of the policymakers. Indeed, the Pigovian model does not address the costs of implementing the corrective policies it recommends, and rarely do Pigovians ask whether the desired policy outcomes are actually achieved. When confronted with evidence that they have not, or that they have but at a cost that far outweighs any conceivable measure of benefits, the usual response is to deplore the unfortunate, but surely unintended consequences, quickly followed by a call for more and "better" intervention.

The interest-group or "capture" theory of government, which provides an alternative to the Pigovian model, has a venerable history in the literature of economics and political science, going back perhaps as far as Knut Wicksell's classic work, "A New Principle of Just Taxation."[3] The interest-group theory rests on two basic premises, the first of which is that the same behavioral model used to explain decision making in ordinary markets applies to decision making in the public sector. Public policymakers are not benevolent maximizers of social welfare, as assumed by the market failure model, but are instead motivated by their own self-interests. Within the political marketplace that generates specific policy outcomes, all of the relevant participants are predicted to behave in the same way they are observed to behave in private markets. Firms seek to maximize profits, consumers seek to maximize utility, and policymakers seek to maximize political support.[4]

The second basic premise of the interest-group theory is that while policy errors are certainly possible, it is not very helpful to rely on error or ignorance as a basis for *explaining* policy outcomes. Instead, and especially when a policy has persisted over an extended period of time, it seems reasonable to assume that the truly intended effects of a policy can be deduced from the actual effects: "The theory tells us to look, as precisely and carefully as we can, at who gains and who loses, and how much, when we seek to explain a . . . policy."[5] Thus, the interest-group theory is not a theory about how government should work, but rather it is a theory about how government does work, based upon the application of the tools of positive economic science to the analysis of political choices. The only important difference between the market for private goods and the market for wealth transfers in this approach to the study of governmental processes consists of differences in the constraints that face self-interested market participants in the two settings. Outcomes differ in political markets not because the goals of individual behavior are different, but because the institutions within which individuals pursue their own gain are different.

THE MARKET FOR WEALTH TRANSFERS

In its simplest form, the interest-group theory of government is usually stated in terms of economic regulation because the theory was first articulated as a way of explaining the wide divergence observed between the actual and intended effects of this type of intervention into the economy. By asking why it is that applying controls on price and entry to decreasing-cost industries rarely seems to benefit consumers, George Stigler formalized the notion that coalitions of producers will often find it profitable to use the apparatus of public regulation for their own gain.[6] This follows because producer groups are typically small enough in number and their financial interests are sufficiently large that the potential benefits from organizing and lobbying for monopoly rights will exceed the associated costs. On the other hand, the more diffuse nature of consumer interests coupled with the fact that each bears only a small share of the regulatory burden means that the relatively high costs of organizing to oppose monopoly-enhancing regulations will exceed the expected gains for such groups. As a result of its lobbying advantage, industry can therefore often successfully use the political process to secure for itself such regulatory favors as direct cash subsidies, control over the entry of new rivals, restrictions on the outputs and prices of complementary and substitute goods, and the legitimization of price-fixing schemes.

The interest group model is much more general, however. It applies to any situation in which the monopoly power of the state can be mobilized selectively to benefit one group at the expense of others. Suppose that we can order the n individuals in the economy into all possible coalitions, running from n coalitions of size one to one coalition of size n.[7] There are $2^n - 1$ such possible groups. We then rank these combinations of individuals, in descending order, in terms of their demand for wealth transfers. That is, we suppose that one dollar is available for transfer, and we ask each group how much it is willing to pay for the right to be the recipient of the transfer. Each group's bid price is determined by netting out from one dollar its costs of organizing (which includes overcoming free-rider problems), becoming informed, and lobbying for the transfer and, so, generally speaking, coalitions having a comparative advantage in collective action will submit the highest bids. Proceeding in this way, subtracting successively each group's costs from one dollar, yields the downward-sloping schedule, D, shown in Figure 2.1. Groups located closer to the origin have lower costs and, hence, higher net demand prices for transfers. The coalition located at the point where D crosses the horizontal axis has organization costs of one dollar; its net demand price is accordingly zero. And, it costs groups even further to the right

Figure 2.1 The Demand for and Supply of Wealth Transfers

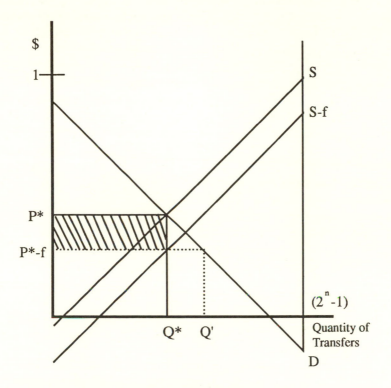

Source: Adapted from Robert E. McCormick and Robert D. Tollison,
*Politicians, Legislation, and the Economy: An Inquiry into the
Interest-Group Theory of Government*
(Boston: Martinus Nijhoff, 1981), p. 20.

more than one dollar to act collectively. The *net* supply curve of transfers, S-f, is the mirror image of the schedule just constructed. Saying that a coalition faces high costs of organizing to demand transfers is the same thing as saying that the group will find it costly to avoid having a portion of its wealth expropriated for transfer to some other group. Just as it is not worth spending more than one dollar for the right to receive one dollar, it is not worth spending more than one dollar to avoid having to pay one dollar. So, we again rank all possible coalitions of individuals, this time in terms of their willingness to supply transfers. That is, we ask each group how much it would pay to avoid expropriation of one dollar. The net supply price for each group is found by netting out from one dollar its costs of collective action. Groups located closer to the origin are those for which the costs of organizing are relatively high, and so they are the coalitions from which one dollar can be expropriated most cheaply. Proceeding in this way, we derive the upward-sloping schedule, S-f.

The role of political representatives in this setting is to match demanders and suppliers of wealth transfers. They perform this function by, for example, levying taxes on wealth suppliers and transferring the proceeds to demanders in the form of a cash grant. (We shall have more to say on this point below.) We assume that the political broker imposes a fee, f, for this service equal to the marginal cost of the real resources consumed in operating the wealth transfer machinery. (For simplicity, we assume that the broker's marginal cost and, hence, the brokerage fee is constant over the relevant range of transactions.) If, finally, we assume that the brokerage fee is collected from the suppliers of wealth transfers, the (gross) supply schedule, S, is nothing more than the inverse demand curve, S-f, plus the brokerage fee.[8] In other words, the supply price of transfers at any point is the (vertical) sum of the amount a given coalition is willing to pay to avoid expropriation of one dollar plus the fixed fee, f, assessed to cover the cost of transferring wealth.

Thus, we have a situation in which some groups in the economy are willing to pay more than others for the right to receive one dollar in transfers. Given the fixed cost of transacting in this setting, there is a single price, P*, that equates quantity demanded with quantity supplied. In political equilibrium, groups with demand prices below P*-f will be net suppliers of transfers at the rate of one dollar per group. Groups that are willing to pay more than P* will receive transfers at the rate of one dollar per group. And, groups with demand prices below P* but above P*-f are unaffected by the wealth transfer process—the real cost of transacting makes it uneconomic for the broker to segregate these coalitions into demanders and suppliers.

Real resources equal to the area of the shaded rectangle in Figure 2.1 are consumed in reaching a market-clearing level of transfer activity. This is the amount received by the broker which, in turn, covers the cost of operating the brokerage house. The costs borne by suppliers and demanders in engaging in transfer activities must be added to this amount in order to arrive at the total value of resources dissipated in the pursuit of transfers. Note that all of the resources consumed in wealth transfer activities are wasted from society's point of view.[9] By their very nature, such activities result in the redistribution of existing wealth; they do not create new wealth. Thus, by redirecting scarce resources away from the production of goods and services that would augment existing wealth, transfer activities make society poorer on balance: The private gains realized by the recipients of transfers are more than offset by the cost to society of transfer activity.

Transactions in this model need not take place in the form of cash. In particular, the transfers received by net demanders might be denominated in terms of any of the favors that can be conferred by selective use of the coercive power of the state. Domestic oil producers benefit from tariffs or import quotas on foreign oil, butter producers benefit from a tax on margarine, commercial airlines benefit from federal subsidies for airport construction, incumbent practitioners benefit from occupational licensing requirements, labor unions benefit from minimum wage laws, and so on.[10] Similarly, the broker's fee may be paid in votes, gifts, travel junkets, or any other convenient form of barter. And, finally, it is worth noting that suppliers receive an indirect benefit from transfer activity denominated in opportunity cost terms. By paying the taxes or higher prices required to finance the transfer of wealth to demanders, they thereby avoid having to bear the organization costs necessary to resist expropriation. All of this goes toward saying that the equilibrium price, P^*, is just a line of demarcation between winners and losers in the market for wealth transfers.

Competitive market forces ensure that P^* is in fact the market equilibrium "price" of transfers. Suppose that for some reason the actual quantity of transfers was less than the market-clearing level, Q^*. Unexploited gains from trade would thereby exist. Transfers would be available for which demanders are willing to pay more to receive than suppliers are willing to pay to avoid. The market is thus out of equilibrium in the sense that brokers are transferring too little wealth. In such a situation, incumbent politicians are vulnerable to entry by brokers who recognize the unexploited transfer opportunities. Incumbents will be voted out of office, political platforms will change, and so on until the amount of transfer activity rises, and price falls, so as to restore the equality between quantity demanded and quantity supplied.

The model outlined above has purposely remained silent on the question of identifying the winners and losers in the wealth transfer process. This is because the key to understanding transfer activity in a representative democracy lies simply in the fact that certain information and transactions costs are associated with collective action. Given the existence of such costs, political representatives themselves have incentives to search for specific issues that provide opportunities for trade between demanders and suppliers of wealth transfers. Although it is often the case that an outsider can only identify the winners and losers *ex post*, after the market has determined who they are, we can make a few general observations about the nature of the information and organization costs that shape collective action.

There are basically two aspects to the information costs involved in transfer seeking. Each participant in the market must first discover the effects of an issue on his or her personal wealth, and then he or she must identify other individuals who have common interests on the issue. Obviously, if the wealth effects are "small," or not easily discovered, it will not pay to bear the costs of becoming informed. Organization costs present a second barrier to collective action. Even after a community of interests has been identified, the individuals who join together on an issue must reach a consensus on a common course of action, marshall their resources in support of lobbying efforts, overcome free rider problems, and so on. Again, collective action becomes worthwhile only if the potential benefits exceed the associated costs.

The existence of a market for wealth transfers derives simply from the fact that some groups will be able to organize and acquire information about transfer activity more cheaply than others. These cost differentials give rise to the demand for and supply of wealth redistributions that are brokered by political representatives. And, generally speaking, the brokers will have incentives to seek out issues on which the prospective winners are well informed and well organized, while the losers remain rationally ignorant about the effects of transfer activity.

For all of the reasons just stated, smaller groups will tend to have a comparative advantage in transfer-seeking activity. Each member thereby has a larger financial stake in a given political issue insofar as the potential gains (or losses) of redistribution are divided among fewer hands. This factor raises the rate of return to acquiring information about the wealth effects of transfer activity. At the same time, smaller groups face lower costs of reaching agreement and of monitoring and controlling free-riding behavior.[11] Taken together, these observations help explain why small, cohesive interest groups are often successful in obtaining transfers at the expense of the general polity, whose interests are more diffuse and whose costs of organizing are relatively high.

In addition, however, it is worth noting that a significant portion of the costs of engaging in transfer-seeking activity are start-up costs. Once they have been borne, the cost of supplying additional collective effort is relatively low. Groups that have already organized for some other purpose therefore have an important advantage in the market for wealth transfers: To the extent that political lobbying is a by-product of performing some other function, these groups can avoid a large part of the initial costs of transfer seeking. Labor unions, industry trade associations, professional societies, corporations, farmer cooperatives, and so on are well situated to act on political issues that affect their wealth precisely because the costs of identifying and organizing a community of interests have already been incurred.

Thus, depending on the configurations of the costs and benefits of collective action, almost any group (or subgroup) within the polity may find it feasible to use the political machinery of the state for its own benefit. The interest-group theory of government is therefore much more general than is implied by the stylized producer-versus-consumer terms in which it was first articulated. Applying the model to the issue of economic regulation is nevertheless instructive.

INTEREST GROUPS AND ECONOMIC REGULATION

The failure of the traditional model of economic regulation to consider the motives of the regulators was perhaps its most crucial defect. Economists accepted uncritically the assumption that the goal of regulatory policy was to promote consumer welfare by correcting the allocative inefficiencies associated with decreasing-cost industries. They went about developing elegant theoretical models to derive socially optimal pricing policies for such firms that could be applied by regulatory authorities to minimize lost consumer surplus and simultaneously guarantee the firms' owners a "fair" return on their investment.

That regulatory policy does not in fact operate according to the public-interest model was first revealed in a body of research showing that government intervention often failed to achieve its announced goals. One early study of public utility regulation, for example, found that it had little or no effect on the level of electricity prices or on the rates of return to investments in that industry.[12] Similarly, purchasers of new stock issues were found to obtain few benefits from the regulatory oversight exercised by the Securities and Exchange Commission.[13] These and other studies producing the same results raised two important questions. If public regulation generates no discernible benefits for consumers, why are such policies adopted? Given the very real costs to taxpayers of supporting the apparatus of regulation, why do such policies persist?

The answer to both of these questions, as we have seen, is that there is a market for regulatory legislation. Certain groups, whose financial interests are sufficiently concentrated and whose costs of mobilizing political influence are relatively low, stand to gain more than others from the controls on price and entry imposed by public regulatory agencies. This creates incentives for such coalitions to use the apparatus of public regulation to increase their own wealth at the expense of other groups that confront relatively high costs of acquiring information and of organizing to oppose regulatory wealth redistribution. The regulators, in turn, serve as brokers of these wealth transfers. Their motivation for doing so also has a self-interest basis grounded on the political support offered by the demanders of regulation.

Sam Peltzman formalized Stigler's hypothesis that private interests—and not the "public interest"—drive regulatory policy in what has become one of the most important contributions to the theory of economic regulation.[14] Peltzman's model posits a vote-maximizing regulator who faces a tradeoff between the gains conferred on producers and the costs imposed on consumers in setting a regulated price. The essential elements of the theory are illustrated in Figure 2.2. For given cost and revenue conditions, the profit "hill" traces out the output price and profit combinations available to the regulated firm. Profit is zero at p_c, the competitive price. Net revenue then rises as price rises, reaches a unique maximum at p_m, and then declines continuously thereafter. Price p_m corresponds to the unregulated monopoly profit maximum.

The "level curves," labeled M_0, M_1, M_2, are derived from the regulator's political support function. Peltzman denominated political support in terms of votes, but the objective could also be thought of as campaign contributions, the regulator's salary, or other budgetary line items appropriated by the legislature, probability of reappointment or other index of job security in cases where the regulator's service in office is at the pleasure of the executive, and so on. In any case, the regulator's objective is to maximize his or her political support subject to the constraint that setting higher regulatory prices generates greater support from producers but antagonizes consumer interests, and vice versa.

Each level curve (Peltzman called them "iso-majority" curves) shows the various combinations of price and profit that are consistent with a given amount of political support for the regulator. (Higher levels of total political support are associated with higher—more northwesterly—iso-majority curves.) These curves are drawn as convex (from below) to indicate diminishing marginal political returns to higher profit or lower price. That is, holding the regulator's political majority constant (moving along a particular iso-majority curve), greater and greater opposition from consumers is brought forth by each successive increment of profit granted to the regulated firm. This follows because the higher prices (and smaller outputs) necessary to generate larger producer profits increase the burden of regulation to consumers, thereby increasing the rate of return to organizing in opposition to regulatory expropriation of wealth. Similarly, greater

Figure 2.2 The Vote-Maximizing Regulatory Price

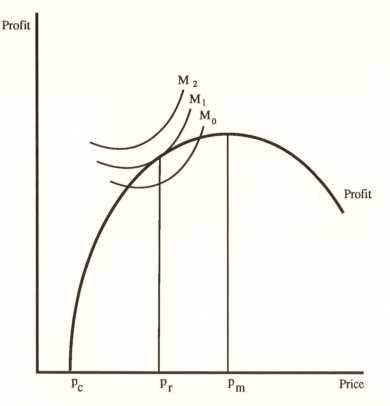

Source: Sam Peltzman, "Toward a More General Theory of Regulation,"
Journal of Law and Economics 19 (August 1976), p. 224.

and greater opposition from producers is brought forth by each successive reduction in price granted to consumers because lower prices increase the cost of regulation to the regulated firms—a cost denominated in terms of the profits foregone as the regulated price is reduced below the monopoly profit-maximizing level.

In Peltzman's model, the regulator selects the price that maximizes his or her political majority subject to the profit constraint. This optimum occurs at the point where an iso-majority curve is just tangent to the profit hill. The political-equilibrium regulatory price is shown as p_r in the diagram. Generally speaking, the more effective producers are in delivering political support to the regulator, the closer will p_r be to p_m. (In the limit, if consumers are completely impotent politically, the iso-majority curves will be horizontal lines and the regulated price will be the monopoly price.) For similar reasons, the more effective consumers are in mobilizing political influence, the closer will p_r be to p_c. However, as long as both groups contribute to the regulator's political majority, neither consumers nor producers will get all that they want from regulation. Pursuing his or her own self-interests under the given constraints, the regulator will rationally set p_r above the competitive price but below the monopoly profit-maximizing level.

There is small but growing literature providing empirical support for the predictions of the Stigler-Peltzman model of regulation.[15] The importance of this work is obvious. It suggests that price regulation does not arise out of public-spirited attempts by government to mitigate the allocative inefficiency of monopoly. The interest-group theory instead argues that the level and pattern of regulatory intervention into the private economy is determined in a political market wherein self-interested regulators serve as brokers between demanders and suppliers of wealth transfers. Among other things, the model implies that it is naive to explain evidence that regulation is ineffective or perverse on the basis of error or ignorance on the part of the regulators. Rather, the apparent anomalies of regulation are understandable, logical outcomes of a political process in which groups having concentrated interests in regulation and facing low organization costs generally prevail over other groups whose interests are diffuse and whose costs of mobilizing political influence are high. The bottom line "is not that the traditional theory of economics is unhelpful in studying regulation but, on the contrary, is most helpful when it is applied directly to the understanding of the regulatory process."[16]

INTEREST GROUPS AND ANTITRUST

In many respects, the attitude of scholars toward antitrust policy in 1990 parallels the conventional wisdom about economic regulation in 1970. In both cases, public policies are assumed to have been enacted and enforced by a fallible, but basically benign, government. Policy failures are ascribed to error or ignorance, and reform proposals stress the need for closer adherence to economic principles. As we have seen, however, a fairly standard characterization of how geographically based representative democracy works in practice suggests that elected representatives receive a higher payoff from promoting local interests than from taking vague positions in support of economic efficiency or the "national interest." Particularly for a member of the

House of Representatives, "the welfare of his constituents may depend disproportionately on a few key industries. The promotion of the industries becomes one of his most important duties as a representative of the district."[17]

To illustrate the potential for using antitrust policy as mechanism for wealth redistribution, suppose that a merger leading to increased economic efficiency is proposed. The shareholders whose wealth will be enhanced and the consumers who will benefit from lower prices are ordinarily not organized into a cohesive interest group and are dispersed geographically. At the same time, the prospective gains for owners and consumers may be accompanied by losses for the managers and employees of the firm targeted for takeover. Jobs may be scheduled for elimination, plans may be drawn up for closing down production plants, abandoning or selling off product lines, moving offices, and so on. These possibilities mean that a merger involving a firm located in a given politician's home district confronts him or her with the prospect of immediate costs, while the benefits are spread more diffusely among shareholders and consumers nationwide. Managers and employees whose jobs are on the line will rationally seek political help to stop the merger from being consummated, and the representative will rationally respond to this demand. Failure to do so will result in a loss of wealth for the district and a loss of votes for the politician.

In short, a political-support–maximizing representative has a clear incentive for seeing that antitrust policy furthers the interests of his or her own constituency. At the same time, the representatives of other districts and states have a much smaller stake in the outcome because the prospective benefits of the merger to their individual constituencies are trivial in relation to the total gains associated with the acquisition. These other representatives may therefore be willing to back the affected politician's opposition to the proposed merger in exchange for a promise of his or her support in the future when one of their own constituencies can benefit from the selective use of the antitrust policy process. The potential for having an impact on a law enforcement agency's decision to oppose the merger will be particularly great for the members of Congress who sit on the committees having budgetary or oversight responsibilities with respect to the Department of Justice and the Federal Trade Commission. Because these committees have authority to control appropriations, confirm the president's political appointees to the agencies, and so on, a legislator in such a position will have "a great deal of power to advance the interests of businesses located in his district however unimportant the interests may be from a national standpoint."[18] As such, antitrust policy would be expected to operate much like regulatory policy in general, with private interests and wealth redistribution being the key to explaining the observed effects of government intervention.

Frank Easterbrook, in fact, has charged that the Department of Justice has purposely used antitrust suits to establish the district courts as de facto regulatory agencies with respect to industries in which the government was convinced that competitive market forces were "unworkable," but in which the political process had not acted to impose formal regulation.[19] That is, antitrust may just be another example of a public policy apparatus designed to facilitate wealth redistribution in the economy. Put another way, antitrust may afford certain well organized interest groups with an alternative mechanism—a mechanism of particular value in sectors of the economy where industry-specific regulatory or legislative constraints do not exist—for obtaining wealth transfers at the expense of other, less well organized groups.

Instigating an antitrust law suit, like efforts to influence a ruling by a public regulatory agency, provides an opportunity for demanders of wealth transfers to win in the courts what they are unable to win in the private marketplace. Antitrust can be employed to restrict the entry of new rivals to an industry, to limit price or nonprice competition, to impose costs on certain members of an industry differentially, and so on. Used strategically in this way, antitrust has several unique advantages over alternative methods of competition. For one, when a public law enforcement agency can be induced to bring suit against an existing or prospective competitor, the costs of litigation are borne by the general taxpayer rather than the benefiting interest group. Moreover, rulings by the courts bring the police power of the state to bear on the tasks of adjusting and monitoring the behavior of rivals. And even an unsuccessful lawsuit can impose a capital loss on the owners of a firm targeted by an antitrust complaint.[20]

Government policies of all sorts continue to survive against overwhelming evidence that their social costs far outweigh any conceivable estimate of the private benefits they confer. Minimum wage legislation, trade protectionism, and agricultural price support programs are just a few examples of public policies that fail such a benefit-cost test. Antitrust policy is not unique in this regard. Where antitrust differs from these other forms of government regulation of the private economy is that its underlying purposes remain almost universally beyond dispute. As a result of the preconception that the primary goal of antitrust is the maximization of consumer welfare, the many defects observed in the enforcement of the antitrust laws are attributed to correctable errors. All that is necessary to improve matters is to have the "right" people in position to enforce the "right" laws.

By contrast, the interest-group theory of government suggests that what the conventional wisdom treats as antitrust policy "failures" are in fact the predictable consequences of self-interest–seeking behavior on the part of rational individuals operating under a particular set of institutional and legal constraints. From an analytical point of view, instigating an antitrust law suit is no different from any other method of transfer seeking through political processes. The actual strategy chosen for pursuing a wealth transfer in any given situation will simply be the one that offers the highest expected rate of return.

NOTES

1. Arthur C. Pigou, *The Economics of Welfare*, 4th ed. (London: Macmillan, 1932).

2. Robert E. McCormick and Robert D. Tollison, *Politicians, Legislation, and the Economy: An Inquiry into the Interest-Group Theory of Government* (Boston, MA: Martinus Nijhoff, 1981), p. 3.

3. Knut Wicksell, *Finanztheoretische Untersuchungen* (Jena, 1896). Portions of this work appear as "A New Principle of Just Taxation" (James M. Buchanan, trans.), in Richard A. Musgrave and Alan T. Peacock, eds., *Classics in the Theory of Public Finance* (London: Macmillan, 1958), pp. 72–118. For a review of the general literature on this subject, see Richard A. Posner, "Theories of Economic Regulation," *Bell Journal of Economics* 5 (Autumn 1974), pp. 335–58.

4. "Political support" is here defined broadly, and may differ according to the identity of the relevant policymaker(s). In the case of the Congress, the maximand is typically assumed to be probability of reelection, a goal that can be achieved by maximizing votes, campaign contributions, or both. Appointed officials maximize probability of reappointment, agency budgets, or expected income after leaving government service; career bureaucrats maximize their promotion prospects; and so on. The point is that policymakers seek to maximize their own private interests and not the "public interest."

5. George J. Stigler, "Supplementary Note on Economic Theories of Regulation (1975)," in George J. Stigler, *The Citizen and the State: Essays on Regulation* (Chicago, IL: University of Chicago Press, 1975), p. 140.

6. George J. Stigler, "The Theory of Economic Regulation," *Bell Journal of Economics* 2 (Spring 1971), pp. 3–21.

7. The following discussion relies on McCormick and Tollison, *Politicians, Legislation, and the Economy*, pp. 18–22.

8. The assumption that the brokerage fee is paid by the suppliers of wealth transfers is arbitrary, but unimportant. Assuming that the fee is paid by demanders, and so subtracting it from the demand schedule, would make no difference to the analysis.

9. Gordon Tullock, "The Welfare Costs of Tariffs, Monopolies, and Theft," *Western Economic Journal* 5 (June 1967), pp. 224–32.

10. Stigler, "Theory of Economic Regulation," pp. 4–6.

11. See, generally, Mancur Olson, *The Logic of Collective Action: Public Goods and the Theory of Groups* (Cambridge, MA: Harvard University Press, 1971).

12. George J. Stigler and Claire Friedland, "What Can Regulators Regulate?: The Case of Electricity," *Journal of Law and Economics* 5 (October 1962), pp. 1–16.

13. George J. Stigler, "Public Regulation of the Securities Market," *Journal of Business* 2 (April 1964), pp. 117–42.

14. Sam Peltzman, "Toward a More General Theory of Regulation," *Journal of Law and Economics* 19 (August 1976), pp. 211–48.

15. See, for example, Ryan Amacher, Richard S. Higgins, William F. Shughart II, and Robert D. Tollison, "The Behavior of Regulatory Activity Over the Business Cycle: An Empirical Test," *Economic Inquiry* 23 (January 1985), pp. 7–19; W. Mark Crain and Robert E. McCormick, "Regulators as an Interest Group," in James M. Buchanan and Robert D. Tollison, eds., *The Theory of Public Choice—II* (Ann Arbor: University of Michigan Press, 1984), pp. 287–304; Michael T. Maloney, Robert E. McCormick, and Robert D. Tollison, "Economic Regulation, Competitive Governments, and Specialized Resources," *Journal of Law and Economics* 27 (October 1984), pp. 329–38; and William F. Shughart II and Robert D. Tollision, "The Cyclical Character of Regulatory Activity," *Public Choice* 45 (1984), pp. 303–11.

16. Stigler, *Citizen and the State*, p. xi.

17. Richard A. Posner, "The Federal Trade Commission," *University of Chicago Law Review* 47 (1976), p. 83.

18. Ibid.

19. Frank H. Easterbrook, "The Limits of Antitrust," *Texas Law Review* 63 (1984), p. 35.

20. For example, see Thomas W. Ross, "Winners and Losers under the Robinson-Patman Act," *Journal of Law and Economics* 27 (October 1984), pp. 243–71, reporting evidence that defendants who have won their contested cases fare as poorly in the capital market as those who lose.

Part II

Private Interests at Work

3

Business Enterprise

Private business firms are the demanders of antitrust wealth transfers, but not as a monolithic interest group whose members have the same single-minded purpose. Indeed, it might well be said that private businesses (and consumers) are harmed overall by the existence of an actively enforced antitrust policy. The important point to recognize, however, is that winners and losers are created whenever government intervenes to correct a perceived antitrust problem, and the prospective gains to the benefitting parties provide incentives for using antitrust processes to their own advantage.

As a wealth transfer mechanism, antitrust policy is particularly valuable insofar as it cuts across the economy, applying to a broad spectrum of business practices. It supplies a general legal framework that can be called upon by many firms in a variety of industries to secure advantages over rivals or to obtain protection from competitive market forces. Thus, the law on mergers can be used by the managers and employees of firms targeted for takeover to prevent acquisitions that might cost them their jobs. The same law can be used by rival firms to block a merger that would result in the creation of a more efficient and, hence, more effective competitor. The law on price discrimination can be used by colluding firms to discipline a coconspirator found cheating on their price-fixing agreement; it can be used by an established firm to prevent the entry of an aggressive price cutter; or it can be used by the entrant to prevent established rivals from responding to new competition with lower prices. The law on vertical restraints of trade can be used by independent retailers to forestall the growth of competitors employing more efficient methods of product distribution. There are many more examples in this regard.

The decision to "invest" in antitrust as a method of competition is no different from any other capital-budgeting problem the firm confronts. Faced with a loss of sales to a new or established rival, the firm can respond by cutting price, improving product quality, increasing its advertising expenditures, or taking any of a number of other actions, or combination of actions, that normally characterize the workings of a competitive market economy. Alternatively, the firm can appeal to government for protection. It can lobby for favorable legislation, it can attempt to influence a bureaucratic ruling, or it can instigate an antitrust lawsuit either on its own or by supplying information about a possible law violation to the public antitrust agencies. Which of these various options is chosen in any given circumstance is simply a matter of selecting the strategy offering the highest expected rate of return to the firm.

In short, the power residing in the antitrust laws to declare illegal certain business practices thought to be anticompetitive is also a power that can be used to subvert the competitive process. A law that declares mergers to be illegal where they would substantially lessen competition or tend to create a monopoly is also a law that can be used to prevent mergers that will make life uncomfortable for rivals by promising to generate substantial cost savings. A law that declares selective price cutting to be illegal where the effect would be to injure competitors unfairly is also a law that can be used against a rival that, by virtue of superior efficiency, is able to offer lower prices to customers.

The interest-group theory outlined in Chapter 2 teaches us that whenever a government policy process can be mobilized to benefit the few at the expense of the many selectively, there will be strategic use of that policy by groups having a stake in its exercise. This is not to say, it is important to emphasize, that such behavior represents a misuse or abuse of the policy process. Rather, the pursuit of wealth transfers (or the defense of existing wealth) through the antitrust laws simply reflects rational, self-interest–seeking behavior under given constraints. Nor is it necessary to inquire into the motives of the framers of antitrust. Whether antitrust was designed purposely as a wealth transfer mechanism or, instead, transfer seeking is an unintended or unforeseen consequence of a policy meant to promote consumer welfare, the fact remains that actual law enforcement efforts have served primarily to redistribute wealth, not enhance it. For every case where the decision of the courts appears to be consistent with a goal of promoting competition in the private economy, there are dozens of cases where the net result was to prevent the benefits of competition from reaching consumers. Indeed, the number of antitrust cases identified in the scholarly literature as being inconsistent with the objective of protecting the interests of consumers is so large that one could reasonably conclude that those that are represent policy mistakes.[1]

It is impossible to enumerate all of the antitrust law provisions and administrative mechanisms that lend themselves to transfer-seeking activity on the part of private firms in the economy. In what follows, however, we discuss three areas of the law that stand out as particularly good examples of the selective benefits available through antitrust processes. These are the law on mergers, the law on price discrimination, and the law on vertical restraints of trade.

THE LAW ON MERGERS

Firms merge in order to increase their profits either by exploiting additional market power or by taking advantage of cost savings, or both. It is the task of the antitrust law enforcement agencies and the courts to identify which of these two effects dominates in any particular case, allowing mergers that promise net economic efficiencies to proceed and forbidding those that will reduce the welfare of consumers on balance.[2]

Merger law enforcement is based upon an "incipiency" doctrine which holds that preventive measures against monopoly are preferable to corrective measures. Today, the law on mergers is the most actively applied of the major provisions of antitrust policy, but this is a relatively recent development. Section 1 of the Sherman Act states that "every contract, combination in the form of trust or otherwise, or conspiracy, in restraint of trade or commerce among the several States, or with foreign nations, is declared to be illegal." It then goes on to specify that

> Every person who shall make any contract or engage in any combination or conspiracy hereby declared to be illegal shall be deemed guilty of a felony, and, on conviction thereof shall be punished by fine not exceeding one million dollars if a corporation, or, if any other person, one hundred thousand dollars, or by imprisonment not exceeding three years, or by both said punishments, in the discretion of the court.

Section 2 follows this up by declaring that "every person who shall monopolize, or attempt to monopolize, or combine or conspire with any other person or persons, to monopolize any part of the trade or commerce among the several States, or with foreign nations, shall be deemed guilty of a felony. . . . " The penalty provisions are the same as for Section 1 violations.[3]

In sum, the Sherman Act declares illegal existing conspiracies and combinations (Section 1) and attempts to create them (Section 2). From an early date, however, it became clear to those favoring an activist antitrust policy that the reach of the Sherman Act was limited. Dissatisfaction with the Justice Department's efforts to enforce the law was almost immediate. Only 16 cases were instituted by federal prosecutors in the first decade following the Sherman Act's passage. Indeed, the department brought an average of just six complaints per year through 1914.[4]

If the Justice Department initially lacked zeal in bringing Sherman Act cases, its inactivity was in part due to the rough going it faced early on in the courts. For one, the "conspiracy" and "combination" language of the law made it impotent against single-firm monopolies. Secondly, judicial interpretations of several key terms limited the Sherman Act's reach, at least temporarily. For example, in *E.C. Knight* Chief Justice Fuller held that the Sherman Act could not be used against the sugar trust because *manufacturing* is not commerce: "Commerce succeeds to manufacture and is not part of it."[5] Similarly, actions by a firm that injured its rivals in the United States were held immune from the law if the acts occurred in a foreign country.[6] Thus, despite some early successes against price fixing by the powerful trusts that dominated the meat packing,[7] oil,[8] and tobacco industries,[9] there was soon a demand for additional legislation that would define more precisely the boundaries of antitrust policy.

There were two divergent viewpoints about how the perceived deficiencies of the Sherman Act might be redressed. In the U.S. House of Representatives, the favored course of action was to enumerate the specific business practices that were to be made unlawful and make them criminal offenses. By contrast, the Senate wanted to reserve the task of identifying unlawful practices for the newly created Federal Trade Commission, which was to be an expert law enforcement body with a broad mandate to attack unspecified "unfair methods of competition." The Clayton Act eventually emerged as a compromise between these two positions. It enumerated specific law violations, but did not subject violators to criminal penalties. Qualifying phrases were inserted in the final version of the statute to provide the FTC with flexibility in enforcing the law.[10]

The Clayton Act declares illegal four specific business practices where the "effect may be to substantially lessen competition or tend to create a monopoly." These are price discrimination (Section 2), exclusive dealing and tying contracts (Section 3), acquisitions of competing companies (Section 7), and interlocking directorates (Section 8).[11] Thus, the Clayton Act responded to the critics of the Sherman Act by providing sharper definitions of unlawful practices and by giving antitrust law enforcers a legal mechanism—Section 7—that could be used to prevent monopoly problems in their incipiency.

Section 7 of the Clayton Act is sometimes referred to as the "holding company" section. It was designed to dismantle the great trusts of the era, which were basically created when holding companies were established to purchase stock (equities) in several independent enterprises, thereby acquiring ownership interests in two or more competing firms within the same industry and, sometimes, across the boundaries of related industries. The original Section 7 read in part:

> That no corporation engaged in commerce shall acquire, directly or indirectly, the whole or any part of the stock or other share capital of another corporation engaged also in commerce, where the effect of such acquisition may be to substantially lessen competition between the corporation whose stock is so acquired and the corporation making the acquisition, or to restrain such commerce in any community, or tend to create a monopoly in any line of commerce.

The silence of Section 7 on means other than stock purchases by which one corporation could gain an ownership interest in another was eloquent. It soon became apparent that mergers carried out through the purchase of physical assets did not offend the Clayton Act, even if stock was also acquired.[12] This glaring loophole, along with subsequent court decisions holding that an acquiring firm could not be compelled to divest the physical assets it had purchased after a merger had been consummated even if the stock acquisition was found to be illegal,[13] made Section 7 virtually impotent.

The omission that permitted mergers involving the purchase of physical assets to escape condemnation was not corrected until 1950. The Celler-Kefauver Act of that year amended Section 7 by adding that "no person . . . shall acquire the whole or any part of the assets of another person also in commerce . . . where . . . the effect of such acquisition may be to substantially lessen competition, or tend to create a monopoly." The amendment was quite effective in strengthening antimerger law enforcement. Until the late 1960s, the government hardly lost a case it brought under Section 7.

The mandate of Section 7 requires the prosecutors and the courts to identify and prohibit those mergers that may "substantially lessen competition, or tend to create a monopoly." Doing so requires first defining a "line of commerce"—the relevant product and geographic markets—within which the competitive effects of the merger are to be analyzed. Does the merger create a firm with such a large share of market sales that the postmerger price is likely to be the monopoly price? Does the disappearance of a former competitor increase the expected gains or reduce the expected costs of collusion among the surviving firms? The answers to both of these questions and, therefore, the decision about whether to challenge the acquisition follow directly from the market definition adopted to delineate the boundaries of effective competition in any particular case.

As it evolved in the case law, merger enforcement has basically become a question of market concentration and market shares.[14] That is, whether or not a particular merger is deemed to violate Section 7 depends mainly upon the degree to which sales or productive assets in the relevant market are concentrated in the hands of a few firms (both pre- and post-merger). This judgment, in turn, depends upon how narrowly or broadly the market boundaries are drawn. Most merger cases are therefore decided in a debate between the plaintiff, who argues for narrow boundaries, and the defendant, who seeks a broad definition, about which products and geographic areas are "in" the market and which are "out."

Instead of being used as a way of summarizing and organizing the information relevant for analyzing the possible competitive effects of merger, market definition has become the principal issue. Moreover, market definition proceeds not with the aid of serious economic analysis, but rather by adopting "the parlance of businessmen ('the Chicago drugstore market,' 'the high-fashion shoe market')."[15] This is so despite the apparent precision of the market share and market concentration standards promulgated by the Department of Justice in order to provide firms with information about the criteria it will apply in deciding whether or not to challenge a particular merger.[16] The market share and market concentration standards are indeed fairly precise, but, clearly, a market will be more or less concentrated and, hence, a merger will or will not go beyond the market share benchmarks required of a prima facie violation of the law, depending upon which products and what geographic areas are or are not included in the numerical calculations.[17]

It should therefore not be surprising that the market definitions adopted in many of the mergers reviewed by the public enforcement agencies seem to have little correspondence with the actual boundaries of effective competition that will constrain any market power created by merger. That is, market definition consists of the conceptually straightforward task of identifying the products and firms that do—or could—offer reasonable alternatives to buyers if they are confronted with an increase in the price of the good sold by the merger partners. Yet, for example, in challenging Nestlé's proposed acquisition of Stouffer, the Federal Trade Commission defined the relevant market as "high-priced, nonethnic, frozen entrees."[18] Other illustrations from mergers reviewed under the 1968 Merger Guidelines include "bagged dry-mix concrete in the Washington/Baltimore area," "beer production and distribution within the state of Kentucky," and "direct contract front-loaded trash removal in Dallas." Antitrust markets have also been defined for "home and office staplers," "traditional department stores in Milwaukee," and "noncarbonated, ready to serve, naturally or artificially flavored fruit drinks, fruit punches, or fruit ades which contain 50 percent or less fruit juice and are customarily sold under refrigeration to the consumer."[19] More recently, a proposed merger was abandoned when the FTC unanimously voted to oppose the acquisition on grounds that it would reduce competition and possibly lead to higher prices in the "gourmet spice market."[20] There are many more examples in this regard—too many, in fact, to believe that narrow market definitions are an aberration rather than the norm in public merger enforcement policy.

Such aberrations are, however, consistent with the private interests at work in the enforcement of the law on mergers. Narrow market boundaries increase the probability that any given acquisition will be challenged by the antitrust authorities. The more merger cases there are to work on, the more opportunities there are for the attorneys employed by the enforcement agencies to build the human capital that will be rewarded when they subsequently take jobs in private antitrust law firms, and the larger and more secure are the antitrust bureaus. The private antitrust bar gets to defend more clients, and economists working as consultants for plaintiffs and defendants earn larger incomes. Thus, the private incentives of a variety of interested parties run strongly in the direction of tight merger guidelines and narrow market boundaries.[21]

More important for our purposes here, vague enforcement standards, which permit arbitrarily narrow market definitions, facilitate the strategic use of merger law by competitors of the firms that seek government's permission to merge. Many mergers result in the closure of outmoded production facilities, the replacement of incumbent managers, the combination of duplicative product distribution networks, and other synergistic effects that promise to reduce costs. Increased economic efficiencies of this sort will increase the wealth of the owners of the firm targeted for takeover and benefit consumers by allowing the product to be produced and sold more cheaply. At the same time, however, rival sellers are faced with the prospect of increased competitive pressures. They can respond by attempting to emulate the organizational innovations the merger partners plan to implement or by taking other steps to lower their own costs. Alternatively, the competitors can complain to the antitrust authorities of a possible violation of the merger law. They will almost surely be joined on the issue by the managers and employees who face the prospect of losing their jobs and by local public officials in the areas where plants are scheduled for closure who face the prospect of employment losses and a smaller tax base. These demands for protectionism can readily be met if the antitrust authorities adopt a sufficiently narrow market definition such that the market shares and market concentration levels involved go beyond the thresholds required for finding a merger law violation.

Of course, it is possible that opposition by competitors to a proposed merger could arise from a public-spirited attempt on their part to check what they believe to be a consumer-welfare–reducing increase in monopoly power. After all, who besides rivals will have access to the specialized information about market conditions necessary to distinguish between efficiency-enhancing and market-power–increasing merger motives? If not, surely the antitrust authorities are able to see through and reject competitors' complaints that are nothing more than self-serving attempts to handicap their rivals.

Neither of these possibilities is supported by the evidence, however. Tests using data from the capital market suggest that the horizontal mergers challenged by the Antitrust Division and the FTC under Section 7 of the Clayton Act have not been anticompetitive, on average.[22] Instead, competitors of the prospective merger partners appear to benefit most from merger enforcement.

The empirical tests that underlie this conclusion are somewhat complex, but worth discussing briefly. Consider the possible effects of a merger announcement on stockholder wealth. Generally speaking, the owners of the firms that intend to combine will enjoy positive "abnormal" returns on their investments relative to those experienced by the owners of other firms in the economy. This effect is independent of the motive for merger. The expectation that increased future cash flows will accrue to the assets of the merging firms, either because the merger will create additional market power or because it will lead to efficiency gains, will increase the present discounted value of an ownership position in the combined firm, and this will induce increases in the share prices of the merger partners. The abnormal returns experienced by the owners of rival firms, on the other hand, will vary according to the capital market's evaluation of the source of the gains accruing to the merging firm's stockholders. If the merger is based on monopoly power, the owners of rival firms will also experience positive abnormal returns. Increased future cash flows to competitors would be expected in this case because rivals could either share in the monopoly profits created by the merger by colluding with the merger partners, or they could expand their share of market sales by undercutting any attempt by the combined firm to raise price. By contrast, the owners of rival firms will experience negative abnormal returns if the merger creates efficiency gains that place them at a competitive disadvantage relative to the merger partners.

Similar considerations apply to the announcement of an antitrust complaint challenging the legality of the proposed merger or a court decision holding the acquisition to be unlawful. Both events will tend to reduce the wealth of the owners of the merging firms insofar as monopoly rents or potential cost savings will be lost. On the other hand, the stock price effects on rival firms associated with an antitrust complaint will again depend on the capital market's evaluation of the competitive impact of the merger. If the acquisition is driven by monopoly power considerations, events like an antitrust challenge that decrease the probability that the merger will be consummated will be associated with negative abnormal returns for competitors because they too will be prevented from sharing in the monopoly rents. By contrast, if the merger is based upon economic efficiency, rivals will avoid being placed at a competitive disadvantage if the merger is blocked, and the owners of these firms will therefore enjoy positive abnormal returns.

Thus, by carefully examining the stock price effects associated with news events related to merger law enforcement, one can gain insights into merger motives and, hence, the impact of law enforcement activities. One such study examined a sample of 82 horizontal mergers challenged by the Antitrust Division and the FTC between January 1963 and December 1981.[23] The researchers found that rivals typically experienced zero or positive abnormal returns as a result of events that reduced the likelihood of mergers being consummated, findings that are inconsistent with the hypothesis that the acquisitions were based upon market power considerations. The authors concluded that "while it is possible that the government's merger policy has deterred some anticompetitive mergers, the results indicate that it has also protected rival producers from facing increased competition due to efficient mergers."[24]

Avoiding a competitive disadvantage through strategic use of the antimerger law is apparently a feasible strategy for rival firms. There is also evidence that it may be a profitable strategy for firms targeted for takeover. A study of one hundred acquisition targets who sued their suitor, charging fraud, antitrust violations, or violations of state or federal tender offer regulations, found that the suits added 17 percentage points, on average, to the initial takeover premium offered to the stockholders of those targets that were eventually acquired.[25] Thus, the antimerger law provides a mechanism through which rivals can avoid being placed at a competitive disadvantage and takeover targets can increase the price at which they are eventually bought out. These prospective benefits provide obvious incentives for private firms to "invest" in antitrust processes for their own gain.

If anything, recent antimerger law enforcement policy changes have increased rather than diminished the opportunities for firms to use antitrust processes strategically. The most important of these policy changes was the establishment of a premerger notification requirement by the Hart-Scott-Rodino (HSR) Antitrust Improvement Act of 1976. The legislation was nominally designed to give the Antitrust Division and the FTC adequate time to assess the competitive effects of proposed acquisitions prior to their consummation. Until its enactment, the two agencies could learn about prospective merger activity only by indirect means. They relied upon reports printed in specialized business publications and the popular press, company news releases, and other publicly available sources to discover information concerning merger plans in the economy. Moreover, there was no assurance that the law enforcement bureaus could act quickly enough to prevent a possibly questionable acquisition from proceeding. The government had no authority to require that a merger be postponed while an investigation was pending. And, although the antitrust laws do not have a statute of limitations as far as federal enforcement efforts are concerned, the inability to delay events meant that many mergers deemed unlawful could only be challenged ex post, requiring the authorities to seek divestiture of illegally acquired assets or attempt by some other means to undo acquisitions already completed.[26]

In order to correct these perceived deficiencies in the merger enforcement process, the Hart-Scott-Rodino Act imposed notification requirements on mergers involving firms above a certain size, and established a 30-day timetable (15 days if the acquiring firm makes a tender offer in the form of cash only) for the agency having jurisdiction to decide if it will oppose the merger.[27] This waiting period can be extended by 20 days (10 days for a cash only transaction) if supplementary information is requested from the prospective merger partners. These notification requirements and waiting periods apply if the firm making the acquisition has total assets worth $100 million or more, or annual sales of at least $10 million, and the company to be acquired has at least $10 million in assets or annual sales. Any transaction meeting these size limits is covered if the acquiring firm will gain control of more than $15 million worth (or 15 percent) of its merger partner's stock or assets.

Although the premerger notification rules that went into effect during the latter part of 1978 provide obvious benefits to the antitrust agencies in terms of supplying them with information about impending mergers in the economy, the HSR requirements may also entail a subtle social cost. Premerger notification essentially imposes a duty on firms to announce publicly that they have discovered the existence of a previously hidden profit opportunity. That is, a company becomes an acquisition target when an outsider forms the opinion that a profit can be made by gaining ownership control of the firm's assets and taking actions, such as replacing incumbent managers, rearranging production lines and distribution channels, closing outmoded plants, selling off high-cost operating divisions, and so on, that will improve the company's performance (make it more efficient). In cases where the proposed acquisition is delayed while the government seeks additional information from the merger partners, other firms, which had been unaware of the existence of undervalued assets, are given time to step forward with takeover offers of their own. The HSR process thus allows these other firms to free ride on the information revealed by the premerger announcement.

There are two reasons why premerger notification has the potential for reducing the efficiency with which resources are allocated in the economy. First, free-rider effects lower the value of information about the existence of profit opportunities, particularly to prospective acquiring firms operating in the same industry as the takeover candidate. The waiting periods imposed may also raise the cost of takeovers by giving target firms the opportunity to prepare and implement defensive tactics, such as repurchasing stock, acquiring debt, or preparing a lawsuit. Both of these factors reduce the incentives of entrepreneurs to search out information about profit opportunities and to exploit it through merger.[28] Second, casual observation suggests that premerger notification promotes conglomerate-type mergers (mergers between firms operating in unrelated lines of business), relative to horizontal mergers, because such acquisitions are less likely to be delayed by the HSR process. The above consequences are costly to the economy because firms are more likely to discover undervalued assets within their own industry and to employ such resources more efficiently when purchased than companies operating outside the relevant market. It is not by accident that in recent years steel companies have acquired oil companies, or that tobacco companies have merged with soft drink manufacturers. Rather, such acquisitions are one effect of a law enforcement mechanism that combines premerger notification with a narrow set of merger guidelines—the firm that typically steps forward when a previously announced merger falls through due to antitrust concerns is one that represents no overlapping markets.[29]

It is conceivable, of course, that the benefits of premerger notification in terms of improved law enforcement are sufficient to offset the associated costs. The hypothesis that the HSR process has improved merger case selection by the Antitrust Division and the FTC has been tested. The findings suggest no such improvement. Indeed, the benefits to *competitors* of merger law enforcement were found to be more significant after the implementation of premerger notification than before. In short, "the additional enforcement powers granted under the HSR Act apparently have not led the agencies to pick cases better."[30]

To summarize, the power residing in the Clayton Act to prevent mergers between firms where they would tend to create a monopoly is also a power that can be used to prevent mergers that will make life uncomfortable for rivals by promising to generate substantial cost savings. The interest-group theory teaches us that whenever a government policy process can be mobilized to benefit one group selectively at the expense of another there will be strategic use of that policy by the prospective beneficiaries. Thus, the pursuit of wealth transfers (or the defense of existing wealth) through the law on mergers simply reflects rational, self-interest–seeking behavior under given circumstances. And, whether the merger law was designed purposely with transfer seeking in mind or, instead, such behavior is merely an unintended by-product of a policy meant to promote consumer welfare is basically irrelevant. The bottom line is that actual law enforcement efforts have served primarily to redistribute wealth, not enhance it. The evidence from a large number of merger case studies, with their aberrant market definitions and *de minimus* market shares, and from systematic analyses of the capital market effects of merger law enforcement suggest strongly that competitors, not consumers, are the principal beneficiaries of the statutory provisions and administrative procedures of the law on mergers.

THE LAW ON PRICE DISCRIMINATION

Section 2 of the Clayton Act, as amended in 1936 by the Robinson-Patman Act, is held in disrepute by virtually all antitrust scholars.[31] In addition to the fact that it prohibits differences in price that might strengthen competitive forces along with those that might be injurious, the law itself is exceedingly difficult to interpret. Moreover, the burden of proof rests entirely with the firm charged with unlawful price discrimination. The act of selling the same commodity at different prices to different customers is presumptively illegal unless the seller can show that price discrimination is justified by actual differences in the cost of supplying different buyers, by the necessity of meeting an equally low price of a competitor, or by the need to dispose of obsolete or perishable goods.

More importantly, Section 2 of the Clayton Act strikes at a business practice that on the whole tends to increase allocative efficiency (improve consumer welfare).[32] That is, it is well established that even though some customers may be made worse off on account of having to pay higher prices while others gain from a reduction in price, on balance price discrimination is more likely to increase total output than to reduce it. Thus, compared to simple monopoly pricing, the introduction of price discrimination improves social welfare by mitigating allocative inefficiency. As such, the generally hostile attitude of public policy toward price discrimination cannot be justified on efficiency grounds. It is certainly true that some degree of market power is necessary for price discrimination to be a feasible business strategy, but condemning the practice of selling the same commodity at different prices to different customers solely on the basis that such a pricing policy would not be possible in a perfectly competitive market overlooks the more critical fact that moving from simple monopoly to discriminating monopoly typically improves the allocation of society's scarce resources.

If the promotion of allocative efficiency cannot explain the Clayton Act's stated goal of eliminating the practice of price discrimination, one must look to distributional effects for a possible rationale. As we have just seen, even when price discrimination leads to an increase in total output over and above the quantity produced under simple monopoly pricing, it creates winners and losers among the class of customers who buy goods at discriminatory prices. Compared with a policy of charging the same price to all buyers, price discrimination redistributes wealth from customers who pay higher prices to those whose prices are reduced. Similarly, rivals who sell in the discriminating firm's lower-priced market face increased competitive pressures as a result of the introduction of this pricing strategy. Thus, one interpretation of the law on price discrimination is that it provides a mechanism whereby the groups that are disadvantaged on account of the redistributive effects of price discrimination can avoid expropriation of their wealth. In short, self-interests and not the public interest may explain the emergence and enforcement of a policy that condemns a business practice that more often than not improves social welfare.

Indeed, the evidence concerning the interest-group basis of the law on price discrimination is virtually definitive. Price discrimination was initially made illegal with passage of the Clayton Act in 1914.[33] But, while the Federal Trade Commission instituted a fairly large number of Section 2 cases early on (one hundred such matters had been prosecuted by the end of 1919),[34] the proscription on price discrimination became a dead letter during the Roaring Twenties. The commission's inability to enforce Section 2 arose from two factors. First, the courts interpreted the law to be concerned mainly with the possible adverse effects of price discrimination on sellers, so-called "primary-line" injury. Indeed, the original intent of Section 2 was to prevent "financially powerful corporations" from using local price-cutting tactics to impair the competitive positions of their smaller rivals.[35] The "secondary-line" injury suffered by buyers who paid higher prices on account of discrimination did not come within the statute's protection until late in the game.[36] Secondly, simple quantity discounts were held not to represent an unlawful form of price discrimination under the original language of Section 2. Defendants naturally availed themselves of this loophole frequently.[37]

At the same time, a revolution was taking place in the distributive trades, particularly so within the grocery business.[38] As early as the late 1850s, chain store systems had begun to replace the traditional method of distributing goods from manufacturer to wholesaler to retailer. The chains were able to achieve substantial economies by integrating the wholesale and retail functions, and their development put great economic pressure on smaller, independent retailers and the wholesalers, brokers, and middlemen who found themselves bypassed by the new operations. In the grocery business, chains like the Great Atlantic and Pacific Tea Company accounted for almost one-third of retail sales nationwide by 1929. Chains made similar strides in other retail fields during the early twentieth century. The first few decades of the 1900s saw the expansion of large chains in apparel (J.C. Penney), drugs (Walgreen), variety (F.W. Woolworth), and department stores (Montgomery Ward).

The established independent wholesalers and retailers fought this development, first, by lobbying for special taxes. During the late 1920s and throughout the 1930s, 28 states passed legislation that provided for graduated annual license fees to be imposed on chain stores.[39] These fees typically started out low, and then increased rapidly as additional stores were added to the chain within a state. Montana's top marginal tax rate of $30 per store, for example, was reached on the eleventh store; the top rate in Texas ($750 per store) was reached on the fifty-first store. That these taxes were punitive in some instances is illustrated by the fact that in 1935, the average annual net profit per store for grocery chains was only $950.[40]

On another front, the Great Depression introduced the National Recovery Administration's (NRA) "Codes of Fair Competition" to the wholesale and retail trades. These codes were designed to limit price competition in a variety of industries under the guise of ridding the economy of the "exploiter of labor" and the "unscrupulous price-cutter."[41] In the drug trade, independent druggists lobbied for state "fair trade" laws authorizing manufacturers to impose minimum resale prices on retailers. (To the extent that the specified minimum retail prices were above those charged by the chains, such laws would tend to eliminate the chains' price advantage.) The National Association of Retail Druggists drafted a model resale price maintenance statute that was adopted in 20 states. Forty-five states eventually passed some sort of fair trade legislation; resale price maintenance imposed by manufacturers under state legal authority was exempted from the antitrust laws in 1937 by the Miller-Tydings Act.[42]

When the NRA codes were declared unconstitutional in 1935, the independent wholesalers and retailers turned immediately to their champion, Representative Wright Patman of Texas, who declared that "there is no place for chain stores in the American system."[43] His bill strengthening Section 2's proscription on price discrimination was introduced on June 11, 1935. (The original bill was actually drafted by an attorney employed by the Wholesale Grocers Association.) A modified version, co-sponsored by Senator Robinson, was enacted the following year.

Evidence from the capital market suggests that passage of the Robinson-Patman Act itself and subsequent enforcement efforts by the Federal Trade Commission have had an important and sizable impact on chains, brokers, and other middlemen.[44] The law was particularly damaging to grocery chains. Publicly traded chain stores as a group suffered a 58 percent decline in equity value relative to the market as a whole over the 31-month period running from June 1935 through December 1937. The six largest grocery chains had earned average after-tax profits of 8.1 percent in 1936; this figure fell to 3.5 percent in 1937. As mentioned earlier, chains accounted for nearly one-third of total retail grocery sales nationwide by 1929. Their market share reached 44 percent in 1933, but as a result of the chain tax movement and Robinson-Patman, independent grocers prospered to the extent that the chains' share declined to 36.7 percent in 1939. Grocery chains still only accounted for 37 percent of national sales in 1948.

The chains lost ground to independent retailers in other fields as well. Their share of total national retail sales (including groceries) was 37 percent in 1933; it was 22.8 percent in 1939, and 22.3 percent in 1948. By contrast, independent food brokers did quite well in the years immediately following passage of the Robinson-Patman Act. Food brokers' commissions had fallen by 39 percent between 1929 and 1935. Between 1935 and 1939, however, their commissions grew by 50 percent—a rate double that of the growth in total retail food sales and more than seven times that of grocery wholesalers' commissions over the same period. The brokers experienced gains totalling $7.1 million, or 19 percent of their total commissions, in 1939 alone.[45]

The FTC's enforcement efforts under Section 2 of the Clayton Act have continued to have an adverse impact on the owners of firms charged with price discrimination violations. The targets of FTC complaints in a sample of Robinson-Patman cases instituted between August 1962 and April 1981 suffered declines in equity value ranging from 2 percent to 9 percent depending on whether the matter went to a hearing before an administrative law judge or was settled by a consent agreement. Interestingly, the size of the negative impact on the wealth of the owners of firms charged with Section 2 violations appears to be independent of the ultimate resolution of the case. Firms against whom the complaints are dismissed fare as badly in the capital market as those which are found guilty of unlawful price discrimination.[46]

In short, the law on price discrimination has a clear private interest basis. The Robinson-Patman Act emerged in 1936 as the principal weapon of wholesalers and independent retailers in their attempt to halt the expansion of larger, more efficient chain store operations. Although the law did not achieve this ultimate goal, it certainly has imposed millions of dollars of losses on retail chains and other business enterprises. Moreover, to the extent that the Robinson-Patman Act has been successful in preventing economies in the distribution of goods from being passed on in the form of lower prices, even larger costs have been imposed on consumers.

Section 2 of the Clayton Act was originally aimed at preventing financially powerful corporations from using local price-cutting tactics to impair the competitive positions of their smaller rivals. The fear was that price discrimination could be used by a firm in a conscious attempt to drive its competitors in a specific geographic area out of business with the object of gaining a monopoly there, which could then be used to restrict output and raise price. Pricing tactics of this sort are known as *predatory pricing*.

Predatory pricing exists when a firm sells at a price below marginal production cost with the express purpose of driving a competitor out of business.[47] If the predator can force a rival to sell below cost, the prey will eventually go bankrupt and exit the industry. As result, the predator secures additional market power which can then be exploited to raise price above the competitive level.

An inconsistency in this scenario is immediately apparent, however. The predatory price war continues until one or more of the predator's rivals have exited the industry. In the next period, the successful predator raises price above marginal cost to begin recouping its earlier losses. But, under the assumption that the predator's rivals, both actual and potential, are equally efficient (have access to the same cost function),[48] any attempt to raise price above marginal cost at this point will invite entry. An outsider knows, of course, that if it enters and the incumbent resumes predation, it would be better not to enter. On the other hand, the potential entrant also knows that if it does enter the incumbent will be better off (will incur smaller losses) by not predating. Thus, it is rational for the outsider to enter and for the incumbent not to predate. But, if entry is rational and predation is irrational in the period following the price war, the same must be true in every previous period. By backward induction at each stage, predation does not pay.[49] In short, the only way that a predator can injure a competitor is to expand its own output so as to take sales away from the prey at the predatory price. It follows that the predator will incur larger losses during the price war than will the firm it hopes to bankrupt.

Thus, while it is certainly true that firms often engage in selective price cutting for a number of reasons, including promotional campaigns to expand sales in a given location, to introduce a new product, or to hold on to an established market position against an aggressive newcomer, using such tactics to gain or maintain a monopoly is self-defeating. Of course, in discussing the origins of the Robinson-Patman Act we have already seen why it might be rational for firms—particularly high-cost, inefficient firms—to complain of predatory pricing and price discrimination on the part of their rivals. They may be able to win in the courts a competitive advantage that they cannot possibly win in the marketplace. What better victory could there be than to have a judicial decree entered against a "predator" to "stop competing, leave your competitors alone, raise your prices?"[50] At worst, even an unsuccessful complaint will impose a capital loss on the rival for the reason that the cost defense permitted by the law is "impossible."[51]

Almost all respectable scholarship concludes that the Robinson-Patman Act is "mistaken in its assumptions and further deformed in its application."[52] But, while enforcement efforts have declined in recent years, price discrimination complaints continue to be issued despite repeated calls for repeal of Section 2.[53] This state of affairs strongly suggests that the Robinson-Patman Act exists solely to facilitate transfer seeking. The law on price discrimination is perhaps the leading example of the argument that antitrust serves private interests, and not the public interests.

THE LAW ON VERTICAL RESTRAINTS OF TRADE

What Oliver Williamson refers to as "nonstandard" business practices—customer and territorial restrictions, tie-in sales, block booking, franchising, vertical ownership integration, and so on—are just beginning to emerge from a long period of inhospitable treatment during which economists and the courts held them to be presumptively anticompetitive.[54] The conventional wisdom invoked monopoly explanations like leverage, market foreclosure, and price discrimination to suggest that rivals, distributors, or customers were injured when nonstandard contracting was employed. This approach was based largely on comparisons with the theoretical model of perfect competition where no such extra-firm restraints are necessary to mediate market exchanges. That view was in turn supported by the belief that all transaction economies are purely technological in nature and can therefore be fully realized within the firm.[55] Hence, Ronald Coase's famous observation that "if an economist finds something—a business practice of one sort or another—that he does not understand, he looks for a monopoly explanation."[56]

The revolution in economic and judicial thinking about nonstandard contracting is far from complete, however. On the one hand, vertical ownership integration through merger of buyer and seller is now rarely held to have anticompetitive purposes and effects. Of late, such mergers are even more rarely challenged in the courts. For example, only 13 of the 119 government merger complaints involving vertical charges issued between 1952 and 1980 were brought after 1970. Indeed, just two mergers that involved only vertical issues were challenged by the antitrust authorities between 1970 and 1980.[57] On the other hand, vertical contracting between buyer and seller which stops short of ownership integration is treated idiosyncratically. Vertical *price* restraints like resale price maintenance, where a manufacturer places limits on the wholesale or retail price of its product, are illegal per se under antitrust laws.[58] This was not always so, however. Between passage of the Miller-Tydings Act in 1937 and its repeal in March 1976, firms operating in states that enacted "fair trade" laws permitting the setting of minimum resale prices were exempt from prosecution under the Sherman Act. (A similar exemption was granted under the Federal Trade Commission Act by the McGuire Fair Act Amendment of 1952; it too was repealed effective March 1976.) By contrast, *nonprice* vertical restraints are generally not presumptively unlawful, but there are exceptions. For example, customer and territorial restrictions, which had long been illegal per se,[59] were held subject to a rule of reason analysis and, in fact, unobjectionable for the case at hand in the *Sylvania* decision.[60] Tying arrangements continue to labor under judicial opprobrium, however.[61]

The inconsistencies in the treatment accorded vertical restraints in the courts reflect the fact that there is as yet no unifying economic theory that serves to explain the purposes and effects of these various business practices. Some general statements about the law and economics of vertical contracting can nevertheless be made at this point. First, economists are beginning to recognize that in many cases, if not all, vertical agreements between buyers and sellers are a *sub-*

stitute for ownership integration. When such a relationship obtains, nonstandard business practices are unlikely to have pernicious effects on competition; indeed, they would be expected to entail the same efficiency consequences now normally attributed to vertical integration. Secondly, because of the mounting evidence suggesting that vertical contracting can have competitive purposes and effects, a policy of per se illegality for these practices can no longer be justified. Although subjecting all buyer-seller agreements to a rule of reason standard might raise the uncertainty and cost of litigation over these issues and increase the incidence of anticompetitive uses of such restraints, far fewer competitive uses of these business practices would be deterred. In a recent study of a large sample of private and government antitrust cases that alleged unlawful resale price maintenance between 1976 and 1982, for example, anticompetitive theories could account for no more than 15 percent of all the cases, and for an even smaller proportion of the private cases.[62] Moreover, even when the use of vertical contracting has the potential for reducing allocative efficiency (for example, resale price maintenance might aid in the enforcement of a collusive price-fixing agreement among manufacturers), it is the underlying market power at the upstream production stage, and not the restriction imposed by sellers on buyers in and of itself, that forms the basis for restraint of trade. The majority of these collusion-type cases can therefore be attacked under existing horizontal price-fixing doctrine. Finally, adopting a uniform policy toward vertical contracts would remove the unfounded legal distinction between price and nonprice restraints. As Judge Bork has observed, "precisely the same analysis may be applied to all vertical restraints."[63] If one of them can be subject to a rule of reason, they all may be.

Because all contractual relationships between buyer and seller can be analyzed in the same way, one example is sufficient to illustrate how the antitrust law in this area can be used for transfer-seeking purposes. Consider the case of exclusive territories and franchise contracts. The assignment by manufacturers of exclusive geographic territories to individual wholesale or retail dealers is a prevalent feature of modern marketing and distribution systems. This practice is employed in the distribution of a variety of goods and services, including automobiles, newspapers, televisions, "fast food," and professional sports. In most of these situations, the manufacturer or franchisor typically promises the downstream firms that no other dealer will be authorized to locate within the specified territory. For example, the relevant clause in the contracts between the White Motor Company and its authorized dealers stated that

> Distributor is hereby granted the exclusive right, except as
> hereinafter provided, to sell during the life of this agreement, in
> the territory described below, White and Auto Car Trucks pur-
> chased from company hereunder.... Distributor agrees to
> develop the aforementioned territory to the satisfaction of Com-
> pany, and not to sell any trucks purchased hereunder except in
> accordance with this agreement, and not to sell such trucks except
> to individuals, firms, or corporations having a place of business
> and/or purchasing headquarters in said territory.[64]

In return, the franchisee or authorized dealer typically agrees to
follow a standardized business operation plan, to purchase certain
inputs only from the franchisor or designated suppliers, to pay royalty
fees for use of the franchisor's brand name, and so on.

Territorial limitations basically insulate dealers from competition
with one another. *Intrabrand* competition is reduced insofar as each
dealer is granted some local monopoly power with respect to that
brand. It was primarily for this reason that, after initially expressing
a willingness to consider the effects of these limitations on a rule of
reason basis in *White Motor*, the Supreme Court reversed itself and
declared territorial restraints illegal per se.[65] As we shall soon see,
however, there is reason to believe that the reduction in competition
among the distributors of a given manufacturer's product which
accompanies a system of exclusive territories helps promote competition between them and the distributors of other manufacturers'
products, that is, reduced intrabrand competition increases *interbrand*
competition. In recognition of this possibility, a subsequent reversal
of *Schwinn* returned territorial restrictions to a rule of reason standard.[66]

Why should manufacturers want exclusive territories? The basic
answer is that territorial limitations are imposed on downstream firms
for many of the same reasons that provide a motive for forward
ownership integration. Manufacturers have an important stake in the
activities of the distributors of their products. The assignment of
exclusive territories offers a contractual alternative to ownership integration that, under certain circumstances, will be the low-cost
method of assuring that the performance of downstream firms is in
the manufacturer's best interest.

The anticompetitive theories of vertical territorial restraints can be
readily dismissed. First, like forward integration, the manufacturer's
designation of exclusive territories for its dealers cannot increase or
extend horizontal monopoly power from the upstream to the
downstream industry. Indeed, territorial limitations represent something of a paradox in this regard. An input monopolist has a strong

interest in promoting competition downstream. This is because the existence of an additional output restriction at the retail level will lower the derived demand for the manufacturer's product and prevent the manufacturer from fully maximizing its profits. Hence, successive monopoly—monopoly at both the upstream and downstream stages—generates a motive for vertical ownership integration which leads to an expansion in final product output and a reduction in final product price. With exclusive territories, however, we have a situation wherein the upstream firm purposely confers local market power on its dealers. Because this action by itself will tend to reduce the manufacturer's profits, it must be the case that territorial restrictions create offsetting benefits in the form of lower transactions costs that make the arrangement economical.

For this reason, and despite the fact that assigning buyers to sellers is an obvious and low-cost method of eliminating secret price cutting,[67] it is highly unlikely that vertical territorial restraints will be employed to support the operation of a manufacturers' cartel. By reducing profits upstream, exclusive territories would frustrate the very purpose of collusion. Similarly, manufacturers would not willingly impose territorial restraints for the purpose of supporting a dealers' cartel. For such a strategy to be profitable downstream, the collusive agreement must include the distributors of all (or most) of the brands of the product in question, an unlikely event in view of the ease of entry into retailing. In short, the use of exclusive territories to reduce competition at either the manufacturer or retail level is highly problematic.

To reiterate, territorial limitations are motivated by many of the same forces that provide an incentive for vertical integration. In contracting with its dealers, the manufacturer agrees to protect each from competition with the others. The promise of local monopoly power (and profits) generates an excess supply of applicants for the dealership rights in each territory. As a result, the manufacturer can afford to screen the candidates, examining their financial records, credit histories, prior business experience, and so on for the purpose of selecting the individual who will most likely maintain some specified level of performance. This selection process is critical because the ultimate value of the manufacturer's product will depend in large part upon the subsequent ability of these distributors to supply pre- and post-sale services, to engage in local promotional activities, to employ pleasant and knowledgeable sales personnel, to maintain an attractive place of business, in short, to be the manufacturer's agent in the retail marketplace. The importance of these considerations can be seen clearly in the case of franchise contracts. There, although the franchisor also typically engages in market research to select the optimal franchise location, helps finance the construction of the retail outlet, and provides the franchisee with a standardized business operation plan, the primary item supplied to the franchisee is the franchisor's trademark. Because the trademark serves as a signal of quality to consumers, the franchisor has a crucial stake in the performance of its distributors. Their actions will have a direct impact on the franchisor's reputation and, hence, on the market value of the licensed trademark.[68]

Although all parties have an interest in maintaining a reputation for quality, each individual distributor has an incentive to cut costs and allow the quality of its own operation to decline. As long as all other distributors hold their standards at the level expected by consumers, the cheater can increase its profits in the short run by free riding on the reputations of the others. Obviously, if one dealer has this incentive, they all do. It is for this reason that exclusive territory contracts typically contain an elaborate system of controls for mitigating the free-rider problem and other agency costs associated with the structure of the manufacturer-dealer relationship.

One way for the manufacturer to assure some specified standard of performance is to require each distributor to pay a nonrefundable, lump sum fee for the exclusive territorial right. If the manufacturer can terminate dealers for nonperformance, the lump sum payment serves as a forfeitable bond which the distributor posts to guarantee noncheating behavior. Other contractual provisions in this regard may include a requirement that the dealer purchase some of its complementary inputs directly from the manufacturer or from a list of authorized suppliers, and a system of royalties in which the dealer agrees to pay a fixed percentage of its profits to the manufacturer. In the former case, the manufacturer gains a greater degree of control over the quality of the downstream product. Output royalties are often used in conjunction with lump sum entry fees when uncertainty about final product demand prevents the manufacturer from fully capitalizing the profits inherent in the local dealer monopoly upfront.[69] Generally speaking, the lump sum entry fee, the royalty payments, the wholesale price of the manufacturer's product, and the prices of any complementary inputs purchased from the manufacturer will be structured in such a way that each dealer earns only a competitive rate of return on his or her investment. The assignment of exclusive territories is a way for the manufacturer to guarantee that one dealer's profits will not be eroded by competition from others. The manufacturer cannot, of course, insulate its dealers from the competition of dealers in the products of other manufacturers, but it can guarantee not to opportunistically locate another of its own distributors within the specified territory.

As we have mentioned, however, each individual dealer has an incentive to behave opportunistically once the upfront investments have been made that establish the dealership as going concern. Because both parties are "locked into" their relationship to a significant degree, the manufacturer is vulnerable to exploitation by its dealer.[70] The manufacturer cannot turn to alternative downstream outlets without incurring substantial costs. The incumbent dealer will have to be terminated, contracts renegotiated, and so on, during which time sales and reputational capital may be lost. The existence of such transaction costs provides the dealer with an opportunity to obtain more favorable contractual terms than had been agreed to initially. That is, the owner of an authorized dealership can expropriate from the manufacturer wealth equal to the cost that would be incurred in switching to an alternative dealer.[71]

The dealer can press for lower prices on inputs purchased from the manufacturer, for lower royalty payments, for a larger exclusive territory, and so forth, all of which would tend to increase his or her own profits at the expense of the manufacturer. Renegotiating the original contract is costly for the dealer as well as for the manufacturer, however, and the manufacturer of course has a strong incentive not to cave in to the dealer's demands. Under such circumstances, antitrust offers an economical method by which the dealer can expropriate wealth from the manufacturer. In particular, rather than bearing the cost of contract renegotiation, the dealer can attempt to void certain contract provisions by complaining that they constitute antitrust law violations. In this way, litigation costs can be shifted to the public law enforcement agencies and if the government's prosecution is successful, which it is especially likely to be when the complaint involves a per se illegal vertical restraint of trade like tie-in sales or requirements contracts, the dealer will win release from contractual terms that the manufacturer was unwilling to revise.

Similar considerations apply in situations where a manufacturer terminates one of its dealers for failure to perform. The dealer can respond by suing for breach of contract if the manufacturer's reasons for termination are unfounded. Alternatively, the dealer can complain that the contract at issue is unlawful by reason of provisions that illegally restrain trade in violation of the antitrust laws. By taking the latter course, the dealer may be able to extract monetary damages from the manufacturer even if he or she ultimately loses the franchise.

Evidence that the antitrust laws are widely used to this effect is provided by a recent study that examined a large sample of private and government cases that alleged unlawful resale maintenance (RPM) between 1976 and 1982.[72] Eighty-seven percent of the private RPM cases that went to trial over this period were initiated by dealers against their own distributors or manufacturers (and most of these by terminated dealers). Although the success rate of the plaintiffs was low—plaintiffs won only 28 percent of the court verdicts in the sample—the evidence also indicated that approximately 70 percent of the complaints filed were settled out of court. This suggests that the defendants acceded at least partially to the plaintiffs' demands in order to avoid the expense of trial. More importantly, however, the author of the study concluded that "based on a reading of the substance of the disputes, many private RPM cases appear to be essentially contract disputes recast as antitrust cases and embellished with a variety of antitrust charges."[73]

To summarize, the power residing in the antitrust laws to declare illegal certain business practices thought to be anticompetitive is also a power that can be used to subvert the competitive process. We have discussed three areas of the law that stand out as particularly good examples of the selective benefits available through antitrust processes. We have seen how the law on mergers can be used to block acquisitions that will make life uncomfortable for rivals by promising to generate cost savings, how the law on price discrimination can be used against a competitor that by virtue of superior efficiency is able to offer lower prices to consumers, and how the law on vertical restraints of trade can be used by buyers to resolve contract disputes with sellers. Although the survey was far from complete, it is sufficient to establish that certain firms and industries stand to gain more (or lose less) than others from an actively enforced antitrust policy. These prospective benefits provide an incentive to "invest" in antitrust as a way of securing competitive advantages over rivals and, moreover, such investment decisions are no different from any other capital-budgeting problem confronted by a firm. Whether or not antitrust processes will be used in this way, as, in fact, a substantial amount of empirical evidence suggests they have, is simply a matter of selecting the investment opportunity that offers that highest expected rate of return.

NOTES

1. That policy failures are the norm in antitrust is a main theme of Robert H. Bork, *The Antitrust Paradox: A Policy at War with Itself* (New York: Basic Books, 1978).

2. See Oliver E. Williamson, "Economies as an Antitrust Defense Revisited," *University of Pennsylvania Law Review* 125 (April 1977), pp. 699–736, which expands upon and corrects Oliver E. Williamson, "Economies as an Antitrust

Defense: The Welfare Tradeoffs," *American Economic Review* 58 (March 1968), pp. 18–36.

3. 26 Stat. 290 (1890), as amended, 15 U.S.C.A. Sections 1–2 (1980). The penalty provisions were changed substantially in 1974 (88 Stat. 1708). Prior to that time, Sherman Act violations were considered to be misdemeanors, and no distinction was made between individuals and corporations. Guilty parties were initially subject to a maximum prison sentence of one year and a $5000 fine, which was raised to $50,000 in 1955 (69 Stat. 282).

4. Richard A. Posner, "A Statistical Study of Antitrust Law Enforcement," *Journal of Law and Economics* 13 (October 1970), p. 366.

5. *U.S. v. E.C. Knight Co.*, 156 U.S. 1 (1895). This interpretation was overturned four years later when Judge Taft declared the manufacture of cast iron pipes to affect commerce. See *U.S. v. Addyston Pipe & Steel Co.*, 85 F. 271 (6th Cir. 1898).

6. In *American Banana Co. v. United Fruit Co.*, 213 U.S. 347 (1909), plaintiff American Banana complained that United Fruit had undertaken predatory acts (including destruction of property) in Central America to preserve its domination of banana exports to the United States.

7. *Swift & Co. v. U.S.*, 196 U.S. 375 (1905).

8. *Standard Oil Co. v. U.S.*, 221 U.S. 1 (1911).

9. *U.S. v. American Tobacco Co.*, 221 U.S. 106 (1911).

10. A.D. Neale and D.G. Goyder, *The Antitrust Laws of the U.S.A.: A Study of Competition Enforced by Law*, 3rd ed. (Cambridge, UK: Cambridge University Press, 1980), pp. 181–82.

11. 38 Stat. 730 (1914), as amended, 15 U.S.C.A. Sections 12–27 (1980).

12. A representative, though much later, case is *U.S. v. Celenese Corp. of America*, 91 F. Supp. 14 (S.D.N.Y. 1950).

13. *Swift & Co. v. FTC*, 272 U.S. 554 (1926).

14. The leading precedents are *U.S. v. Columbia Steel Co.*, 334 U.S. 495 (1948), a pre-1950 Section 7 case that established "percentage command of a market" as a crucial element of merger analysis; *U.S. v. E.I. du Pont de Nemours & Co.*, 351 U.S. 377 (1966), which created a "reasonable interchangeability" standard for defining relevant markets that stressed the availability of alternative commodities for buyers; and *Brown Shoe Co. v. U.S.*, 370 U.S. 294 (1962), which enumerated "practical indicia," like the product's peculiar characteristics and uses, unique production facilities, distinct customers, and distinct prices, for drawing the boundaries of relevant antitrust markets.

15. Franklin M. Fisher, "Horizontal Mergers: Triage and Treatment," *Journal of Economic Perspectives* 1 (Fall 1987), p. 23.

16. U.S. Department of Justice Merger Guidelines, *Trade Regulation Reporter* 1 (May 1968), par. 4510. Revisions to the guidelines were issued as U.S. Department of Justice Merger Guidelines, 14 June 1982; the guidelines were revised again in 1984.

17. An even more basic issue is whether the merger guidelines are really guidelines at all. One study has shown that about 21 percent of the merger cases brought under the 1968 guidelines fell *below* the announced market share and market concentration thresholds. Almost none of these below-guidelines matters could be explained by the exceptions to the numerical criteria provided in the

Justice Department's merger enforcement policy statement. The author of the study concluded that "the guidelines have not been a reliable signal of the enforcement policies of either the Antitrust Division or the Federal Trade Commission." See Robert A. Rogowsky, "The Justice Department's Merger Guidelines: A Study in the Application of the Rule," in Richard O. Zerbe, Jr., ed., *Research in Law and Economics*, vol.6 (Greenwich, CT: JAI Press, 1984), pp. 135–66.

18. Franklin M. Fisher, "Diagnosing Monopoly," *Quarterly Review of Economics and Business* 19 (Summer 1979), pp. 7–33.

19. Rogowsky, "Justice Department's Merger Guidelines," pp. 155 and 166.

20. The case involved McCormick & Company's attempt to purchase the assets of Spice Islands, a competitor in the spice and seasonings business. According to one food industry source, the difference between "gourmet" and regular spices "is that one comes in a fancy bottle and is sold in upscale stores, and the other is sold in cans at your local Safeway." See Warren Brown, "Faced with Lawsuit, McCormick Drops Bid for Spice Islands," *Washington Post*, May 24, 1988, p. C1.

21. See Malcolm B. Coate, Richard S. Higgins, and Fred S. McChesney, "Bureaucracy and Politics in FTC Merger Challenges," Center for Policy Studies Working Paper No. 48, Clemson University, November 1988, and the discussion in later chapters, especially 4, 5, and 7.

22. B. Espen Eckbo, "Horizontal Mergers, Collusion, and Stockholder Wealth," *Journal of Financial Economics* 11 (1983), pp. 241–73; Robert Stillman, "Examining Anti-Trust Policy Towards Horizontal Mergers," *Journal of Financial Economics* 11 (1983), pp. 225–40; and B. Espen Eckbo and Peggy Wier, "Antimerger Policy Under the Hart-Scott-Rodino Act: A Reexamination of the Market Power Hypothesis," *Journal of Law and Economics* 28 (April 1985), pp. 119–49.

23. Eckbo and Wier, "Antimerger Policy Under the Hart-Scott-Rodino Act."

24. Ibid., p. 121.

25. Gregg A. Jarrell, "The Wealth Effects of Litigation by Targets: Do Interests Diverge in a Merge?," *Journal of Law and Economics* 27 (April 1985), pp. 151–77.

26. For a good discussion of the practical difficulties of requiring ex post divestiture as compared with ex ante prohibition of mergers, see Richard A. Posner, *Antitrust Law: An Economic Perspective* (Chicago, IL: University of Chicago Press, 1976), pp. 78–95.

27. The notification requirements actually took effect on September 5, 1978, with the publication of Premerger Notification Rules, *Federal Register* 43 (1978), pp. 33–450.

28. In this regard, premerger notification is likely to generate adverse capital market effects similar to those associated with the disclosure requirements imposed on cash takeover bids by the Williams Act. See Gregg A. Jarrell and Michael Bradley, "The Economic Effects of Federal and State Regulation of Cash Tender Offers," *Journal of Law and Economics* 23 (April 1980), pp. 371–407.

29. There is an even more direct cost of premerger notification in that the burden of complying with "second requests" can be immense. For example, in responding to the FTC's subpoena concerning Kohlberg Kravis Roberts (KKR) & Company's acquisition of RJR Nabisco, KKR's attorneys amassed 680 cartons

of company documents. In order to meet the FTC's submission deadline for this quantity of materials, which required the services of 150 lawyers to assemble, the law firm "discovered that the cheapest way to get everything there was to rent a DC-9." See "For Further Details, See Carton No. 587," *Wall Street Journal*, March 15, 1989, p. B1.

30. Eckbo and Wier, "Antimerger Policy Under the Hart-Scott-Rodino Act," p. 121.

31. See, for example, Bork, *Antitrust Paradox*, pp. 382–401, and Richard A. Posner, *The Robinson-Patman Act: Federal Regulation of Price Differences* (Washington, DC: American Enterprise Institute, 1976).

32. Joan Robinson, *The Economics of Imperfect Competition*, 2d ed. (London: Macmillan, 1969), p. 203.

33. Section 2 of the Clayton Act made price discrimination an antitrust offense. Railroad rate discrimination (paying rebates to "favored" shippers and discriminating among commodities and places) had been outlawed in 1887 by the Interstate Commerce Act. See Clair Wilcox, *Public Policies Toward Business*, 3d ed. (Homewood, IL: Richard D. Irwin, 1966), pp. 389–90

34. Posner, "Statistical Study of Antitrust Enforcement," p. 370.

35. Phillip Areeda, *Antitrust Analysis: Problems, Text, Cases*, 3d ed. (Boston, MA: Little, Brown, 1981), p. 1061.

36. *George Van Camp & Sons Co. v. American Can Co.*, 278 U.S. 245 (1929).

37. *Goodyear Tire & Rubber Co. v. FTC*, 101 F.2d 620 (6th Cir.), cert. denied, 308 U.S. 557 (1939). Although this decision was rendered after passage of the Robinson-Patman Act, the case was initiated under the original language of Section 2.

38. The following discussion is based upon Thomas W. Ross, "Winners and Losers under the Robinson-Patman Act," *Journal of Law and Economics* 27 (October 1984), pp. 243–71.

39. Thomas W. Ross, "Store Wars: The Chain Tax Movement," *Journal of Law and Economics* 29 (April 1986), pp. 125–37.

40. Ibid., pp. 126–27.

41. Ellis W. Hawley, *The New Deal and the Problem of Monopoly: A Study in Economic Ambivalence* (Princeton, NJ: Princeton University Press, 1966), p. 19.

42. Ross, "Winners and Losers under the Robinson-Patman Act," p. 248.

43. Ibid., p. 249.

44. Ibid., p. 252–71.

45. Ibid., p. 258.

46. Ibid., p. 271.

47. Phillip Areeda and Donald F. Turner, "Predatory Pricing and Related Practices under Section 2 of the Sherman Act," *Harvard Law Review* 88 (February 1975), pp. 697–733.

48. This is the only case in which predation makes sense. Setting price below cost is unnecessary if rivals are less efficient, and illogical if rivals are more efficient.

49. R. Mark Issac and Vernon L. Smith, "In Search of Predatory Pricing," *Journal of Political Economy* 93 (April 1985), p. 342.

50. James C. Miller III and Paul A. Pautler, "Predation: The Changing View in Economics and the Law," *Journal of Law and Economics* 28 (May 1985), p. 498.

51. Posner, *Robinson-Patman Act*, p. 30.

52. Bork, *Antitrust Paradox*, p. 384.

53. In December 1988, the FTC issued a Robinson-Patman complaint against six major book publishers, charging them with offering discriminatory discounts to several large retail bookstore chains. See Monica Langley, "FTC Charges Six Publishers with Price Bias," *Wall Street Journal*, December 23, 1988, p. B4.

54. Oliver E. Williamson, *The Economic Institutions of Capitalism: Firms, Markets, Relational Contracting* (New York: The Free Press, 1985), pp. 19–20 and 370–73.

55. Ibid., pp. 370–71.

56. Ronald H. Coase, "Industrial Organization: A Proposal for Research," in Victory R. Fuchs, ed., *Policy Issues and Research Opportunities in Industrial Organization* (Cambridge, MA: National Bureau of Economic Research, 1972), p. 67.

57. Alan A. Fisher and Richard Sciacca, "An Economic Analysis of Vertical Merger Enforcement Policy," in Richard O. Zerbe, Jr., ed., *Research in Law and Economics*, vol. 6 (Greenwich, CT: JAI Press, 1984), p. 59.

58. *Dr. Miles Medical Co. v. John D. Park & Sons Co.*, 220 U.S. 373 (1911).

59. *U.S. v. Arnold Schwinn & Co. et al.*, 388 U.S. 365 (1967).

60. *Continental T.V. Inc. et al. v. GTE Sylvania, Inc.*, 433 U.S. 36 (1977).

61. *Northern Pacific Railway Co. v. U.S.*, 336 U.S. 1 (1958).

62. Pauline M. Ippolito, *Resale Price Maintenance: Economic Evidence from Litigation* (Washington, DC: Federal Trade Commission, 1988).

63. Bork, *Antitrust Paradox*, p. 289.

64. *White Motor Company v. U.S.*, 372 U.S. 253 (1963).

65. *U.S. v. Arnold Schwinn & Co.*, 388 U.S. 365 (1969).

66. *Continental T.V., Inc. v. GTE Sylvania, Inc.*, 433 U.S. 36 (1977).

67. George J. Stigler, "A Theory of Oligopoly," *Journal of Political Economy* 72 (February 1964), pp. 44–61. Secret price cutting is deterred if price reductions can only be offered to the firm's own assigned customers. For cheating to be profitable, the firm must take sales away from other members of the cartel. But the loss of assigned customers will provide an immediate signal that secret price concessions are being offered, helping the cartel to identify and discipline members not adhering to the price-fixing agreement.

68. For an introduction to the literature on franchising that stresses the efficiency aspects of franchise contracts, see Richard E. Caves and William F. Murphy II, "Franchising Firms, Markets, and Intangible Assets," *Southern Economic Journal* 42 (April 1976), pp. 572–86; Paul Rubin, "The Theory of the Firm and the Structure of the Franchise Contract," *Journal of Law and Economics* 21 (April 1978), pp. 223–33; Benjamin Klein, "Transaction Cost Determinants of 'Unfair' Contractual Arrangements," *American Economic Review Papers and Proceedings* 70 (May 1980), pp. 356–62; and Roger D. Blair and David L. Kaserman, "Optimal Franchising," *Southern Economic Journal* 49 (October 1982), pp. 494–505. An opposing view is given by Frederick S. Inaba, "Franchising: Monopoly by Contract," *Southern Economic Journal* 47 (July 1980), pp. 65–72.

69. Blair and Kaserman, "Optimal Franchising."

70. These incentives for opportunistic behavior are symmetric in the sense that the manufacturer can take advantage of its dealers by attempting to obtain more favorable terms (higher royalty payments, higher prices for complementary

inputs, and so on) than had been agreed to initially. However, we focus on dealer opportunism because it appears to be more prevalent empirically. See below.

71. See Benjamin Klein, Robert G. Crawford, and Armen A. Alchian, "Vertical Integration, Appropriable Rents, and the Competitive Contracting Process," *Journal of Law and Economics* 21 (October 1978), pp. 297–326.

72. Ippolito, *Resale Price Maintenance*, pp. 88–89.

73. Ibid., p. 89.

4

The Antitrust Bureaucracy

The public law enforcement agencies—the Antitrust Division of the Department of Justice and the Federal Trade Commission—serve as the agents-in-place of the political representatives who broker antitrust wealth transfers in the economy. Their incentive for doing so derives from the fact that the agencies' operating budgets, power, and prestige are determined directly by the political representatives who have been elected by the various interest groups who have a stake in antitrust policy. That is, given that Congress has authority to appropriate funding for the antitrust agencies, to confirm the president's appointees to policymaking positions, and to exercise oversight responsibilities with respect to their law enforcement activities, the Antitrust Division and the FTC have strong incentives to enforce the antitrust statutes in the way that Congress wants them enforced, regardless of how the resulting enforcement activities comport with the "public interest" in some abstract sense.

In addition, however, because Congress cannot monitor the antitrust bureaucracy costlessly—to do so, agency records must be examined, oversight hearings must be held, and, most importantly, congressional attention must be redirected away from other pressing policy matters—the agencies themselves have some freedom in determining the level and mix of antitrust cases they will institute during any particular period of time. How this discretion will be used depends largely on the private benefits and costs of various possible enforcement activities that are perceived by the rational, self-interest-seeking individuals employed by the antitrust bureaus. This is not to say that all, or even most, of observed antitrust decision making is driven by the private interests of those charged with law enforcement responsibilities. But, given that enforcement resources are scarce, that congressional oversight is imperfect, and that the antitrust agencies must choose at the margin between, say, bringing an extra merger case or issuing one more price discrimination complaint, the private incentives of public prosecutors play a role in explaining actual enforcement decisions.

The influence of private incentives on public decisions to prosecute holds an important lesson for the normative critics of antitrust policy. In particular, "better" antitrust enforcement is not simply a matter of appointing "better" law enforcement personnel. It is not a lack of zeal for promoting consumer welfare, ignorance of economic principles, or other character flaws that are responsible for the antitrust policy failures so often identified and debated in the normative literature. Instead, these "failures" are explained in part as rational responses to the constraints imposed by the organizational structures of the enforcement agencies themselves, the value placed on "visible" case output by upper-level agency officials and Congress, and the rewards offered by private industry and the private antitrust bar for experience in trying cases. Thus, "better" antitrust policy, in whatever sense that phrase may be used, does not require changing the identities of the people charged with implementing it. Effective reform instead requires changing the constraints under which the enforcement bureaus and their employees operate.

THE JUSTICE DEPARTMENT'S ANTITRUST DIVISION

The Antitrust Division of the Department of Justice is headed by an assistant attorney general who has responsibility for overall division policy and reports directly to the attorney general. It resides squarely within the executive branch of government and so the top officials are appointed by and serve at the pleasure of the president.

In recent years, the Antitrust Division's legal staff has been organized into three main subdivisions, each headed by a deputy assistant attorney general. The principal one of these subdivisions responsible for antitrust investigations is further divided into sections according to areas of specialization, which include consumer affairs, energy, foreign commerce, regulated industries, and transportation. In addition, a separate Economic Policy Division advises on the technical aspects of the division's enforcement activities. The division has grown substantially in size over the years. In the early 1980s it employed some 450 lawyers and 45 economists, with a budget approaching $45 million.[1]

Table 4.1 provides some basic information on the budgetary resources available to the Antitrust Division and its enforcement activities through 1981.[2] Generally speaking, the division was relatively quiescent until 1939. Prior to that time it instituted an average of only about eight cases per year; in no year during this early period did it bring more than 23 antitrust complaints. Afterwards, its level of enforcement activity increased by more than five times (to an average of just

Table 4.1 Antitrust Division Budget and Enforcement Activity, 1890–1981

Year	Budget[a] ($000)	Cases	Year	Budget[a] ($000)	Cases	Year	Budget[a] ($000)	Cases
			22	–	17	55	3,148	34
1890	–	1	23	–	8	56	3,396	30
91	–	0	24	–	13	57	3,539	38
92	–	5	25	–	12	58	3,912	47
93	–	1	26	–	9	59	4,131	46
94	–	2	27	–	13	1960	4,500	35
95	–	1	28	–	17	61	5,074	47
96	–	3	29	–	8	62	5,873	56
97	–	2	1930	–	7	63	6,218	26
98	–	0	31	–	3	64	6,599	51
99	–	1	32	204	5	65	7,072	35
1900	–	0	33	150	9	66	7,175	36
01	–	0	34	154	6	67	7,495	34
02	–	3	35	415	4	68	7,820	47
03	–	2	36	420	5	69	8,352	43
04	–	1	37	435	7	1970	10,026	54
05	–	5	38	414	10	71	11,079	43
06	–	14	39	789	31	72	12,268	72
07	–	10	1940	1,309	65	73	12,836	47
08	–	7	41	1,324	71	74	14,790	46
09	–	3	42	2,325	46	75	18,253	39
1910	–	15	43	1,800	22	76	22,239	45
11	–	23	44	1,760	19	77	27,706	40
12	–	20	45	1,540	20	78	32,371	43
13	–	22	46	1,875	37	79	37,508	33
14	–	11	47	2,089	25	1980	43,544	50
15	–	7	48	2,400	44	81	44,862	18
16	–	2	49	3,572	31			
17	–	21	1950	3,750	48			
18	–	10	51	3,750	42			
19	–	3	52	3,421	27			
1920	–	8	53	3,200	18			
21	–	20	54	3,500	24			

Sources: For the 1890-1969 period, the case data are from Richard A. Posner, "A Statistical Study of Antitrust Enforcement," *Journal of Law and Economics* 13 (October 1970), p. 366; they are from Joseph C. Gallo, Joseph L. Craycraft, and Steven C. Bush, "Guess Who Came to Dinner: An Empirical Study of Federal Antitrust Enforcement for the Period 1963-1984," *Review of Industrial Organization* 2 (1985), p. 109, for the remaining years. Appropriations were obtained from the *Budget of the United States Government*, respective years.

[a]Unavailable prior to 1932.

Table 4.2 Classification of Justice Department Antitrust Charges, 1963–84

Nature of Charge	Number	Percent
Horizontal Conspiracy	759	50.0
Monopolizing	83	5.5
Acquisition Short of Monopoly	235	15.0
Boycott	36	2.4
Resale Price Maintenance	33	2.2
Vertical Integration	29	2.0
Tying Arrangement	34	2.2
Exclusive Dealings	27	2.0
Territorial and Customer Limitations	185	12.2
Violence	4	0.3
Price Discrimination	12	0.8
Other Predatory or Unfair Conduct	50	3.3
Interlocking Directorates	6	0.4
Clayton Act Sec. 10	2	0.1
Labor Cases	3	0.2
Patent and Copyright Cases	24	1.6
TOTAL	1,522	100.0

Source: Joseph C. Gallo, Joseph L. Craycraft, and Steven C. Bush, "Guess Who Came To Dinner: An Empirical Study of Federal Antitrust Enforcement for the Period 1963-1984," *Review of Industrial Organization* 2 (1985), p. 128.

over 41 cases per year). This expansion in case loads coincided with what was happening to the division's funding levels. Appropriations rose by nearly two-thirds between 1939 and 1940. They fell somewhat during World War II, then recovered to their prewar high in 1948. Since that time the division's budgetary resources have risen fairly steadily, with the largest increases occurring during the inflationary period of the late 1970s.

The Antitrust Division focuses the bulk of its efforts on attacking horizontal conspiracies, a category that includes simple price fixing as well as collusion on nonprice terms, exchanges of information, territorial or product market division, and so on. As Table 4.2 shows, such allegations have accounted for fully one-half of the Justice Department's antitrust charges in recent years.[3] (The number of violations alleged exceed the number of cases instituted in a given year because a single case may involve more than one defendant and each defendant may be charged with more than one infraction.) This emphasis on horizontal matters is especially striking in 1981–84, when bid-rigging cases against government contractors accounted for nearly all of the cases instituted by the Antitrust Division.[4]

Next in frequency are acquisitions short of monopoly, which entail possible violations of the merger proscriptions (Section 7) of the Clayton Act, followed by allegations involving unlawful territorial and customer limitations. This latter category represents one member of the class of so-called "vertical restraints." When combined with other examples of this sort (boycotts, resale price maintenance, vertical integration, tying arrangements, and exclusive dealing), such violations become the second most important area of Antitrust Division enforcement activity.

The distribution of Justice Department antitrust charges during the two decades ending in 1984 represents somewhat of a departure from historical enforcement patterns. Allegations involving horizontal conspiracies accounted for just over 36 percent of the charges filed by the Antitrust Division between 1890 and 1969.[5] More emphasis was placed on monopolizing (14 percent of the allegations), boycotts (9 percent), exclusive dealing (5 percent), and price discrimination (5 percent) matters in this earlier period, and merger violations were charged much less frequently because of the loopholes in the original language of the Clayton Act.[6] Overall, the division has stepped up its enforcement efforts substantially in recent years. It brought more than half as many antitrust charges between 1963 and 1984 as were filed in the first 75 years following passage of the Sherman Act.

The Antitrust Division's record of success in the matters it initiates has improved markedly over time as well. It prevailed in 86 percent of the 842 cases reaching some sort of resolution between 1963 and 1984;[7] convictions were obtained in 92 percent of the matters involving criminal charges during the same period.[8] This compares with an overall success rate of about 80 percent through 1964, which includes figures as low as 38 to 55 percent during a number of five-year intervals early on in the division's history.[9]

From whence does the Antitrust Division's enforcement activity arise? It would be mistakenly optimistic to suppose that after Congress determines a funding level, Division personnel take the initiative to search over the economy for possible sources of allocative inefficiency, rank them in terms of their welfare cost to consumers, and then initiate cases in order of importance until the current antitrust budget is exhausted. Rather, much of the day-to-day routine involves the investigation of matters brought to the division's attention through the premerger notification process and the complaints of antitrust infractions made by outsiders, most of whom are either rivals, customers, or suppliers of the alleged violator. Once a complaint has been received, an investigation into the merits of the allegation is begun, supplementary information is obtained from the relevant parties either voluntarily or by subpoena, and if warranted, a legal action is subsequently instituted which is ultimately settled by litigation or, more commonly, by an out-of-court agreement between the Justice Department and the defendant(s). About one-third of the cases are resolved within six months after initiation;[10] the remainder take longer, sometimes dragging on for years. The investigation phase that preceeds the decision to issue a formal complaint can be quite protracted as well.

Of course, the statistics of antitrust are only half of the story. Equally important are the actual effects of enforcement, if any, on the extent of monopoly or other unlawful business practices in the economy. We have noted previously (see Chapter 1) that many individual antitrust cases have been criticized severely for their failure to incorporate sound economic principles. A limited amount of additional evidence on this score is available from a small number of studies that analyze the effectiveness of antitrust enforcement with respect to certain types of violations.

Hay and Kelley, for example, examined a sample of horizontal price-fixing cases brought by the Antitrust Division.[11] They looked at "all Section 1 criminal cases which were filed *and* won in trial or settled by *nolo contendere* pleas from January 1963 to December 1972,"[12] comparing the facts in each case with the factors economic theory suggests may facilitate collusion between rivals. Their findings indicated that "industries colluding at one point in time often can be found to be colluding at later points in time, in spite of Antitrust action in the interim." These results led Hay and Kelley to recommend stiffer penalties "to raise further the perceived cost of violating the antitrust laws and thus force compliance by firms in industries prone to conspiracy."[13]

U.S. manufacturing firms named as parties to horizontal conspiracy suits from 1958 to 1967 were found to be "consistently less profitable" than noncolluders by Asch and Seneca.[14] They interpreted this evidence as suggesting either that low profits motivate firms to enter into collusive agreements, or that the antitrust authorities more often prosecute unsuccessful cartels. Similarly, Palmer found that firms having below-average growth rates during the 1966–70 period were disproportionately represented in antitrust suits charging horizontal restraint of trade.[15]

The effectiveness of relief measures in merger cases has been examined by Kenneth Elzinga.[16] His data consisted of a sample of 39 Clayton Act Section 7 cases filed by 1960, and settled by the end of 1964. By Elzinga's reckoning, the remedial measures were "unsuccessful" in 21 of the cases and "deficient" in eight others. When he expanded his evaluative criteria to include the time elapsed between the date of the acquisition and issue of the relief order, 35 out of the 39 cases ended in less than "sufficient" relief. An expanded version of this study produced similar results on a sample of 104 merger cases filed in 1968 or later by the Federal Trade Commission or the Justice Department, in which relief was accomplished by 1981.[17] The analysis showed that

> substantial structural relief was achieved in roughly one-third of the cases examined. Of these, more than 70 percent presented no likelihood of a substantial lessening of competition. Fewer than a dozen of the 104 cases in the sample remain to which, pending further scrutiny, some consumer welfare gain might be attributed.[18]

George Stigler assessed the general effects of the antitrust laws on aggregate concentration, on the frequency of merger, and on the prevalence of collusion.[19] Using data covering roughly 1890 to 1960, and contrasting market share figures in selected U.S. industries with corresponding U.K. statistics, Stigler found that the Sherman Act had had only modest effects on aggregate concentration. He did conclude, however, that Section 7 of the Clayton Act had been a powerful discouragement to horizontal mergers following its amendment in 1950 by the Celler-Kefauver Act, and that the Sherman Act appeared to have reduced the availability of certain methods of collusion.

All in all, the statistical studies of enforcement by the Antitrust Division paint a picture that is largely one of policy failure. Although the agency can be judged "successful" on its own terms, that is, having issued a significant number of antitrust complaints in which the government prevails, these cases often involve firms operating in unconcentrated industries where the likelihood of consumer injury is low, and impose penalties that are unlikely to have substantial deterrent effects. This latter point is especially important because a large part of the argument in favor of an antitrust policy is that one case not only remedies unlawful practices by a single firm or industry, but also can deter many other firms from committing similar violations: "The ghost of Senator Sherman is an ex officio member of the board of directors of every large company."[20] Yet the evidence presented by the economists who have studied the effects of antitrust enforcement suggests that even the convicted firms themselves may not be deterred from repeating earlier violations. This would seem to weaken the support for a vigorous antitrust policy.

THE FEDERAL TRADE COMMISSION

The FTC is an independent agency established in 1914 to enforce the provisions of the Federal Trade Commission Act and the Clayton Act.

It is headed by five commissioners who are appointed by the president to staggered seven-year terms. (No more than three of the commissioners can at any one time be members of the same political party.) Since 1950, the president has selected one of the commissioners to serve a four-year term as chairman of the Federal Trade Commission, with authority to appoint the directors and other top managers of the commission staff.[21]

The FTC's antitrust mandate combines broad investigative, prosecutorial, and adjudicative functions. The commission can institute investigations of possible law violations either on its own initiative or in response to allegations of unlawful conduct brought to its attention by outsiders, issue complaints if warranted, and impose orders to cease and desist on parties determined to be engaged in "unfair methods of competition." The great majority of the commission's antitrust matters are settled by consent agreements, but if necessary formal hearings on the charges can be held before an administrative law judge, who is in the FTC's employ and whose findings of fact and decision in the matter are then confirmed or denied in whole or in part by the commission. Any party determined to be in violation of the law in such proceedings may appeal the decision to the federal courts. If no appeal is sought or if the commission's order is subsequently upheld, the FTC's decision becomes final and must be obeyed. The commission may impose fines or other civil penalties on firms that do not comply with its orders. At each stage of the enforcement process, the decision to go forward must be confirmed by a majority vote of the commissioners.

To assist it in carrying out its law enforcement duties, the commission employs a large professional staff, composed recently of around 500 attorneys and in excess of 90 economists.[22] The legal staff is divided about equally between the FTC's antitrust mission (these are assigned to the Bureau of Competition) and the consumer protection matters that the commission enforces under the "unfair or deceptive acts or practices in commerce" language of Section 5. The Bureau of Competition staff is further subdivided along lines of specialization, including sections devoted to health care, petroleum, and food. A separate Bureau of Economics advises the commission on the technical aspects of its enforcement activities. It too is compartmentalized according to areas of specialization like antitrust, consumer protection, industry analysis, and regulatory analysis. The commission's budget now exceeds $70 million annually, a figure that is more than 1.5 times larger than the resources available to its counterparts in the Antitrust Division, reflecting the wide-ranging nature of the FTC's mandate.[23]

Table 4.3 FTC Budget and Antitrust Enforcement Activity, 1914–81

Year	Budget ($000)	Cases[a]	Year	Budget ($000)	Cases[a]	Year	Budget ($000)	Cases[a]
1914	–	–	38	1,996	28	62	10,345	15
15	184	0	39	2,283	31	63	11,472	9
16	431	1	1940	2,346	33	64	12,215	12
17	567	20	41	2,300	32	65	13,475	18
18	1,609	64	42	2,360	16	66	13,863	19
19	1,754	121	43	2,050	14	67	14,378	9
1920	1,306	18	44	2,083	8	68	15,281	15
21	1,032	26	45	2,059	6	69	16,900	15
22	1,026	32	46	2,174	9	1970	20,889	11
23	974	50	47	2,975	11	71	22,490	25
24	1,010	51	48	2,970	11	72	25,189	16
25	1,010	21	49	3,621	10	73	28,974	26
26	1,008	4	1950	3,723	5	74	32,496	20
27	997	8	51	3,892	18	75	38,983	20
28	984	10	52	4,314	16	76	47,199	24
29	1,163	17	53	4,179	7	77	54,680	16
1930	1,496	12	54	4,054	11	78	62,100	14
31	1,863	4	55	4,129	29	79	65,300	30
32	1,817	3	56	4,529	22	1980	66,059	28
33	1,427	4	57	5,550	16	81	70,774	19
34	1,314	14	58	6,186	13			
35	2,097	30	59	6,488	12			
36	2,035	33	1960	6,840	26			
37	1,939	18	61	8,010	7			

Sources: For the 1914-1969 period, the case data are from Richard A. Posner, "A Statistical Study of Antitrust Enforcement," *Journal of Law and Economics* 13 (October 1970), p. 369; they are from Joseph C. Gallo, Joseph L. Craycraft, and Steven C. Bush, "Guess Who Came to Dinner: An Empirical Study of Federal Antitrust Enforcement for the Period 1963-1984," *Review of Industrial Organization* 2 (1985), p. 109, for the remaining years. Appropriations were obtained by the author from the Office of the Secretary of the Federal Trade Commission.
[a]Restraint-of-trade cases only.

Table 4.3 presents information on the commission's budget and law enforcement activities through 1981. The case data reported there include only those matters involving restraint-of-trade charges brought under Section 5 of the FTC Act. They do not count the false advertising, deception, fraud, and mislabeling cases that account for the bulk of the commission's Section 5 workload.[24]

By and large, the FTC was much more active on the antitrust front during its early history than the Department of Justice had been. The Antitrust Division instituted an average of only about 8 cases per year between 1890 and 1938 (see Table 4.1). By contrast, the commission brought an average of over 24 restraint-of-trade cases annually until the end of the Great Depression. The pattern then reversed. The fivefold expansion in the Antitrust Division's enforcement activities that began in 1939 was accompanied by a drop in the FTC's restraint-of-trade case load to an average of just over 16 matters per year.

This reversal coincided almost precisely with the enactment of the Robinson-Patman Amendment to Section 2 of the Clayton Act in 1936. Although the commission had instituted a fairly large number of Section 2 matters in its early days, the price discrimination proscription of the law was virtually unenforced from the early 1920s until the mid 1930s. As shown in Table 4.4, the situation changed dramatically within one or two years after the Robinson-Patman Act was placed on the books. The commission brought 124 price discrimination cases during the five-year interval running from 1935 to 1939 (75 of these were instituted between 1936 and 1939), compared with only seven matters in the preceding decade. It became particularly active in this area beginning in the mid 1950s. Over one-half of all the Section 2 cases the commission has ever instituted were brought during the decade running from 1955 to 1964 (234 such matters were initiated in 1963 alone). In short, the Robinson-Patman Act ushered in a period in which the FTC specialized somewhat in charging firms with price discrimination violations, leaving the more traditional areas of antitrust enforcement to its counterparts in the Department of Justice. The commission's Robinson-Patman activities declined significantly in the 1970s and 1980s, however. This decline was due partly to the increasing criticism of the statute by economists, and partly because of the emphasis placed on industry-wide rulemaking activities prompted by the Magnuson-Moss Warranty/Federal Trade Commission Improvement Act of 1976.

The FTC has focused the bulk of its restraint-of-trade enforcement efforts in recent years on mergers and acquisitions. This is shown in Table 4.5, which indicates that 42 percent of the antitrust charges brought by the commission between 1963 and 1984 involved possible violations of Clayton Act Section 7 ("acquisition short of monopoly"). This represents a significant departure from earlier years when horizontal price fixing was the most frequent (22 percent) of the FTC's restraint-of-trade allegations.[25] Like the Antitrust Division, vertical restraints (resale price maintenance, tying, exclusive dealing, and so on) represent an important area of commission enforcement activity. But, unlike its counterpart antitrust agency, the overall level of the commission's enforcement efforts (measured in terms of the number of restraint-of-trade charges made) has not changed markedly in recent years.[26]

Table 4.4 FTC Cases under Clayton Act Section 2, 1914–81

Interval	Number
1914-1919	100
1920-1924	42
1925-1929	5
1930-1934	2
1935-1939	124
1940-1944	106
1945-1949	94
1950-1954	66
1955-1959	227
1960-1964	545
1965-1969	102
1970-1974	45
1975-1979	19
1980-1981	4
TOTAL	1,481

Sources: Richard A. Posner, "A Statistical Study of Antitrust Enforcement," *Journal of Law and Economics* 13 (October 1970), p. 370 (1936-1969); Office of the Secretary of the Federal Trade Commission (1914-1935 and 1970-1981).

Table 4.5 Violations Alleged in FTC Restraint-of-Trade Cases, 1963–84

Nature of Charge	Number	Percent
Horizontal Price Fixing	36	9.0
Monopolization	26	6.0
Acquisition Short of Monopoly	178	42.0
Resale Price Maintenance	55	13.0
Tying	12	3.0
Exclusive Dealing	26	6.0
Price Discrimination[a]	21	5.0
Patents	4	1.0
Labor	2	0.5
Interlocking Directorates	13	3.0
Boycott	10	2.0
Reciprocity	3	0.7
Restrictive Leasing	11	3.0
Other	22	5.0
TOTAL	419	100.0

Source: Joseph C. Gallo, Joseph L. Craycraft, and Steven C. Bush, "Guess Who Came To Dinner: An Empirical Study of Federal Antitrust Enforcement for the Period 1963-1984," *Review of Industrial Organization* 2 (1985), p. 129.
[a]Includes only those Robinson-Patman cases in which predatory price discrimination was charged.

The FTC's record of success in antitrust matters has improved significantly over time, however. Before 1963, the commission won just over one-half (51 percent) of its restraint-of-trade cases. Since then it has prevailed in 90 percent of them.[27] But FTC matters take substantially longer to resolve, on average, than do the cases instituted by the Antitrust Division. In excess of 90 percent of the commission's restraint-of-trade cases do not reach a settlement within six months; 14 percent of the matters initiated after 1963 lasted more than six years.[28]

The Federal Trade Commission is perhaps the most intensively studied federal agency.[29] With its broad mandate of antitrust and consumer protection enforcement, the commission has attracted considerable attention from scholars interested in evaluating the performance of government bureaus. One of the more important issues addressed is the desirability of having the antitrust laws enforced by two separate agencies with overlapping jurisdictions. The quality of antitrust output is often discussed in this literature, where quality refers to the relative number of "good" and "bad" cases under dual enforcement compared with some idealized benchmark that might exist if there was only a single antitrust agency. Much weight is placed on the fact that the FTC's authority under Section 5 is ill defined, and that the commission is both prosecutor and judge.[30] Importance is also attached to the FTC's status as an independent agency, in contrast to the Antitrust Division's position as a line item in the executive branch budget.

Like its companion agency, many of the individual cases brought by the commission have been dissected and criticized.[31] But unlike the analysis of the Antitrust Division's enforcement activities, research on the FTC has paid particular attention to its ties to the Congress. What is becoming increasingly apparent is that the FTC, rather than operating as the independent, expert law enforcer it was conceived as being, has followed policies that are in many respects consistent with and responsive to the political preferences of its overseers in Congress.[32] This sort of behavior is entirely understandable. If the commission's budgetary appropriations are tied to the number of cases it brings, regardless of the benefits to consumers, the agency will have an incentive to ignore the returns to society of antitrust law enforcement.[33] One explanation for observed enforcement patterns, therefore, is that the potential benefits to consumers of the complaints brought by the commission receive less weight in the case selection process than the "private" benefits to the FTC. Thus, the commission enforces the laws Congress wants it to enforce, whether or not those statutes or the cases brought under them comport with economic efficiency in some abstract sense.

DUAL ENFORCEMENT

An important issue in antitrust policy concerns the desirability of having the laws enforced by two separate agencies having overlapping jurisdictions.[34] Antitrust is unique among federal government policy programs in terms of the degree to which it is administered by autonomous bureaus. This system has been criticized almost since it was created by the passage of the Federal Trade Commission Act in 1914. Many of these criticisms are not leveled at dual enforcement, per se, but rather represent attacks on the nature of the FTC's organizational structure and its broad enforcement authority. There is, however, a long history of concern about the potential waste of public resources associated with having two governmental agencies perform essentially the same function.

The debate over the extent to which dual enforcement leads to resource waste began as early as 1925. In that year, the National Industrial Conference Board complained that the commission's vigorous program of resale price maintenance prosecutions had encroached on an area of antitrust law enforcement activity that Congress had not intended to be in its purview. The board went on to recommend that

> in order to bring about a more logical and efficacious distribution of functions, and thereby contribute to the expedition of Federal Trade Commission procedure *in its proper sphere*, [it seems necessary] to provide by law that whenever the commission secures evidence pointing to a violation of the Sherman Act it shall transmit the same to the Department of Justice, with such recommendations as it may deem suitable.[35]

Criticisms such as this apparently had little practical effect on interagency rivalry. The independence of the two agencies prior to 1948 is illustrated by the confrontation that occurred between the commission and the Justice Department in their separate investigations of the Aluminum Company of America (Alcoa) during the mid 1920s.[36] In October 1924, the FTC wrote to the attorney general advising him of evidence in its possession that Alcoa was in violation of a consent decree the firm had entered into with the Justice Department in 1912. Because the statute of limitations would become operative within one year, the commission initiated its own investigation, but when the evidence the FTC had uncovered was requested by the attorney general, "it was refused unless *written* consent was given by the Aluminum Company."[37] After Alcoa failed to give its permission, the Justice Department began an investigation, but by the time the interagency dispute had gone on for two months, the Senate intervened to halt any inquiry into Alcoa's alleged violations. In January 1926, the Senate Judiciary Committee began an investigation of the two agencies' handling of the case, an event that has been described as "the amazing spectacle of a congressional committee's investigation of the Department of Justice's investigation of the Federal Trade Commission's investigation of the Aluminum Company of America."[38]

Similar examples pointing to duplication of efforts by the two enforcement agencies could be recounted.[39] The lack of coordination was in part due to the fact that the FTC's authority with respect to Sherman Act violations was unclear until 1948. A Supreme Court decision in that year held that the commission could bring suit against contracts, combinations, or conspiracies "in restraint of trade" under Section 5 of the FTC Act.[40] Mutual action to delimit their respective fields of authority immediately followed this decision. In June 1948, an interagency liaison agreement established a formal mechanism for allocating cases among the two law-enforcement bodies.[41] The principal features of the 1948 accord provide a division of enforcement authority according to industry of respondent and, to a lesser extent, according to type of violation. The major areas of responsibility outlined in Table 4.6 are suggestive of the rather detailed allotments made under the liaison agreement. Case allocations are handled through a procedure in which one agency grants "clearance" to the other to pursue a particular investigation. In the liaison process, consideration is usually given to prior experience with the industry or firm in question, with the exception that criminal charges are handled exclusively by the Justice Department.

The FTC-Antitrust Division case allocation system is not without its critics. One commentator believes that the exchange of information about possible law violations taking place within the liaison framework "raises substantial constitutional questions, including issues of due process and self-incrimination."[42] Another cites instances in which the interagency competition for cases has caused unwarranted administrative delays.[43] But the liaison system is more usually described as a "well-established mechanism for avoiding duplication."[44]

The historical development of U.S. antitrust institutions supplies the conditions for a unique natural experiment in which the effects of dual enforcement can be tested. Prior to 1948, the Justice Department and FTC "competed" in producing similar "output" that might be thought of as antitrust cases instituted. Since that time, the two agencies have colluded much like a private cartel by dividing up their areas of enforcement responsibility. The coordination of activities under the liaison agreement effectively creates a single antitrust law enforce-

Table 4.6 Industry and Violation Allocations under the 1948 Liaison Agreement

FTC	Antitrust Division
Brewing: monopolization and price discrimination	Brewing: acquisitions
Auto parts: monopolization and acquisitions	Automobile industry: monopolization and dealer relations
Tires, batteries, and accessories: distribution	Tires: manufacturing
Cement	Steel
Shopping centers: trade restraints	Aviation
Department stores: acquisitions	Newspapers: acquisitions
Health care	Aluminum
Food and food distribution	Patents and know-how
Petroleum: monopolization	Communications
Copiers and business machines	Banking and securities
Franchising	Computers
Textile mill products: acquisitions	International agreements
Dairy industry: acquisitions	

Source: David L. Roll, "Dual Enforcement of the Antitrust Laws by the Department of Justice and the FTC: The Liaison Procedure," *The Business Lawyer* 31 (July 1975), p. 2080.

ment apparatus. If we suppose that each bureau receives budgetary appropriations in proportion to its share of total antitrust output and simplify things in other ways, including making the assumptions that the Antitrust Division and the FTC seek to maximize their own budgets and behave according to Cournot output conjectures, then we can derive some predictions about the cost of enforcement under the two regimes. In particular, independent dual enforcement should lead to more output (and more output per budget dollar) than collusive dual enforcement.[45]

Mean annual case output, real budgets, and output per thousand budget dollars are shown for two time periods, 1932–48 and 1949–81, in Table 4.7.[46] The comparison is striking. Although total antitrust activity remained roughly the same (239 cases per year in 1932–48, and 249 cases per year in 1949–81), average cases per thousand budget dollars fell dramatically after 1948. The liaison agreement appears to have cut antitrust output per thousand budget dollars in half. Put another way, the average cost per FTC case rose from about $31,000 to $64,000 (1972 dollars) between the two periods; the cost of an average Justice Department case rose from $123,000 to $204,000. This suggests that following the 1948 accord, the Antitrust Division and the FTC employed relatively more attorneys, economists, and other

Table 4.7 Antitrust Cases and Appropriations, Annual Averages, 1932–81

Time Period	Federal Trade Commission			Antitrust Division		
	Cases	Real Budget[a]	Cases per thousand dollars	Cases	Real Budget[a]	Cases per thousand dollars
1932-1948	214.2	6,401.38	0.0319	25.1	3,110.18	0.0081
1949-1981	199.5	19,188.30	0.0157	49.2	10,798.40	0.0049

Source: Richard S. Higgins, William F. Shughart II, and Robert D. Tollison, "Dual Enforcement of the Antitrust Laws," in Robert J. Mackay, James C. Miller III, and Bruce Yandle, ed., *Public Choice and Regulation: A View from Inside the Federal Trade Commission* (Stanford: Hoover Institution Press, 1987), p. 174.
[a]Thousands of 1972 dollars.

bureaucratic inputs per case than might have been used in the absence of collusion.[47] The implication is that the liaison agreement, and not dual enforcement per se, may be responsible for the resource waste claimed to follow from having a system in which the antitrust laws are enforced by two separate agencies.

Some critics have argued that the potential for wasted resources is less serious than the uncertain legal standards that businesses face because of dual enforcement: Dual antitrust policies force "the business community to risk being caught between two conflicting federal agencies."[48] This matters because if the alleged violator "happens to draw the Justice Department, he will be accorded a federal court trial and due process, but if he draws the FTC, he will be relegated to a quasi-judicial procedure, where his rights are not so great."[49]

In sum, major questions about the purposes and effects of dual antitrust law enforcement remain unresolved. Important clues may be found in the differing organizational structures of the two bureaus. One study, for example, has shown that the case "output" of the five-member FTC displays less variability over time than that of its counterpart agency operating under the proximate control of a single administrator.[50] The commission may in fact be less "independent" than is commonly assumed. The important point, however, is that positive economics has much to say about the behavior of the antitrust agencies.

BUREAUCRATIC INCENTIVES

Of course, the crux of the matter at hand is to ask how the private incentives of law enforcement personnel and the organizational con-

straints imposed by the structures of the bureaus themselves affect
public antitrust enforcement activities. An early step toward the positive analysis of this question was taken by Suzanne Weaver in her
study of decision making within the Justice Department's Antitrust
Division.[51] Weaver's main contribution was to elicit information about
the private incentives faced by public antitrust prosecutors. Based
upon the results of interviews conducted during 1971 with some one
hundred agency staff members, private antitrust attorneys, and other
observers of the division, she sought to answer the question, "Why
does the division choose to bring any particular case?"[52] According to
Weaver, events taking place during the early 1950s, including passage
of the Celler-Kefauver Amendment to Section 7 of the Clayton Act and
the indictment of the leading manufacturers of electrical equipment
for price fixing, made "antitrust expertise a more valuable commodity
to the business community and to law firms serving it."[53] Because of
this increased demand, "experience in the Antitrust Division became
newly valuable to a young lawyer who wanted eventually to work in
private practice. . . . " And, the specific experience wanted was trial
experience in the federal courts.[54] Thus, the attorneys employed by the
Antitrust Division began to view "government service not as an ultimate career objective, but as a means to an end—a career in the
private bar."[55]

Weaver's work thus suggests that, at the margin, the self-interested
goal of getting to trial may win over the merits of a particular case in
the decision to prosecute. Unfortunately, her study suffers from the
faults common to all research based upon evidence derived from
interviews—what people say often diverges from what they actually
do. Weaver was also an "outsider" and was therefore unable to obtain
access to internal Antitrust Division documents. Her research nevertheless sheds light on the workings of the public antitrust bureaucracy.
It suggests that private incentives may play an important role in
explaining public policy.

The incentive structure faced by Federal Trade Commission attorneys has been examined by Robert Katzmann, who also noted that the
ultimate career goal of many members of the legal staff is a job with a
prestigious private law firm.[56] Such goals mean that upper-level
managers will find that complicated "structural matters and industry
wide cases threaten the morale of the staff because they often involve
years of tedious investigation before they reach the trial stage." As a
result, commission policymakers have an incentive to support "the
opening of a number of easily prosecuted matters, which may have
little value to the consumer . . . in an effort to satisfy the staff's perceived needs."[57] To quote one FTC attorney, "For me, each complaint
is an opportunity, a vehicle which someday could take me into the

courtroom. I want to go to trial so badly that there are times when I overstate the possibilities which the particular matter might offer."[58]

Katzmann's main point is that one cannot explain the FTC's case selection process entirely on the basis of industry economic characteristics, which might serve as a proxy for antitrust's potential for improving social welfare. Rather, the decision to prosecute is dominated by factors internal to the commission—staff career objectives, the availability of enforcement resources, and so on. Another observer of the FTC agrees:

> The principal attraction of Commission service to lawyers who wish to use it as a steppingstone to private practice lies in the opportunities it affords to gain trial experience. . . . It is the experience of trying cases, the more the better, not the social payoff from the litigation, that improves the professional skills and earning prospects of FTC lawyers.[59]

The turnover rates among the attorneys employed by the public enforcement agencies reported by Weaver and others bear these conclusions out. For example, between 1970 and 1976, some 13 to 25 percent of the FTC's attorneys departed annually; 90 percent of the legal staff had been with the commission four years or less. At the end of fiscal year 1976, only 20 of the nearly 200 attorneys who had joined the FTC in 1969 were still on board. Eighty-nine percent of all of the lawyers who began work at the commission between 1972 and 1975 expected (in July 1976) to leave within two years.[60] In 1949, no attorney departing the Antitrust Division was recorded as having left for private law firms or industry; in 1959, the figure was four out of 17 and by 1964, 16 of 21 attorneys left for the private bar.[61]

The research by Kenneth Clarkson and Timothy Muris on the FTC similarly focuses on internal organizational conflicts, staff incentives, and external constraints.[62] They suggest, for example, that in the early 1970s, the commission shifted its enforcement efforts away from Robinson-Patman price discrimination matters in favor of cases attacking industry structure in order to minimize the tension between FTC attorneys and economists, and because the increased complexity of the agency's caseload provided human capital benefits to the legal staff. In addition, Clarkson and Muris attribute the FTC's lack of zeal for bringing price-fixing cases to a desire on the part of the commission's attorneys to differentiate themselves in the post-government job market from their counterparts in the Antitrust Division.

More recently, Robert Rogowsky used the incentive system facing government attorneys and agency managers to explain the ineffectiveness of the remedies imposed in merger cases.[63] Drawing on a theory of government enterprise,[64] which suggests that "visible" output will be favored over "invisible" output, Rogowsky argues that, because the personal reward structure facing them pushes the government's antitrust attorneys in the direction of generating new complaints and trying new cases, remedy tends to become an incidental aspect of the law enforcement process. Once the liability phase of an antitrust proceeding has been "won," staff attorneys and upper-level bureau managers have an incentive to resolve the relief issue quickly in order to move on to other investigations that hold the promise of going to trial. A "weak" remedy may therefore be proposed by the prosecutors (or accepted when offered by the defendant) simply to get the negotiations over with quickly and a final judgment entered closing out the case. Alternatively, Rogowsky suggests that remedies tend to be ineffective because the allegations made in many of the government's complaints tend to be weak or meritless. Insofar as cases are selected for prosecution not because of their social payoff but because of their potential for being settled expeditiously either in trial or through negotiations with the defendant that lead to a consent order, weak allegations can be disposed of quickly with weak remedies.

Taken as a group, these few studies of organizational behavior point to the conclusion that the antitrust bureaucracy does not select cases to prosecute on the basis of their potential net benefit to society. Instead, the managers and staff of the Antitrust Division and the Federal Trade Commission use the discretion at their disposal partly to further their own private interests rather than those of the public at large.

NOTES

1. See A. D. Neale and D. G. Goyder, *The Antitrust Laws of the U.S.A.: A Study of Competition Enforced by Law*, 3d ed. (Cambridge, UK: Cambridge University Press, 1980), p. 373; and George J. Stigler, "The Economists and the Problem of Monopoly," *American Economic Review Papers and Proceedings* 72 (May 1982), p. 10.

2. The Antitrust Division did not become a separate line item in the Department of Justice budget until 1932.

3. Joseph C. Gallo, Joseph L. Craycraft, and Steven C. Bush, "Guess Who Came to Dinner: An Empirical Study of Federal Antitrust Enforcement for the Period 1963–1984," *Review of Industrial Organization* 2 (1985), p. 128.

4. Ibid., p. 126.

5. Richard A. Posner, "A Statistical Study of Antitrust Enforcement," *Journal of Law and Economics* 13 (October 1970), p. 398.

6. Ibid.

7. Gallo, Craycraft, and Bush, "Guess Who Came to Dinner," p. 114.

8. Ibid., p. 119.

9. Posner, "Statistical Study of Antitrust Enforcement," p. 381.

10. Gallo, Craycraft, and Bush, "Guess Who Came to Dinner," p. 110.

11. George A. Hay and Daniel Kelley, "An Empirical Study of Price-Fixing Conspiracies," *Journal of Law and Economics* 17 (April 1974), pp. 13–38.

12. Ibid., p. 18. Emphasis in original.

13. Ibid., p. 28.

14. Peter Asch and Joseph J. Seneca, "Is Collusion Profitable?," *Review of Economics and Statistics* 58 (February 1976), pp. 1–10.

15. J. Palmer, "Some Economic Conditions Conducive to Collusion," *Journal of Economic Issues* 6 (June 1972), pp. 29–38.

16. Kenneth G. Elzinga, "The Antimerger Law: Pyrrhic Victories," *Journal of Law and Economics* 12 (April 1969), pp. 43–78.

17. Robert A. Rogowsky, "The Economic Effectiveness of Section 7 Relief," *Antitrust Bulletin* 31 (Spring 1986), pp. 187–233.

18. Ibid., p. 228.

19. George J. Stigler, "The Economic Effects of the Antitrust Laws," *Journal of Law and Economics* 9 (October 1966), pp. 225–58.

20. George J. Stigler, "Monopoly and Oligopoly by Merger," *American Economic Review Papers and Proceedings* 40 (May 1950), p. 32.

21. See Bruce Yandle, "Chairman Choice and Output Effects: The FTC Experience," in Robert J. Mackay, James C. Miller III, and Bruce Yandle, eds., *Public Choice and Regulation: A View from Inside the Federal Trade Commission* (Stanford, CA: Hoover Institution Press, 1987), pp. 283–94. Prior to 1950, the chairman was little more than presiding officer at commission meetings, and the slot was rotated annually among the commission members. The change in the method used for selecting FTC chairmen (as well as the chairs of independent commissions governmentwide) followed the recommendations of the Hoover Commission report of 1949. Because of the political nature of their appointment, FTC chairmen have traditionally resigned that office (but not necessarily their position as commissioner) following presidential elections so that the new president has the freedom to designate a new chairman.

22. Neale and Goyder, *Antitrust Laws of the U.S.A.*, p. 383; Stigler, "Economists and the Problem of Monopoly," p. 10.

23. Budget data were obtained by the author from the Office of the Secretary of the Federal Trade Commission.

24. In addition to the FTC and Clayton Acts, the commission enforces a long list of specialized statutes. These include the Truth-in-Lending, Fair Credit Reporting, Fair Debt Collection, Fair Credit Billing, and Fair Credit Opportunity Acts. Other laws enforced by the FTC are the Trademark Act, the Export Trade Act, the Fair Packaging-Labeling Act, the Consumer Leasing Act, the Hobby Protection Act, the Textile Act, the Wool Act, and the Fur Act.

25. Posner, "Statistical Study of Antitrust Enforcement," p. 408.

26. This is a consequence of the differing organizational structures of the two agencies. See William F. Shughart II, Robert D. Tollison, and Brian L. Goff, "Bureaucratic Structure and Congressional Control," *Southern Economic Journal* 52 (April 1986), pp. 962–72.

27. Gallo, Craycraft, and Bush, "Guess Who Came to Dinner," p. 113.

28. Ibid., p. 112.

29. See Robert J. Mackay, James C. Miller III, and Bruce Yandle, "Public Choice and Regulation: An Overview," in Mackay, Miller, and Yandle, eds., *Public Choice and Regulation*, p. 3.

30. See Chapter 6.

31. One of the many examples in this regard is Ernest Gellhorn, "Regulatory Reform and the Federal Trade Commission's Antitrust Jurisdiction," *Tennessee Law Review* 49 (1982), pp. 471–510.

32. Such a conclusion was drawn by William E. Kovacic, "The Federal Trade Commission and Congressional Oversight of Antitrust Enforcement: A Historical Perspective," in Mackay, Miller, and Yandle, eds., *Public Choice and Regulation*, pp. 63–120. Evidence concerning the links between Congress and the FTC is discussed in Chapter 5.

33. On the incentives of government bureaus to produce "visible" output that can be readily monitored by congressional oversight committees, see Cotton M. Lindsay, "A Theory of Government Enterprise," *Journal of Political Economy* 84 (October 1976), pp. 1061–76.

34. This section draws heavily on Richard S. Higgins, William F. Shughart II, and Robert D. Tollison, "Dual Enforcement of the Antitrust Laws," in Mackay, Miller, and Yandle, eds., *Public Choice and Regulation*, pp. 154–80.

35. Emphasis added. Quoted in Gilbert H. Montague, "The Commission's Jurisdiction over Practices in Restraint of Trade: A Large-Scale Method of Mass Enforcement of the Antitrust Laws," *George Washington Law Review* 8 (January-February 1940), pp. 385–86.

36. Described by Thomas C. Blaisdell, *The Federal Trade Commission: An Experiment in the Control of Business* (New York: Columbia University Press, 1932).

37. Ibid., p. 90. Emphasis in original.

38. Ibid., p. 241.

39. Blaisdell observes that "the lack of coordination of Commission activities with those of the Attorney General have never appeared to worse advantage" than in their contemporaneous investigations of RCA during the 1920s. Ibid., p. 243.

40. *FTC v. Cement Institute*, 333 U.S. 683 (1948).

41. David L. Roll, "Dual Enforcement of the Antitrust Laws by the Department of Justice and the FTC: The Liaison Procedure," *The Business Lawyer* 31 (July 1975), p. 2075.

42. J.B. Sloan, "Antitrust: Shared Information Between the FTC and the Department of Justice," *Brigham Young University Law Review* 4 (1979), p. 883.

43. Roll, "Dual Enforcement of the Antitrust Laws."

44. Neale and Goyder, *Antitrust Laws of the U.S.A.*, p. 373.

45. This model is developed fully by Higgins, Shughart, and Tollison, "Dual Enforcement of the Antitrust Laws," pp. 160–69.

46. The budget of the Antitrust Division is not available prior to 1932.

47. Holding constant both the volume of cases instituted and the growth in real GNP over the period (a factor that explains about 60 percent of the variation in the budgets of the two agencies between 1932 and 1981), the liaison agreement

still had a significantly positive impact on antitrust enforcement budgets. See Higgins, Shughart, and Tollison, "Dual Enforcement of the Antitrust Laws," pp. 173–75.

48. T.J. McGrew, "Antitrust Enforcement Has More Staff Than Policy," *Legal Times of Washington* 4 (October 12, 1981), p. 11.

49. Vaill, "Federal Trade Commission," p. 764.

50. Shughart, Tollison, and Goff, "Bureaucratic Structure and Congressional Control."

51. Suzanne Weaver, *The Decision to Prosecute: Organization and Public Policy in the Antitrust Division* (Cambridge, MA: MIT Press, 1977).

52. Ibid., p. 66.

53. Ibid., pp. 38–40. Following entry of the final judgment in the electrical equipment conspiracy case, private litigants filed some 2,200 treble damage suits against the coconspirators.

54. Ibid.

55. Ibid., p. 76.

56. Robert A. Katzmann, *Regulatory Bureaucracy: The Federal Trade Commission and Antitrust Policy* (Cambridge: MIT Press, 1980).

57. Ibid., p. 83.

58. Ibid., p. 61.

59. Richard A. Posner, "The Federal Trade Commission," *University of Chicago Law Review* 37 (1969), p. 86.

60. Kenneth W. Clarkson and Timothy J. Muris, "Commission Performance, Incentives, and Behavior," in Kenneth W. Clarkson and Timothy J. Muris, eds., *The Federal Trade Commission Since 1970: Economic Regulation and Bureaucratic Behavior* (Cambridge, UK: Cambridge University Press, 1981), p. 300.

61. Weaver, *Decision to Prosecute*, p. 185.

62. Clarkson and Muris, "Commission Performance," pp. 303–4.

63. Rogowsky, "Pyrrhic Victories of Section 7."

64. Lindsay, "Theory of Government Enterprise."

5

The Congress

A fairly standard characterization of how geographically based representative democracy works in practice suggests that legislators receive a higher payoff from promoting local interests than from taking vague positions in support of economic efficiency or the "national interest." For example, individual legislators work hard to attract military construction projects to their states and districts (and strongly oppose decisions to close existing facilities) not because such spending programs are social welfare maximizing, but rather because they generate direct benefits for their own constituents, while the cost is borne by the general taxpayers, most of whom reside—and vote—in other jurisdictions.[1] Antitrust policy is not fundamentally different in this regard. Given that private firms, who have incentives to use antitrust processes to obtain protection from competitive market forces, are also in a position to provide political support (votes, campaign contributions, and so on) to their elected representatives, these representatives have strong incentives to supply such protection. The individuals sitting on congressional committees having budgetary and oversight responsibilities with respect to the Federal Trade Commission and the Department of Justice are particularly well situated to influence these agencies to adopt law enforcement strategies that selectively benefit the firms and industries located within the boundaries of their own districts and states.

Writing in 1969, Richard Posner advanced such an "antitrust pork barrel" hypothesis with respect to the FTC.[2] Posner charged that the commission was significantly impaired in its task of promoting the public interest by its dependence upon Congress. He emphasized that each member of Congress is obligated to protect and further the provincial interests of the citizens of the jurisdiction he or she has been elected to represent. Specifically, "the welfare of his constituents may depend disproportionately on a few key industries. The promotion of the industries becomes one of his most important duties as a representative of the district." Moreover, because congressional authority regarding the commission's budget and confirmation of political appointees to the agency is concentrated in the hands of members of certain committees and subcommittees of Congress, a legislator in such a position will have "a great deal of power to advance the interests of businesses located in his district however unimportant the interests may be from a national perspective." Posner concluded that a major reason that FTC investigations are seldom in the public interest is that many are initiated "at the behest of corporations, trade associations, and trade unions whose motivation is at best to shift the costs of private litigation to the taxpayer and at worst to harass competitors."[3]

The antitrust porkbarrel hypothesis thus rests on three basic propositions. The first is that a geographically based system of representation confronts the legislator with a high payoff from representing local interests in the legislature, and little or no payoff from voting in terms of economic efficiency or the national interest. This asymmetry in the payoffs facing the legislator is based partly on the fact that insofar as the prospective largess will be shared by relatively few individuals, voters have greater incentives to become informed about and to lobby for localized benefits. By contrast, the bulk of the cost of financing transfers to a given political jurisdiction will be borne by greater numbers of nonresident taxpayer-consumers, most of whom will rationally find it not worth their while to organize in opposition to wealth expropriation. A political-support–maximizing legislator will accordingly search for vote-trading bargains that can be struck with the representatives of other constituencies that provide benefits to the local interests he or she represents at the expense of taxpayer-consumers in general. This is just another way of stating the obvious point that the representatives of rural districts will tend to promote farm interests in the national legislature, that the representatives of districts where the local work force is heavily unionized will tend to promote labor's interests, and so on.

The second element of the antitrust porkbarrel hypothesis is that antitrust processes afford wealth transfer opportunities to firms and industries in the economy. Antitrust actions always create winners and losers in the sense that they benefit one set of firms at the expense of others. For example, a law enforcement agency's decision to oppose a proposed efficiency-enhancing merger redistributes wealth from the merger partners' stockholders to the owners of rival firms. Similarly, the issue of an antitrust complaint challenging the legality of a particular business practice imposes a capital loss on the owners of the targeted firm, even if the firm's defense is ultimately successful. Given that antitrust can help or hurt selected business interests, the business sector has incentives to offer political support (votes, campaign contributions, and so forth) to its elected representatives in exchange for the representatives' influence in securing favorable antitrust treatment or defeating unfavorable treatment. The representatives, in turn, have strong motives for responding to this demand so long as the increment in political support supplied by the prospective beneficiaries is greater than the support that will be withdrawn by the prospective losers.

The final link in the antitrust porkbarrel hypothesis is an empirical question concerning whether Congress, in fact, exercises influence over the agencies charged with antitrust law enforcement responsibilities in a way that leads these agencies to promote local interests rather than the public interest. It is to an examination of this question that we now turn.

CONGRESS AND THE ANTITRUST BUREAUCRACY

The influence of ordinary politics on public antitrust enforcement is most evident in the case of the Federal Trade Commission, perhaps the most intensively studied (and most heavily criticized) federal agency. What is becoming increasingly apparent is that the commission, rather than operating as the "independent," expert law enforcement body it was initially conceived as being, has followed policies that are in many respects consistent with and responsive to its overseers in the U.S. Congress. Of course, this sort of behavior is entirely understandable within the context of the interest-group model of government. On a general level, for example, if the FTC's budgetary appropriations are tied to the number of antitrust cases it brings, regardless of the benefits of those cases to consumers, the agency will rationally ignore the potential social welfare gains of its law enforcement activities.[4] One explanation for observed enforcement patterns, therefore, is that the potential benefits to consumers of the complaints issued by the commission receive less weight than the "private" benefits to the FTC of bringing large numbers of cases. In other words, the commission brings the number and types of cases Congress wants it to bring, whether or not those cases comport with economic efficiency in some abstract sense.

More to the point, however, is the question concerning whether the FTC's enforcement activities benefit the firms and industries Congress wants to benefit. The preferences of each member of the legislature help determine the direction taken by the bureaucracy on any policy issue, including antitrust, but because the range of issues is large and all require the acquisition of specialized knowledge about programs and policy options, the Congress has established an elaborate system of committees and subcommittees, each of which is charged with the task of monitoring specific agencies and policy areas, allowance being made for inevitable overlapping committee jurisdictions. It is the membership of each of these committees that exercises proximate control over the agencies within its domain. The committee holds oversight hearings to evaluate agency performance, wields veto power over presidential appointments to agency policymaking positions, makes funding recommendations for various agency programs, and so on.

By and large, these committees are composed of members to whom the policies established or enforced by the agencies they oversee are important electorally. Thus, we normally observe agricultural committees to be dominated by representatives from rural constituencies, maritime committees dominated by members from coastal areas, and so forth. The interest-group model suggests that the position taken by each committee member on any given issue is chosen so as to maximize the political support received from his or her constituency. It therefore becomes the committee's task to search for the particular policy position, or set of policy positions, that is consistent with overall political equilibrium. In other words, through vote trading and compromise, the committee attempts to arrive at a set of policy objectives that *jointly* maximizes the membership's political support.

Once political equilibrium is attained, the committee must then see to it that the policies actually undertaken by the bureaucracy are consistent with its own preferences. To do so, the committee employs the aforementioned margins of control, using its power to hold oversight hearings, to review and recommend changes in the agency's authorization legislation, to confirm political appointees, and to adjust funding levels so as to assure that the agency is responsive to congressional wishes.[5]

Anecdotal evidence regarding the influence of Congress on bureaucratic decision making, including antitrust policymaking, is well documented.[6] More critical to the pork barrel hypothesis, however, is the question concerning whether the geographic distribution of antitrust cases differs systematically from the pattern one would observe in the absence of congressional influence on public law enforcement activities. Specifically, does antitrust enforcement selectively favor the firms and industries that operate in the states and districts represented by the members of Congress who sit on the committees having oversight responsibilities with respect to the antitrust bureaucracy?

This question was addressed in an important study of the FTC's case-bringing activities over the years 1961 through 1979.[7] After identifying the committees and subcommittees of the House and Senate having jurisdiction over the FTC, the authors tallied the number of antitrust actions against firms headquartered in the constituencies of the committee members that were *dismissed* relative to the total number of actions brought against these firms. They then tested whether this ratio was significantly different from the fraction of actions dismissed involving firms headquartered in jurisdictions not represented by committee members.

The basic results are summarized in Table 5.1. For each of two subperiods, 1961–69 and 1970–79,[8] and for each of the two Senate committees, one Senate subcommittee, and five House subcommittees sharing FTC budget and oversight authority, the table shows the ratios of dismissals to complaints issued within and without the jurisdictions represented by committee members as well as the z-statistic that tests for a difference in the two proportions.[9] As can be seen, the results suggest that FTC complaints issued against firms headquartered in the jurisdictions represented by the relevant committee members— particularly so in the case of the companies headquartered in the districts represented by the members of key House subcommittees— were more likely to be dismissed than complaints involving firms headquartered elsewhere. On the basis of this evidence of geographic bias, the authors concluded that "representation on certain subcommittees is apparently valuable in antitrust proceedings," a finding that lends strong support "to a private-interest theory of FTC behavior."[10]

Political influence on the FTC apparently goes beyond its antitrust mission. One study suggests that the commission drew back from an activist regulatory posture in late 1979 because of turnover among key congressional subcommittee members in the 1976 and 1978 elections.[11]

During most of the 1970s, the commission was a major participant in the "consumerist" movement, bringing large numbers of enforcement actions under various statutes such as the Truth-in-Lending Act and the Truth-in-Packaging Act as well as initiating many industrywide rule-making proceedings aimed at imposing regulations on, among others, the insurance industry, used car dealers, and undertakers.[12] In late 1979, however, the FTC was suddenly blasted by Congress as a runaway bureaucracy, an out-of-control agency that had "roamed far beyond its congressional mandates with a shotgun attempt to regulate all kinds of business activities that should not be the concern of the government." After a series of hearings in September 1979, which Senator Durkin described as "shock therapy for bureaucrats," a chastened commission systematically watered down or halted outright most of its controversial activities.[13]

There are two alternative explanations for this dramatic shift in regulatory activism at the FTC. One interpretation is that congres-

Table 5.1 Ratios of Dismissals to FTC Complaints, 1961–79

Congressional Committee or Subcommittee	1961-1969			1970-1979		
	Within Congressional Areas	Outside Congressional Areas	z-Statistic	Within Congressional Areas	Outside Congressional Areas	z-Statistic
U.S. Senate:						
Committee on Interior and Insular Affairs	17/64 0.2656	148/515 0.2874	0.36	8/23 0.3478	56/173 0.3237	0.23
Committee on Commerce, Science, and Transportation	32/140 0.2286	133/439 0.3030	1.70*	25/64 0.3906	39/132 0.2954	1.33
Subcommitee on Antitrust and Monopoloy of the Judiciary Committee	60/163 0.3681	105/416 0.2524	2.77***	7/24 0.2917	57/172 0.3314	0.39
U.S. House:						
Subcommittee on Independent Offices and the Dept. of Housing and Urban Development of the Appropriations Committee	14/26 0.5385	151/533 0.2730	2.93***	6/6 1.0000	58/190 0.3052	--a
Subcommittee on Agriculture and Related Agencies of the Appropriations Committee	38/110 0.3454	128/469 0.2708	1.56	0/0 --	64/196 0.3776	--a
Subcommittee on State, Justice, Commerce, and the Judiciary and Related Agencies of the Appropriations Committee	60/198 0.3030	105/381 0.2756	0.69	19/38 0.5000	45/158 0.2848	2.54**
Subcommittee on Oversight and Investigations of the Interstate and Foreign Commerce Committee	4/20 0.2000	161/559 0.2880	--a	6/11 0.5454	58/185 0.3135	1.59
Subcommittee on Monopolies and Commercial Law of the Judiciary Committee	62/176 0.3523	103/403 0.2556	2.37**	18/25 0.7200	46/171 0.2690	4.49***
All five House Committees	84/234 0.3590	81/345 0.2348	3.25***	29/55 0.5273	35/141 0.2651	3.74***

Source: Adapted from Roger L. Faith, Donald R. Leavens, and Robert D. Tollison, "Antitrust Pork Barrel," *Journal of Law and Economics* 15 (October 1982), pp. 337 and 341.
aInsufficient number of observations.
Notes: Asterisks denote significance at the 1 percent (***), 5 percent (**), and 10 percent (*) levels.

sional inattention during the 1970s had given the commission freedom to pursue its own policy agenda, but that once it had gone too far, Congress stepped in to halt the agency's excesses. The other explanation is that the FTC was consistently following the wishes of Congress throughout the 1970s and early 1980s. What occurred in the late 1970s was simply the disappearance of congressional support for an activist FTC:

> This resulted from the nearly complete turnover of those on and in control of the relevant Senate oversight subcommittee. None of the senior members of the subcommittee responsible for major FTC legislation and direction for the previous decade returned after 1976. Those previously in the minority took control of the subcommittee and began reversing the policies initiated by their predecessors. The 1979 and 1980 hearings were simply the most visible culmination of this process.[14]

The hypothesis that congressional influence plays an important role in explaining FTC decision-making receives further support from evidence that the political preferences of the members of relevant oversight committees affect the mix of enforcement actions brought by the commission. Using a sample of cases considered by the FTC between 1964 and 1976, Barry Weingast and Mark Moran reported results showing that the FTC's enforcement activities in four areas (merger, credit reporting, textile labeling, and Robinson-Patman cases) were significantly related to the scores assigned by the Americans for Democratic Action (ADA) to the committee members' voting records. To the extent that higher ADA scores, which indicate more "liberal" voting records, imply greater preferences for FTC activism, this finding suggests that the commission was pursuing— rather than ignoring—congressional interests during the 1970s.[15]

Additional support for the proposition that congressional influence, and not the sudden reining in of a runaway bureaucracy, explains the policy reversals at the FTC in the late 1970s is that because of turnover in oversight committee membership, the mean ADA score of the commission's overseers fell dramatically, particularly so in the Senate. Between 1977 and 1979, the overall mean Senate ADA score fell from 45.5 to 37.5 (out of a possible one hundred). On the Subcommittee on Consumer Affairs of the Senate Commerce Committee, the body having jurisdiction over the FTC's consumer protection mission, the mean ADA score fell from 57.7 to 26.4, and the average ADA score of the chairman of that subcommittee fell from 65 to 32.[16] In short, when congressional support for regulatory activism evaporated, the FTC rationally reversed course.

Subsequent research also suggests that political pressure is important in explaining the FTC's enforcement activities under Section 7 of the Clayton Act, but that antitrust policymaking is influenced by other factors as well.[17] The study examined internal commission records associated with all "second requests" issued under the Hart-Scott-Rodino Premerger Notification Act between June 14, 1982 and January 1, 1987.[18] The resulting sample included 70 FTC decisions. In 27 cases, the commission issued a complaint challenging the merger under Section 7; in the other 43 cases, the merger was allowed to proceed.[19]

A regression model designed to explain the commission's decision concerning whether or not it would challenge a particular merger was specified that included variables measuring the extent of agreement between the staff attorneys and economists assigned to the case respecting market concentration, barriers to entry, and the likelihood of collusion in the relevant industry. The model also included measures of the amount of political pressure placed on the commission regarding the merger. This pressure was proxied by two variables—the amount of news coverage relating to the acquisition and the number of times commission officials were called to testify before congressional committees during the 12-month period centered on the date of the second request.

All of these variables had a statistically significant influence on the commission's decision to prosecute. In particular, mergers were more likely to be challenged the higher the existing level of concentration in the relevant market (i.e., the more narrowly the boundaries of the relevant market were drawn), the higher the barriers to entry were thought to be, and the greater the perceived likelihood of collusion. (Interestingly, when the FTC's lawyers and economists disagreed on these issues, the commission typically sided with their attorneys.) Moreover, greater political pressure—more news coverage and more calls to appear before Congress—was found to cause the FTC to vote to challenge more mergers. Overall, the authors concluded from this evidence that

> there is a constellation of identifiable interests who benefit from the FTC's stopping mergers. Politicians, their organized constituents opposed to mergers, and agency attorneys apparently are among the principal beneficiaries. . . . [T]his combination of personal interests creates an upward bias in the way the Merger Guidelines are applied, resulting in a greater propensity to challenge mergers in the marginal case. Greater appreciation of the ways that antitrust works, and in particular the role of politics in the process, should begin to dispel the notion that antitrust can

be viewed as driven simply by Congressional and bureaucratic concerns for competition.[20]

These few studies of policymaking at the FTC suggest that Congress exercises a powerful influence over antitrust enforcement activities. And, given the institutional features and incentives created by geographically based political representation, a large part of this influence is directed at furthering the interests of local constituents. At the same time, however, antitrust policy consists of a complicated body of law with wide-ranging effects on the private economy. It is therefore unlikely to have a single purpose or to serve a single set of special interests.

CONGRESS AND THE SPECIAL INTERESTS

If Congress has an important influence on antitrust policy, what specific interests does it see are promoted by the bureaucracy's law enforcement activities? One popular view holds that small business is an important beneficiary of antitrust. As we have seen (Chapter 1), a number of leading jurists and other commentators have argued forcefully that the antitrust laws were primarily designed to prevent the aggregation of economic power in the hands of large firms, thereby preserving for its own sake and in spite of higher costs and prices a place for small business in the U.S. economy.

Some support for the small business hypothesis has been found in a study of the FTC's enforcement efforts under the Clayton Act, with particular reference to cases instituted charging violations of Section 2.[21] The commission was found to be much more vigorous in making allegations of unlawful price discrimination during periods of general economic recession than during upturns in the business cycle.

This result is consistent with a prediction of the interest-group theory of government, which suggests that regulatory agencies generally will not force any one group to bear the full adjustment costs associated with variations in the business cycle. That is, the interest-group model predicts that regulatory agencies will redistribute the gains and losses accompanying fluctuating economic conditions by supplying more "producer protection" during contractions and more "consumer protection" during expansions. In other words, regulatory activity that reduces consumer welfare will tend to be countercyclical, intensifying when aggregate demand falls and abating as demand increases.

Consider Sam Peltzman's formulation of the interest-group model.[22] Suppose that aggregate demand falls, decreasing "the total surplus ... over which the regulator might have control and, *pari passu*, the political payoff for its redistribution."[23] (In Peltzman's model, such an event is represented by a downward shift in the "profit hill.") Producer profits decline and increased incentives to cut price are created. Consumers thus tend to benefit at the expense of producers as the economy moves into recession, but to the extent that the regulator receives political support from both constituencies, he or she "will, in general, not force the entire adjustment onto one group." Instead, Peltzman's regulator will call on consumers to "buffer some of the producer losses" by not allowing prices to fall by as much as they would in an unregulated setting.[24] Similarly, when aggregate demand rises, regulatory agencies will redistribute some of producers' gains to consumers. Thus, the regulated price will not be increased by as much as it would rise in an unregulated setting.

Antitrust cases instituted under the Robinson-Patman Act represent a type of regulation that is widely perceived to be anticonsumer. Two hypotheses about the economic effects of the law on price discrimination are relevant in this regard. First, there is a large literature suggesting that cartel cheating increases when aggregate demand declines relative to normal demand.[25] According to this hypothesis, private price-fixing agreements are more difficult to sustain during economic contractions because excess production capacity generates powerful incentives for cartel members to cheat by secretly cutting price. Thus, the demand for Robinson-Patman cases rises during recessionary periods because more vigorous enforcement will limit price cutting and thereby help stabilize private cartels. Second, the downward pressure on price and profit accompanying recession would fall particularly heavily on smaller, high-cost firms in the economy. Such firms would rationally demand increased Robinson-Patman enforcement activity in order to restrict price cuts by larger firms that they are unable to match. Both of these hypotheses suggest that the demand for Robinson-Patman cases will abate during expansionary phases of the business cycle because above-normal demand alleviates price-cutting incentives.

In sum, the demand for Robinson-Patman enforcement activity (and for other types of regulation limiting price cutting) is predicted to increase during recessions so as to mitigate the redistribution of income away from private cartels and small business that would occur in an unregulated market setting. If the FTC is responsive to these demands, its Section 2 caseload would be expected to increase during downturns in the business cycle and to decline during upturns. This is precisely what the study found, a result that the authors concluded "can be rationalized under the view that the FTC is in the business of transferring wealth from consumers either to protect small business or to shore up cartels."[26]

Several other studies have identified a constituency for antitrust among small business interests.[27] A small business theory of antitrust is appealing for a number of reasons, not the least important of which is the fact that small businessmen and women are typically well situated to supply lobbying effort in their own behalf through trade associations and other business organizations at the local, state, and national political levels. For example, political opposition from the small business community has been instrumental in blocking efforts to reform or repeal the Robinson-Patman Act.[28]

Yet, it bears repeating that because antitrust policy consists of a complicated body of laws and administrative procedures with wide-ranging effects on the private economy, it is unlikely to have a single purpose or to serve a single set of special interests. This is particularly true in the case of the FTC, whose legislative mandate gives the agency broad authority to condemn unspecified "unfair methods of competition . . . and unfair or deceptive acts or practices in or affecting commerce." The latter charge, which establishes a consumer protection mission for the FTC, provides an opportunity for gaining further insights into the nature of the private interests served by the antitrust bureaucracy. In particular, the commission's enforcement activities in the area of consumer protection suggest that small business is not the only interest Congress wants the agency to promote.

Indeed, a wealth transfer favoring large firms has been identified in a study of the civil penalties imposed on violators of the commission's cease and desist orders.[29] (Although the FTC has authority to seek civil penalties in district court against firms that do not comply with certain antitrust orders, monetary fines have heretofore been assessed by the commission only in consumer protection matters.) The provisions of the law that authorize such penalties (Section 5(m)(1)(c) of the FTC Act, as amended) are vague with respect to how the commission should go about determining the size of the fine it assesses in any particular case. These provisions state only that penalties shall not exceed $10,000 for each violation, each day of noncompliance constituting a separate violation. In arriving at the total amount, the commission is instructed to consider "the degree of culpability, history of prior such conduct, ability to pay, effect on ability to continue business, and such other matters as justice may require." In short, the FTC has substantial discretion in using monetary fines as an enforcement tool.

The study examined data from 57 civil penalty cases considered by the commission between 1979 and 1981. A regression model designed to explain the variation in civil penalty amounts suggested that fines are a positive function of firm size as measured by sales and are also affected by mitigating and aggravating circumstances reflecting company financial condition, degree of culpability, imposition of other remedial measures, and institutional factors associated with statutory authority and type of violation. Interestingly, however, the commission's stated opinion concerning the degree of consumer injury caused by a particular violation had no impact on the size of the fine assessed, other things being equal. (In fact, when any judgment was made about the significance of consumer injury, whether large or small, fines were *lower* by more than 60 percent, on average, than when the subject was not addressed by the commission at all.) Moreover, although the majority of the variation in civil penalty amounts was accounted for by variations in firm size, an increase in firm size was found to result in a less than proportional increase in the size of the fine, ceteris paribus. In other words, everything else being the same, the fines levied by the commission on small firms constituted a greater proportion of their total sales than did the penalties assessed on large firms. This finding suggests that the fines levied by the FTC operate as a regressive tax on law violators, transferring wealth from small firms to large. Such a result casts some doubt on the popular view that small business is the FTC's main constituency.

Distributional gains and losses from the FTC's advertising substantiation program have also been noted.[30] Case selection decisions under this program, which requires advertisers to possess a reasonable basis for their claims prior to making them, do not appear to follow a "public interest" model. Instead, the commission has targeted its enforcement activities on industries where the potential for transferring wealth is the greatest, that is, industries populated by firms with disparate market shares and reputations. Moreover, evidence from the capital market indicates that the introduction of the FTC's substantiation program had a positive and significant effect on the stock prices of large advertising agencies, suggesting that these agencies were the intended beneficiaries of ad substantiation.

Additional evidence favoring the private interest model of ad substantiation derives from the fact that these regulations are strongly supported by the advertising industry's trade associations, who are themselves deeply involved in "self-regulation." Several months prior to the FTC decision that established substantiation requirements for advertisers,[31] a group of three advertising trade associations, the Association of National Advertisers, the American Association of Advertising Agencies, and the American Advertising Federation, jointly created the National Advertising Division (NAD) of the Council of Better Business Bureaus to monitor its members' advertising campaigns.[32] In addition to operating its own monitoring program, the

NAD accepts complaints about national advertising from any source, including consumers, competitors, and local Better Business Bureaus. The NAD then investigates the complaints, most of which involve allegations of inadequate substantiation, and, when it finds the complaints to be valid, orders modification or withdrawal of the offending ads. Adverse determinations of this sort can be appealed to the National Advertising Review Board (NARB) of the Council of Better Business Bureaus, which attempts to arbitrate the dispute. Cases that cannot be resolved internally are referred by the NARB to the FTC for further action.[33]

The NAD/NARB review process looks suspiciously like a cartel enforcement mechanism that relies on the FTC to discipline recalcitrant members. Between July 1971 and April 1980, for example, 931 of the 1697 complaints received by the NAD came either from member advertising agencies or from its own monitoring program.[34] Coupled with evidence that firms whose advertising claims are challenged successfully by the FTC are significantly impaired in their ability to attract first-time buyers (indeed, an adverse determination by the commission may destroy the entire brand name capital of the advertised product),[35] and reinforced by the potentially high cost of complying with substantiation requirements,[36] the conclusion that the ad substantiation program is a competitive weapon existing to benefit large advertising agencies and their clients is virtually definitive. It should not be surprising, then, that when the chairman of the FTC proposed modifying the ad substantiation program in 1982, he was told in no uncertain terms by representatives of the NAD that "the industry is not interested in anything which questions the advertiser's responsibility to have prior substantiation in hand."[37]

In the interest-group theory of government, the role of the legislature is to establish a political equilibrium level and pattern of wealth transfers by matching demanders and suppliers of redistribution. Its incentive to do so has a self-interest basis grounded in the objective of maximizing political support. Given a geographically based system of representation, such behavior will generally lead individual politicians to favor programs and policies that generate concentrated benefits for their own local constituencies while the costs are spread more diffusely over many jurisdictions. But, the interest-group model also suggests that deals will be struck in the legislature for transferring wealth whenever the incremental gain in political support supplied by the winners exceeds the marginal reduction in support from the losers. As such, there are a myriad of redistribution opportunities that can be exploited by politician-brokers. This market for wealth transfers derives simply from the fact that some groups in the polity are able to organize and acquire information about transfer activity more cheaply than others.

Antitrust, as this chapter has argued, is simply one example, albeit an important one, of a public policy apparatus that affords a mechanism for matching demanders and suppliers of wealth transfers. Antitrust is particularly valuable in this regard because it cuts across the economy, applying not to a specific industry as do more traditional forms of government regulation, but rather to specific business practices used in many industries. Thus, antitrust can be employed to selectively benefit one firm in an individual representative's home district, or it can be used to confer benefits on an entire class of firms (small business, for example).

The tools of positive economics analysis are only just beginning to be applied to study the impact of interest-group politics on antitrust processes. The wealth transfers associated with public law enforcement activities identified thus far are therefore more suggestive than definitive. Moreover, while it is by now fairly well established that the policies followed by the Federal Trade Commission are in many respects consistent with and responsive to its overseers in Congress, no evidence yet exists on the nature and extent of political influences on the other major public law enforcement agency, the Justice Department's Antitrust Division. Consistent with the insights of the interest-group theory of government, however, enough evidence on the links between Congress and the antitrust bureaucracy has been marshalled to explain why antitrust intervention so often fails to promote competition: Congress is (rationally) less interested in enhancing wealth than it is in redistributing it.

NOTES

1. See, generally, R. Douglas Arnold, *Congress and the Bureaucracy: A Theory of Influence* (New Haven, CT: Yale University Press, 1979).

2. Richard A. Posner, "The Federal Trade Commission," *University of Chicago Law Review* 37 (1969), pp. 47–89.

3. Posner is not the only FTC critic to stress the influence of ordinary pork barrel politics on antitrust enforcement activities. Consider the following two comments by other students of the commission:

According to Joseph W. Shea, Secretary of the FTC, any letter the commission gets from a Congressman's office is specially marked with an expedite sticker. The sticker gives the letter high priority, assuring the Congressman of an answer within five days. No distinction is made between letters— whether from complaining constituents, which Congressmen routinely "buck" over to the FTC, or those from the Congressmen themselves [Edward F. Cox, Robert C. Fellmeth, and John E. Schulz, *The Nader Report on the Federal Trade Commission* (New York: Richard W. Baron, 1969), p. 134].

In September 1969, despite vigorous dissents from his colleagues, Commissioner Elman supported Baum's analysis. He told a Senate group that congressional pressure "corrupts the atmosphere" in which his agency works. He charged that congressmen make private, unrecorded calls on behalf of companies seeking FTC approval of million-dollar mergers [Susan Wagner, *The Federal Trade Commission* (New York: Praeger, 1971), p. 211].

For a detailed legal and historical examination of the FTC's relationship with Congress, see William E. Kovacic, "The Federal Trade Commission and Congressional Oversight of Antitrust Enforcement: A Historical Perspective," in Robert J. Mackay, James C. Miller III, and Bruce Yandle, eds., *Public Choice and Regulation: A View from Inside the Federal Trade Commission* (Stanford, CA: Hoover Institution Press, 1987), pp. 63–120.

4. "[One] yardstick that the [Appropriations] subcommittee uses in judging how well the commission is performing has to do with case-load statistics." See Robert A. Katzmann, *Regulatory Bureaucracy: The Federal Trade Commission and Antitrust Policy* (Cambridge, MA: MIT Press, 1980), p. 146.

5. For a discussion of how the institutional structure of the commission facilitates congressional oversight of its enforcement activities, see William F. Shughart II, Robert D. Tollison, and Brian L. Goff, "Bureaucratic Structure and Congressional Control," *Southern Economic Journal* 52 (April 1986), pp. 962–72.

6. During the early years of the Reagan administration, for example, Congress consistently appropriated more money for the FTC than the agency had requested in order to prevent the closure of several regional offices of the FTC and to signal to the commission the desire of Congress for more active enforcement of the Robinson-Patman Act. See Bruce Yandle, "Regulatory Reform in the Realm of the Rent Seekers," in Mackay, Miller, and Yandle, eds., *Public Choice and Regulation*, pp. 121–42.

7. Roger L. Faith, Donald R. Leavens, and Robert D. Tollison, "Antitrust Pork Barrel," *Journal of Law and Economics* 15 (October 1982), pp. 329–42.

8. The sample was divided into two subperiods in order to test whether or not congressional influence over antitrust was affected by significant reform measures implemented at the FTC following the publication in 1969 of two highly critical studies of the commission's policies and procedures. These were American Bar Association (ABA), *Report of the American Bar Association Commission to Study the Federal Trade Commission* (Chicago, IL: ABA, 1969) and Cox et al., *The Nader Report on the Federal Trade Commission*.

9. Complaints include all formal actions initiated by the FTC against firms that are resolved either by an order to cease and desist when the defendant is found guilty or by an order to dismiss. Similar results were obtained when the definition of enforcement actions was expanded to include matters settled by consent decree.

10. Faith, Leavens, and Tollison, "Antitrust Pork Barrel," p. 342.

11. Barry R. Weingast and Mark J. Moran, "Bureaucratic Discretion or Congressional Control? Regulatory Policymaking by the Federal Trade Commission," *Journal of Political Economy* 91 (October 1983), pp. 765–800.

12. The commission's rule-making authority was established by the Magnuson-Moss Warranty/Federal Trade Commission Improvement Act of 1976.

13. Weingast and Moran, "Bureaucratic Discretion or Congressional Control?," p. 776, quoting James Singer, "The Federal Trade Commission—Business's Government Enemy No.1," *National Journal*, October 13, 1979, pp. 1676–80.

14. Ibid., p. 777.

15. Ibid., pp. 788–91.

16. Ibid., pp. 782–83.

17. Malcolm B. Coate, Richard S. Higgins, and Fred S. McChesney, "Bureaucracy and Politics in FTC Merger Challenges," Center for Policy Studies Working Paper No. 48, Clemson University, November 1988.

18. "Second requests" are authorized in cases where the commission believes that a proposed merger may entail anticompetitive consequences and seeks additional data from the merger partners for the purpose of evaluating the acquisition in more detail. See Chapter 3 for a discussion of the premerger notification process mandated by the Hart-Scott-Rodino Act.

19. Coate, Higgins, and McChesney, "Bureaucracy and Politics," p. 11.

20. Ibid., pp. 23–24.

21. Ryan C. Amacher, Richard S. Higgins, William F. Shughart II, and Robert D. Tollison, "The Behavior of Regulatory Activity Over the Business Cycle: An Empirical Test," *Economic Inquiry* 23 (January 1985), pp. 7–20.

22. Sam Peltzman, "Toward a More General Theory of Regulation," *Journal of Law and Economics* 19 (August 1976), pp. 211–40. The interest-group model is presented in Chapter 2.

23. Ibid., pp. 224–25.

24. Ibid., p. 225.

25. On the incentives for price-fixing cartels to seek government protection during economic contractions, see, for example, Ellis W. Hawley, *The New Deal and the Problem of Monopoly* (Princeton, NJ: Princeton University Press, 1966); Thor Hultgren and Merton R. Peck, *Costs, Prices, and Profits: Their Cyclical Relations* (New York: Columbia University Press, 1965); Fritz Machlup, *The Political Economy of Monopoly* (Baltimore, MD: Johns Hopkins University Press, 1952); and Fritz Voight, "German Experience with Cartels and Their Control During Pre-War and Post-War Periods," in J.P. Miller, ed., *Competition, Cartels, and Their Control* (Amsterdam: North-Holland, 1962), pp. 169–213.

26. Amacher et al., "Behavior of Regulatory Activity," p. 16.

27. Thomas W. Ross, "Winners and Losers Under the Robinson-Patman Act," *Journal of Law and Economics* 27 (October 1984), pp. 243–71 and George J. Stigler, "The Origin of the Sherman Act," *Journal of Legal Studies* 14 (January 1985), pp. 1–12.

28. James C. Miller III, "Comments on Baumol and Ordover," *Journal of Law and Economics* 28 (May 1985), p. 269.

29. Phyllis Altrogge and William F. Shughart II, "The Regressive Nature of Civil Penalties," *International Review of Law and Economics* 4 (June 1984), pp. 55–66.

30. Richard S. Higgins and Fred S. McChesney, "Truth and Consequences: The Federal Trade Commission's Ad Substantiation Program," *International Review of Law and Economics* 6 (1986), pp. 151–68.

31. *Pfizer, Inc.*, 81 FTC 23 (1972).

32. Higgins and McChesney, "Truth and Consequences," pp. 153–54. Also see William F. Shughart II and Robert D. Tollison, "Antitrust Recidivism in Federal Trade Commission Data: 1914–1982," in Mackay, Miller, and Yandle, eds., *Public Choice and Regulation*, pp. 276–77.

33. Priscilla LaBarbera, "Advertising Self-Regulation: An Evaluation," *MSU Business Topics* (Summer 1980), pp. 55–63 and Richard A. Posner, *Regulation of Advertising by the FTC* (Washington, DC: American Enterprise Institute, 1973).

34. LaBarbera, "Advertising Self-Regulation," p. 59.

35. Sam Peltzman, "The Effects of FTC Advertising Regulation," *Journal of Law and Economics* 24 (December 1981), pp. 403–48.

36. In *American Home Products Corp. v. FTC*, 695 F.2d 681 (3rd Cir. 1982), for example, the court held advertising claims to be unsubstantiated unless supported by the results of at least *two* controlled clinical studies.

37. "Ad Industry Goes Only Partway with Miller," *Advertising Age*, November 1, 1982, p. 40.

6

The Judiciary

Probably no institution of democratic government is held as being more a thing apart from the political process than the judiciary. In the U.S. political system, the relative independence of judges is an article of faith for both critics and defenders of judicial decision making. Most observers would agree that the courts are effectively insulated from the influence of ordinary politics as a consequence of constitutional provisions that tend to limit the ability of other government branches to sway their decisions. At the federal level, for example, judges are granted life tenure and can only be removed from the bench by means of impeachment; at the state level, most judges serve for more limited periods but generally enjoy a high level of security insofar as they are difficult to remove from office prior to the expiration of their terms. Both state and federal judges face heavy sanctions in cases of detected corruption, and so it is not surprising that bribery is generally thought to play a negligible role in judicial decision making. In short, the conventional wisdom is that the judiciary is—and, indeed, should be—above the fray of interest-group politics.

There are three major noneconomic views concerning the nature and consequences of judicial independence. The independence of the judiciary is sometimes portrayed as necessary to ensure that this branch of government functions as an effective counterweight to the legislative and executive branches. Put in simple terms, the role of the judiciary is to protect society from unconstitutional encroachments by the other branches, and judges are motivated to perform this function by concern for the public interest. Second, the independent judiciary is sometimes regarded as an agent not of the "general interest" but of the interests of groups (minorities) that are otherwise unrepresented (or underrepresented) in other political forums. Third, the independent judiciary is sometimes regarded as something of a "loose cannon." Richard Posner, for example, has argued that because judges receive no monetary gain from the way they decide cases, there is no incentive for them to slant their decisions in favor of any particular interest group.[1] He therefore concluded that there are no pecuniary or political factors that motivate judicial behavior. That is, judicial decision making cannot be explained on the basis of the personal economic interests of judges. Instead, Posner suggested that judges seek to maximize their own utility by deciding cases in ways that impose their personal preferences and values on society.[2]

In an important contribution to the interest-group theory of government, William Landes and Richard Posner argued that these popular models of the functioning of the independent judiciary are ad hoc and unconvincing.[3] They proposed an economic theory in which the role of the judiciary is to provide greater durability for wealth transfers purchased from the legislature by special interest groups. By reason of its effective independence of the existing legislature and by its practice of interpreting laws on the basis of the intent of the enacting legislature, the judiciary confers on legislation something of the character of a binding long-term contract. Wealth transfers enacted by previous legislatures are not overturned simply because the "political winds" have shifted. By following this methodology, the judiciary increases the durability of legislative contracts in general. Hence, legislation is worth more to interest groups than if it were vulnerable to changes in the political composition of the legislature. By providing this security in legislation over time, the independent judiciary makes legislated wealth transfers more valuable and, hence, raises the "price" interest groups are willing to pay to secure redistributions in their own favor.

Landes and Posner offered some limited empirical tests of their model (which was expressly formulated with respect to the federal judiciary), and several subsequent articles have provided evidence consistent with the main implications of the theory.[4] In other words, there are fairly strong indications that the independent judiciary actually functions in the way Landes and Posner predicted.

This chapter considers the implications of the Landes-Posner theory of the independent judiciary as it pertains to judicial decision making in the area of antitrust. To do so, we first lay out the Landes-Posner theory in slightly more detail. We then proceed to a discussion of the role played by the judiciary in the enforcement of the antitrust laws, and present some limited evidence suggesting that the self-interests of judges influence their decisions in antitrust proceedings.

At the outset, it is worth emphasizing that the private interests of the judges who resolve antitrust complaints are less obvious and, therefore, less well understood than those of other groups with a stake in antitrust policy outcomes. This lack of understanding concerning what motivates judicial decision making is partly due to the fact that economists have only recently begun to apply their model of rational choice to the third branch of government. However, the importance of the judiciary's role in antitrust—interpreting the language of the antitrust statutes, determining the boundaries of what constitutes unlawful behavior, setting antitrust penalties, and so on—establishes a prima facie case for asking whether private interests are at work in the courtroom as they are in the legislature and the antitrust bureaucracy.

THE INDEPENDENT JUDICIARY IN AN INTEREST-GROUP PERSPECTIVE

A large literature has arisen in recent years that argues that legislatures can be usefully modeled as "firms" supplying wealth transfers to competing interest groups in the form of legislation.[5] In other words, legislatures assign property rights in wealth transfers to the highest bidder by means of legislative contracts (laws).

But while there are many similarities between legislative "markets" and ordinary markets, the two differ in at least one important respect, namely the mechanisms available for enforcing contracts once they have been negotiated. There are basically two types of mechanisms for enforcing contracts in private markets. One is enforcement by a third party. In this case, the contracting parties rely upon some third party—an arbitrator or the courts—to resolve disputes and to sanction non-compliance. Alternatively, when explicit contracts are absent or incomplete by reason of being costly to negotiate, self-enforcing mechanisms help maintain a transactional relationship. That is, each party relies upon the threat of withdrawal of future business to assure that implicit agreements will be honored.[6] In political markets, however, contracts can in principle be broken by the legislature whenever it so chooses, and the affected party has no immediate avenue of redress. An interest group cannot bring suit against the legislature when an existing contract has been rescinded following a shift in the political winds.

At the same time, however, it is obvious that the value of a legislative wealth transfer to the benefitting interest group will in part be a function of the expected duration of the contract. Uncertainty with respect to the duration of the contract (or a reduction in its expected duration) will tend to lower the present value of the transfer. Given that the composition of the legislature can shift unpredictably over time, and that individual legislators face the necessity of frequent electoral challenge (and consequently have limited tenure of office), markets for legislative wealth transfers would not function very efficiently or, in the limit, would not emerge at all without institutional mechanisms capable of mitigating contractual instability. Simply put, interest groups are not likely to expend resources to secure the passage of legislation if, once enacted, laws are easily altered or repealed. Hence, it is not surprising that wealth-maximizing legislatures have instituted various measures designed to improve the stability of legislative contracts over time and thereby increase the demand for legislative output.

Landes and Posner argued that these institutional arrangements fall into two major categories.[7] The first is comprised of the various procedural rules of the legislature itself, which serve to increase the continuity, regularity, and, hence, stability of legislative operations over time. The constitutive rules of the legislature on such matters as bill introductions, committee hearings, floor action, and majority voting are examples in this regard. By making it more difficult to enact legislation in the first place, such measures serve the purpose of making it more difficult to amend or repeal existing laws.[8]

The second mechanism for promoting the durability of legislative contracts is the existence of an independent judiciary. Legislation is not self-enforcing; recourse to the courts is necessary to give effect to statutory language. If the judiciary acted at the behest of the current membership of the legislature in its decision making with respect to legislation enacted in some previous session of the legislature, decided cases with an eye toward protecting otherwise unrepresented interest groups, or simply based its decisions on personal preferences, it might refuse to enforce those laws. Such judicial behavior would have the effect of rendering contracts between previous legislatures and benefiting interest groups null and void. Landes and Posner offered an example in which the dairy industry "buys" a large tax on margarine production in one session of Congress, but in the next session the margarine producers "buy" the removal of the tax.[9] Similar consequences would arise if the dairy industry buys a tax on margarine production in one session of Congress, but the courts subsequently hold the tax to be unconstitutional.

Of course, an existing legislature might itself simply decide to repeal previously passed legislation. But, as we have mentioned, strong impediments exist to rapid legislative action of this sort, most importantly including the costs associated with achieving majority support for such a repeal in the legislature, along with the various other institutional mechanisms that restrict such behavior (bicameralism, the committee system, and filibusters, for example). A court challenge may for these reasons represent a low-cost means by which existing legislative contracts can be abrogated, given a nonindependent judiciary. At least, litigation represents an alternative margin on which existing wealth transfers can be competed away.

Assume, however, that the judiciary is independent of the (sitting) legislature. If this independence means that judges can be relied upon

to interpret and enforce legislation in accordance with original legislative intent, the independent judiciary will tend to function to protect
the integrity of previous legislative contracts. By doing so, the value
of present and future legislation to interest groups is enhanced, and
the practice of interest-group politics is therefore facilitated. If instead
the legislative marketplace approximated Hobbesian anarchy, that is,
if existing legislatures were unconstrained in their efforts to overturn
previously established contracts between earlier legislatures and interest groups, such contracts would be worth little, and wealth transfer activity by government would be greatly diminished as a result.
When there is no honor among thieves, the level of theft tends to
decline, as it were.

In the Landes-Posner model, then, the courts are considered to be
producers of legislative durability. By virtue of its independence of
the existing legislature and by following the practice of interpreting
legislation in accord with the intent of the enacting legislature, the
judiciary functions to increase the expected present value of legislative wealth transfers. As Landes and Posner explained, however, the
value of the courts to the legislature in this regard and, hence, the
ability of the judiciary to retain its independence, depend upon how
well the courts perform the function assigned to them. This is because
the current legislature, and not previous ones, makes decisions about
the level of judges' salaries and appropriations to the judicial branch
generally. The current legislature is thus in a position to reward
cooperative, and to sanction uncooperative, judicial behavior. And so,

> [i]f the courts are not valued highly, the imposition by the current
> legislature of coercive measures that impair the courts' effective
> functioning will not be perceived as highly costly, and such
> measures will therefore be imposed more often. The value . . . of
> courts is a function in major part of the predictability of their
> decisions, and decision according to the original meaning of a
> statute rather than according to the ever-shifting preferences of
> successive legislatures is probably an important source of that
> predictability, in part because such a decision is based on
> materials (for example, the congressional debates) available to all
> to study and base predictions of judicial behavior on. In short,
> the ability of courts to maintain their independence from the
> political branches may depend at least in part on their willingness
> to enforce the "contracts" of earlier legislatures according to the
> original understanding of the "contract."[10]

Thus, judicial "independence" is a subtle concept indeed. Within
the context of the interest-group model, institutional features like life

tenure that increase the degree of independence of the judiciary from ordinary politics do not place the court system outside the market for wealth transfers but rather provide that market with a contract enforcement mechanism that helps assure its efficient operation. At the same time, the judiciary's ability to maintain its independence is partly a function of its continuing willingness to enforce contracts on the terms agreed to initially in the legislative marketplace.

Unfortunately, Landes and Posner failed to provide an evidentiary link between their interest-group theory of the independent judiciary and actual judicial systems in operation. They showed how legislatures might benefit from the behavior of an independent judiciary but not why judges themselves would benefit from maintaining their independence in the face of political pressure. One recent study has offered evidence for such a link by examining the relationship between measures of judicial independence and judges' salaries.[11] Using data from the state courts, the researchers found that, holding other important factors constant, legislatures appear to reward judicial systems that display a greater degree of independence with higher salaries. That is, the enhanced durability—and, hence, value—imparted to legislative contracts by the independent judiciary seems to be reflected in the pecuniary rewards of judicial office. The authors concluded from this evidence that "self-interested judges can be shown to behave in a manner consistent with the functioning of efficient markets for coercive wealth transfers for the same reasons that other participants in those markets participate—wealth maximization."[12]

The role assigned to the independent judiciary by Landes and Posner offers important insights into the workings of the market for wealth transfers. More important, perhaps, is the fundamental assumption underlying the economic approach to the analysis of judicial behavior, which holds "that judges, like other people, seek to maximize a utility function that includes both monetary and nonmonetary elements (the latter including leisure, prestige, and power)."[13] Of course, not even the most imperialistic of economists would argue that the private interests of judges are the sole determinant of judicial behavior. Just as obviously, however, it is facile to assume that because judges are "independent" they do not respond to incentives and constraints. Indeed, the hypothesis that private interests influence judicial decision making is beyond dispute, but because research in this area is only just beginning, a clear understanding of the variables that enter into judges' utility functions has not yet emerged.[14] What is becoming increasingly apparent, however, is that enforcement of legislative wealth transfers, and not some independent conception of the "public interest," motivates judicial decision making in a large number of cases.[15]

THE JUDICIARY AND ANTITRUST POLICY

The judicial branch plays an obviously important role in the enforcement of antitrust policy insofar as it represents the final arbiter of disputes regarding what specific business practices constitute violations of the Sherman, Clayton, and Federal Trade Commission Acts. It performs this function in two basic settings. The first involves the resolution of complaints issued by the two federal law enforcement agencies; the other consists of private antitrust litigation, which in terms of sheer numbers of suits accounts for the bulk of the judiciary's caseload.

According to the interest-group theory of government, judicial decision making is not guided by some abstract conception of the "public interest." The judiciary instead serves as an agent of the legislature and its principal objective is to impart durability to the private interest bargains struck in the political marketplace. It does so by interpreting legislation according to the intent of the enacting legislature, a practice that is reflected in, and reinforced by, the importance assigned to precedent in judicial decisions.

Whether or not the judiciary actually functions in the way predicted by the interest-group model remains an open question as far as antitrust policy is concerned, however. No direct tests of the theory's implications for judicial behavior in the area of antitrust have yet been formulated. But several observations about actual antitrust enforcement do not refute the hypothesis that the courts function to promote private interests and not the public interest. For one, if, as much of the evidence on the effects of antitrust policy suggests, the laws themselves serve not to enhance economic efficiency but to restrain output and retard the growth of productivity,[16] then the judiciary has obviously contributed to this outcome. That is, in the case of antitrust the courts have neither functioned as an effective counterweight to the legislature nor have they acted to protect the interests of at least one group—consumers—that are underrepresented in other political forums.

Additional insights into the judiciary's role in antitrust policy can be deduced from its decisions with respect to the cases instituted by the federal law enforcement agencies. As we have seen (Chapter 5), the policies followed by these bureaus, particularly those of the FTC, tend to be consistent with and responsive to the preferences of the legislature. Thus, if the antitrust enforcement agencies bring the cases

Congress wants them to bring, regardless of how these enforcement actions comport with economic efficiency, then one implication of the interest-group theory is that the courts should do little to interfere with these efforts. That is, the interest-group theory predicts a high success rate in the federal courts for the Justice Department and the FTC.[17]

This is in fact what the data show, but it is important to note that the role of the federal courts in antitrust policy varies greatly depending upon the source of the complaint. All Justice Department antitrust complaints are resolved in the courts; almost none of the FTC's are. This difference arises from peculiarities in the institutional structures of the two agencies.

The Department of Justice is an agency of the executive branch of government. It accordingly has no adjudicative powers and must therefore appeal to the courts for authority to enforce the antitrust laws against persons or firms it alleges to have violated them. When the Justice Department files a complaint, usually but not always in the District Court of the District of Columbia, the defendant has three basic options. It can enter a plea of guilty (or, more typically, nolo contendere) and accept the penalty imposed by the court; it can plead innocent and contest the charges at trial; or, as happens most often, it can negotiate an out-of-court settlement with the Justice Department, which will then be submitted for judicial approval in the form of a consent order. (Indeed, such negotiations usually take place in advance of the complaint being filed so that the court is presented with a fait accompli.) In such settlements, the defendant typically agrees to plead nolo contendere in exchange for a penalty less severe than it would expect to be asked for and imposed if found guilty at trial. Thus, no matter how they are ultimately resolved, the federal courts are involved directly in all antitrust enforcement actions brought by the Justice Department.

By contrast, like most so-called independent agencies of the federal government,[18] the FTC's mandate combines prosecutorial and adjudicative functions. Complaints issued by the commission in its prosecutorial role are, if contested by the defendant, first litigated before an administrative law judge (ALJ), a hearing examiner who is in the FTC's employ. If the defendant is found guilty at this stage, the decision is automatically appealed to the five-member commission, which then acts as judge. By majority vote, the commissioners decide whether or not to uphold the ALJ's ruling in whole or in part, and assess the penalty, if any.[19] If the commission determines that a law violation has occurred, only then may the defendant appeal the FTC's decision to the federal courts.[20] At any point in this process, the defendant has the option of negotiating a settlement with the commission's attorneys. By definition, such consent orders, which like all other FTC actions, including decisions to open formal investigations and issue complaints, must be approved by majority vote of the commissioners, never find their way into the federal courts.[21] In short, the judiciary becomes involved in antitrust complaints issued by the commission only if, after being tried before an FTC hearing examiner and found guilty by the commission, the defendant exercises its right of appeal.

One important consequence of the commission's joint prosecutorial and judicial roles is that the arrangement appears to lengthen the law enforcement process significantly and, hence, raise the cost of antitrust litigation to the defendants. In essence, alleged antitrust violators face additional proceedings before the FTC that they would not face if the same practices were challenged by the Justice Department. Richard Posner, for example, has concluded that "the use of administrative proceedings to enforce the antitrust laws has not contributed to expedition—rather the contrary." Examining all federal antitrust cases instituted and settled between 1930 and 1964, he discovered that "the average length of FTC cases in which the respondent exercised his right of judicial review is far greater than the average length of litigated Department of Justice cases; and the length of FTC cases reviewed by the Supreme Court is greater than that of Department of Justice cases reviewed by the Court."[22] A more recent study has shown that while nearly one-third of the Justice Department's antitrust cases are settled in six months or less, in excess of 90 percent of the FTC's enforcement actions last *more* than six months.[23]

Perhaps more critical is the potential conflict of interest facing the FTC's commissioners in their dual role of prosecutor and judge. Succinctly put, "FTC cases are tried largely within the FTC itself, with five commissioners first bringing the charges and later adjudging guilt or innocence."[24] Conflicts are most likely to arise in so-called test cases where attempts are made to create new law. In the words of former commissioner Philip Elman, "while there is no bias or prejudgment of guilt in the classic sense, there is an inescapable predisposition in favor of the agency position, as set forth in the complaint. . . . While a test case may be and usually is vigorously contested, the result—at least in the agency phase—is likely to be a forgone conclusion."[25] Richard Posner's judgment is more harsh:

> It is too much to expect men of ordinary character and competence to be able to judge impartially in cases that they are responsible for instituting in the first place. An agency that dismissed many of the complaints it issued would stand condemned of having squandered the taxpayer's money on meritless causes.

Besides, commissioners who lack the tenure, the high status, and the freedom from other duties that federal judges enjoy cannot realistically be expected to perform the judicial function as well; and they do not.[26]

To the criticism that the commission's dual mandate creates an inescapable conflict of interest between its prosecutorial and judicial functions, FTC supporters respond that because the federal courts ultimately determine the legal standards applied to antitrust law violators, aberrant decisions by the commission will never attain the status of enforceable precedent.[27] The fact of the matter is, however, that fewer than 10 percent of the FTC's antitrust cases are ever heard by the courts and those that are appealed are almost always upheld.

Table 6.1 shows the disposition of the complaints issued by the FTC in its antitrust mission between 1963 and 1982.[28] What stands out immediately in the data is that the vast majority of the commission's antitrust charges are settled by consent decree. Over the entire period considered, nearly 65 percent of the complaints issued were resolved in this manner; only about one in three complaints were contested before a FTC hearing examiner (compare columns 3 and 4 with column 2). It is also apparent that the FTC rarely dismisses the complaints it votes to issue when serving in its prosecutorial role. Only 39 (or 7 percent) of the 549 complaints voted out during the 18 years covered in the table were not upheld by a majority of the commissioners. And, of the 481 complaints not dismissed during this period, just 48 decisions were appealed to the federal courts. The FTC's decision was reversed in only 12 of these 48 appeals, the latter figure representing about one-quarter of the cases litigated at the commission. The FTC's success rate at the Supreme Court was even more impressive. The commission lost only one of the 14 of its antitrust cases reviewed by the Court between 1963 and 1984.[29] In short, if we define "success" to represent those orders and decisions issued by the FTC and not appealed by respondents, as well as those upheld by the federal courts if appealed, then the commission was successful in about 85 percent of the antitrust cases it instituted during a recent 18-year period (columns 6 plus 8 plus 10, divided by column 2).

The FTC's record of success in antitrust cases is virtually identical to that of the Department of Justice, which is shown in Table 6.2. Between 1963 and 1984, the Antitrust Division prevailed in 86 percent of the complaints it filed. (Its success rate in criminal cases, which account for about 44 percent of the total, was even higher—convictions in criminal cases were obtained 92 percent of the time.)[30] The Justice Department's record at the Supreme Court was not quite as

Table 6.1 Disposition of FTC Unfair Competition Complaints, FY 1965–82

Fiscal Year (1)	Total Complaints Issued (2)	Settled by Consent Order (3)	Litigated (4)	Dismissed (5)	FTC		Court of Appeals		
					Not Dismissed Not Appealed (6)	Not Dismissed was Appealed (7)	FTC Upheld (8)	FTC Reversed (9)	Mixed (10)
1965	25	17	8	3	19	3	2	0	1
1966	95	81	14	2	88	5	4	1	0
1967	24	17	7	1	19	4	2	0	2
1968	16	10	6	0	15	1	1	0	0
1969	28	19	9	0	24	4	3	0	1
1970	24	12	12	8	13	3	2	0	1
1971	31	19	12	3	25	3	2	1	0
1972	33	15	18	8	20	5	3	2	0
1973	31	20	11	2	28	1	0	1	0
1974	24	13	11	2	16	6	2	3	0
1975	30[a]	14	16	2	22	5	4[b]	1	0
1976	37	24	13	2	29	6[c]	3	2	0
1977	29[d]	18	11	3	23	2[e]	0	1	0
1978	12[f]	6	6	2	7	0	0	0	0
1979	37[g]	26	11	3	29	0	0	0	0
1980	34[h]	21	13	0	27	0	0	0	0
1981	23[i]	16	7	0	18	0	0	0	0
1982	16[j]	8	2	0	11	0	0	0	0
Totals	549	356	187	39	433	48	29	12	5

Source: Evaluation Office, FTC Bureau of Competition.
[a] Includes one case in which litigation was pending as of March 1983.
[b] Includes one case in which appeal to Supreme Court pending.
[c] Includes one case which was remanded to the FTC by the Court of Appeals.
[d] Includes five "Transition Quarter" cases of which one was pending.
[e] Includes one case in which a proposed merger was abandoned while on appeal.
[f] Includes three matters pending at the FTC.
[g] Includes five matters pending at the FTC.
[h] Includes seven matters pending at the FTC.
[i] Includes five matters pending at the FTC.
[j] Includes two pending matters and three cases in which mergers were abandoned after the FTC filed a preliminary injunction.

Table 6.2 The Department of Justice Won-Lost Record in Antitrust Cases, 1963–84

Year in which case was Instituted (1)	Total Cases[a] (2)	Cases Won[b] (3)	Percent Won (4)
1963	26	20	77
1964	51	43	84
1965	29	25	86
1966	36	35	97
1967	34	29	85
1968	47	38	81
1969	43	40	93
1970	54	43	80
1971	43	34	79
1972	72	60	83
1973	47	37	79
1974	46	41	89
1975	39	33	85
1976	45	39	87
1977	40	34	85
1978	41	38	93
1979	33	28	85
1980	38	34	89
1981	16	14	88
1982	20	17	85
1983	25	21	84
1984	17	17	100
Totals	842	720	86

Source: Joseph C. Gallo, Joseph L. Craycraft, and Steven C. Bush, "Guess Who Came to Dinner: An Empirical Study of Federal Antitrust Enforcement for the Period 1963-1984," *Review of Industrial Organization* 2 (1985), p. 114.
[a]Excludes ongoing cases.
[b]Includes consent orders and cases won at trial.

good as that of the FTC, but was still impressive: It won 25 (71 percent) of the 35 cases reviewed by the Court between 1963 and 1984.[31]

The data thus suggest that the courts tend not to interfere much with the law enforcement activities of the federal antitrust bureaucracy. On average, the judiciary sides with the defendants in public antitrust cases only about 15 percent of the time. Is this a little or a lot? More to the point, are the evidently high success rates of the antitrust bureaus in the courts consistent with the interest-group hypothesis of judicial behavior?

Complete answers to the foregoing questions are unfortunately not available. Much more research is required, particularly of the antitrust complaints *not* upheld by the courts. Are public antitrust cases overturned when they would break bargains struck in the legislative marketplace? That is, does the judiciary act to void the antitrust charges brought by the Department of Justice and the FTC when these bureaus for some reason fail to protect the interests of groups (not including consumers) the antitrust laws were designed to protect? Without knowing more about the characteristics held in common, if any, by the public antitrust cases the courts reverse, no conclusions about the judiciary's function can be drawn. We can say, however, that if the antitrust bureaus serve as the agents of Congress, whose role is to enforce a certain set of contracts between the legislature and private interest groups, then the judiciary appears to aid in this enforcement effort by upholding the cases brought by these agencies much more often than not.

The limited data available are thus broadly consistent with the function assigned to the judicial branch by the interest-group theory of government. Judicial decision making in the area of antitrust may also be influenced by more immediate personal interests. Based upon information derived from more than 600 criminal indictments for Sherman Act violations handed down from 1955 through 1980, Mark Cohen recently reported evidence suggesting that, other things being the same, jail sentences imposed on defendants tend to be longer, fines tend to be higher, and nolo contendere pleas are less likely to be accepted over the government's objection when the judge hearing the case perceives an increased opportunity for promotion to a higher court.[32] (Promotion opportunities were measured in terms of vacancies on the appeals court in the sentencing judge's district, his or her experience on the bench, and whether or not the judge was of the same political party as the president.) Cohen also found that the defendants who choose to contest criminal antitrust charges at trial and are subsequently convicted receive heavier penalties, on average, the more crowded is the court docket of the judge who hears the case. This result implies that judges may use the discretion available to them in determining sentences partly to ease their own workloads. That is, by levying stiffer penalties on convicted violators, some of the defendants awaiting trial are induced to settle out of court, thereby reducing the case backlog on the judge's calendar.

In sum, the small amount of evidence generated by applying the economic model of rational behavior to the third branch of government suggests that private interests do play a role in explaining judicial decision making in the area of antitrust. How significant this role may be remains a critical topic for future research.

NOTES

1. Richard A. Posner, *Economic Analysis of Law*, 3rd ed. (Boston: Little, Brown, 1986), pp. 505–07.

2. See, however, Mwangi S. Kimenyi, William F. Shughart II, and Robert D. Tollison, "What Do Judges Maximize?," *Economia Delle Scelte Pubbliche* (1985), pp. 181–88, suggesting that judges are motivated by pecuniary factors.

3. William M. Landes and Richard A. Posner, "The Independent Judiciary in an Interest-Group Perspective," *Journal of Law and Economics* 18 (December 1975), pp. 875–901.

4. W. Mark Crain and Robert D. Tollison, "Constitutional Change in an Interest-Group Perspective," *Journal of Legal Studies* 8 (January 1979), pp. 165–75; W. Mark Crain and Robert D. Tollison, "The Executive Branch in the Interest-Group Theory of Government," *Journal of Legal Studies* 8 (June 1979), pp. 55–89; W. Mark Crain, William F. Shughart II, and Robert D. Tollison, "Legislative Majorities as Nonsalvageable Assets," *Southern Economic Journal* 55 (October 1988), pp. 303–14; Gary M. Anderson, William F. Shughart II, and Robert D. Tollison, "On the Incentives of Judges to Enforce Legislative Wealth Transfers," *Journal of Law and Economics* 32 (April 1989), pp. 215–28; and Gary M. Anderson, Delores T. Martin, William F. Shughart II, and Robert D. Tollison, "Behind the Veil: The Political Economy of Constitutional Change," in W. Mark Crain and Robert D. Tollison, eds., *Predicting Politics: Essays in Empirical Political Economy* (Ann Arbor: University of Michigan Press, forthcoming).

5. See Robert E. McCormick and Robert D. Tollison, *Politicians, Legislation, and the Economy: An Inquiry into the Interest-Group Theory of Government* (Boston, MA: Martinus Nijhoff, 1981), for example, and Chapter 2 for a summary of this model.

6. Benjamin Klein and Keith B. Leffler, "The Role of Market Forces in Assuring Contractual Performance," *Journal of Political Economy* 89 (August 1981), pp. 615–41.

7. Landes and Posner, "Independent Judiciary."

8. A related institutional mechanism for promoting the stability of legislative contracts is the political party. Insofar as such organizations have longer time horizons than their individual members, they have strong interests in maintaining reputations for not reneging on bargains struck with interest groups in the past. One way political parties can provide some assurance to interest groups that they will not arbitrarily void existing legislative contracts is to invest in super-majorities (majorities larger than the minimum necessary for simple control) in the legislature. In essence, the majority party is a supplier of legislative output, and the value of its brand name capital is a function of how well it keeps its word. If the party cheats on its commitments to interest groups, this capital is depreciated. This means that in future elections it will be harder for the party to sell its program to prospective supporters. A larger-than-minimum majority is one way that a party signals that it has more to lose by cheating in terms of its investment in brand name capital, that is, cheating would mean that the party would incur losses in excess of short-run gains. Control of the legislature by

larger-than-minimum majorities is thus analogous to the use of implicit mechanisms for enforcing contracts in ordinary markets. See Crain, et al., "Legislative Majorities as Nonsalvageable Assets."

9. Landes and Posner, "Independent Judiciary," p. 879.

10. Ibid., p. 885.

11. Anderson, et al., "Incentives of Judges to Enforce Legislative Wealth Transfers."

12. Ibid., p. 227.

13. Posner, *Economic Analysis of Law*, p. 505.

14. Richard Higgins and Paul Rubin, for example, tested Richard Posner's conjecture that because judges might aspire to hold higher judicial appointments, they would display "extreme sensitivity to reversal." Higgins and Rubin hypothesized that judges' sensitivity to reversal would tend to decline (and their decisions would therefore be more likely to be overturned) as they grow older and their promotion prospects diminish. However, the researchers did not find a statistically significant relationship between judges' reversal rates and either age or seniority in their study of a small sample of U.S. district court judges of the Eighth Circuit. See Posner, *Economic Analysis of Law*, p. 505, and Richard S. Higgins and Paul H. Rubin, "Judicial Discretion," *Journal of Legal Studies* 9 (January 1980), pp. 129–38.

15. For an extensive discussion of the judiciary's history of declining to interfere with the private interest bargains struck in the legislature, including a large number of examples from the case law, see Peter H. Aranson, "Judicial Control of the Political Branches: Public Purpose and Public Law," in James A. Dorn and Henry G. Manne, eds., *Economic Liberties and the Judiciary* (Fairfax, VA: George Mason University Press, 1987), pp. 47–110.

16. See, for example, Dominick T. Armentano, *Antitrust and Monopoly: Anatomy of a Policy Failure* (New York: Wiley, 1982); Robert H. Bork, *The Antitrust Paradox: A Policy at War with Itself* (New York: Basic Books, 1978); Yale Brozen, *Concentration, Mergers, and Public Policy* (New York: Macmillan, 1982); Richard A. Posner, *Antitrust Law: An Economic Perspective* (Chicago, IL: University of Chicago Press, 1976); and the discussion in Chapter 1.

17. Of course, such an observation is consistent with other hypotheses about judicial behavior, including the proposition that the courts defer to the expertise of the antitrust bureaus when confronted with cases involving complicated matters of law and economics. This alternative view of a passive judiciary, however, is also an admission that the conventional theories of the judiciary serving as an effective counterweight to the executive and legislative branches do not apply in the area of antitrust.

18. "Independence" here refers to budgetary independence of the executive branch.

19. Generally speaking, the commission's remedial actions are in the form of an order to cease and desist an unlawful practice. It may do more in certain types of cases, however. In merger cases, for example, the commission may order partial divestiture of assets (and, indeed, may require that the assets be sold to a specific purchaser) or it may place a ban on future acquisitions. The commission does not itself have authority to impose fines or jail sentences, however.

20. Note only that the defendant may exercise the right of appeal at any stage of the law enforcement process. If the hearing examiner or the commission itself rules against the FTC, the matter is closed.

21. Except if the defendant subsequently violates the terms of the consent order. In such cases the commission has authority to seek civil penalties in district court against the violator. See Chapter 5.

22. Richard A. Posner, "A Statistical Study of Antitrust Enforcement," *Journal of Law and Economics* 13 (October 1970), pp. 377–81.

23. Joseph C. Gallo, Joseph L. Craycraft, and Steven C. Bush, "Guess Who Came to Dinner: An Empirical Study of Federal Antitrust Enforcement for the Period 1963–1984," *Review of Industrial Organization* 2 (1985), p. 112.

24. E.E. Vaill, "The Federal Trade Commission: Should It Continue as Both Prosecutor and Judge in Antitrust Proceedings?," *Southwestern University Law Review* 10 (1978), p. 764.

25. Ibid., p. 770. Several examples belie Elman's assumption of no prejudgment. General Mills, a defendant in the commission's infamous (and ultimately dismissed) "shared monopoly" case, moved to disqualify then FTC chairman Michael Pertschuk on the basis of a public statement he made suggesting that "winning the cereal case would be an enormous help." Although the commission subsequently voted to deny General Mills' motion, Pertschuk was later disqualified from participating in the FTC's children's advertising rule-making proceedings after the District Court of the District of Columbia found that he had "conclusively prejudged factual issues." Similarly, in January 1979 a FTC cease-and-desist order against the American General Insurance Company was overturned because of "Commissioner Colliers' adjudicative participation in the case." Collier had served as a FTC attorney in *American General Ins. Co. v. FTC*, 496 F.2d 197 (5th Cir. 1974) and as commissioner in *American General Ins. Co. v. FTC*, 589 F.2d 462 (9th Cir. 1979). See Vaill, "Federal Trade Commission," pp. 765–66.

26. American Bar Association (ABA), *Report of the American Bar Association Commission to Study the Federal Trade Commission* (Chicago: ABA, 1969), p. 440.

27. Thomas Kauper, for example, sees advantages in the FTC's dual functions in that "as an enforcement agency, as well as an adjudicator, the commission makes policy decisions and provides both the opportunity for judicial actions and input to the judicial process." See Thomas E. Kauper, "Competition Policy and the Institutions of Antitrust," *South Dakota Review* 23 (Winter 1978), pp. 17–18.

28. These data were collected by the author in March 1983. They accordingly include a small number of cases that were pending at the time, and whose subsequent resolution could not be determined.

29. Gallo et al., "Guess Who Came to Dinner," p. 117.

30. Ibid., pp. 118–19.

31. Ibid., p. 116.

32. Mark A. Cohen, "Toward an Economic Theory of Judicial Discretion: The Case of Sentencing Criminal Antitrust Offenders," Owen Graduate School of Management Working Paper, Vanderbilt University, October 1988; and Mark A. Cohen, "The Role of Criminal Sanctions in Antitrust Enforcement," *Contemporary*

Policy Issues 7 (October 1989), pp. 36–46. Cohen has also found evidence supporting a private interest theory of judicial behavior in a study of decisions concerning the constitutionality of the U.S. Sentencing Commission. See Mark A. Cohen, "Explaining Judicial Behavior, or, What's 'Unconstitutional' about the Sentencing Commission?," Owen Graduate School of Management Working Paper, Vanderbilt University, July 1989.

7

The Private Antitrust Bar

Under both the Sherman Act and the Clayton Act, "[a]ny person who shall be injured in his business or property by reason of anything forbidden in the antitrust laws ... shall recover three-fold the damages by him sustained, and the cost of suit, including a reasonable attorney's fee."[1] Standing to sue under the antitrust laws is defined broadly. In addition to private individuals, the term "person" includes corporations, partnerships, and other business entities; municipalities;[2] states;[3] and foreign governments.[4] (But, for purposes of treble-damage actions, the U.S. government is not a "person.")[5]

The right of private parties to sue under the antitrust laws was limited somewhat by two important court decisions imposing the requirement that the antitrust injury sustained be "direct."[6] That is, third parties who pay higher prices or are otherwise damaged by the "passing on" of anticompetitive acts or practices do not have a cause for action.[7] Further limitations regarding the right to sue for treble damages deny standing to purchasers from fringe firms who charge the cartel price but are not themselves directly party to a price-fixing conspiracy;[8] to competitors injured by the lower prices made possible by a merger, even if the merger itself is held unlawful;[9] and to states claiming antitrust injury in the form of diminished tax receipts and other economic damage.[10]

Despite these qualifications, by almost any standard private suits are where the action is in antitrust, or at least it has been so since the early 1960s. It must be said, however, that the available data with respect to private antitrust litigation are very poor. Indeed, except for matters in which there is a reported decision, no record of the private cases filed exists prior to 1938.[11] By most accounts, though, private antitrust suits were rare before 1960, and few plaintiffs were successful. One estimate suggests that a decision was reached in a total of only 158 private damage suits between 1890 and 1940;[12] another places this number at 175.[13] A total of perhaps 423 private cases were initiated over this entire period, with plaintiffs prevailing in only 13 of the reported decisions. Similarly, there were 619 private cases reported as being filed between 1940 and 1959; the plaintiff was successful in just 20 of the 144 private antitrust decisions recorded between 1952 and 1958.[14]

Nothing in the historical data presaged the explosion in private antitrust litigation that occurred beginning in 1960. Since that year, the number of private cases filed annually has consistently outpaced government law enforcement efforts by a factor of 20 or more. Indeed, in excess of 1000 private antitrust suits have been commenced in every year since 1971 (see Table 7.1; compare Tables 6.1 and 6.2).

The reasons for this dramatic increase in private antitrust litigation are not well understood. Treble damages have been held partly responsible, but this remedy was available from the beginning. Several procedural changes were adopted during the 1960s, including the rules governing class action suits,[15] which reduced the burden on plaintiffs, but these changes do not seem to have been significant enough to have triggered a sudden rise in private litigation.[16]

One consideration worth noting is that many private antitrust suits are follow-ons to successful government prosecutions; a single government case often spawns a large number of private damage suits against the same defendant. The leading example in this regard occurred during the 1960s after entry of the final judgment in the electrical equipment conspiracy case.[17] Private litigants filed 2233 treble-damage actions against the coconspirators in the wake of the government's victory.[18] This situation seems to be typical. Two-thirds (986 out of 1456) of the private antitrust cases commenced between 1946 and 1963 were preceded by an Antitrust Division judgment involving the same defendant(s).[19] In other words, private plaintiffs often free ride on public law enforcement efforts by suing for treble damages after the respondents have been found guilty in a government antitrust case. Section 5(a) of the Clayton Act in fact declares that a "final judgment or decree . . . to the effect that a defendant has violated" the antitrust laws "shall be prima facie evidence against such defendant" in subsequent private suits. As such, much private antitrust litigation does not involve proof of liability, but instead centers on resolving claims of injury and the calculation of consequent monetary damages. Moreover, because a single government case may give rise to a large number of private actions, "one does not know how many [separate] violations have been attacked by private suits."[20]

Enough is known about private antitrust suits, however, to make them a growing cause for concern. Richard Posner, for example, has written that the "burgeoning of the private antitrust action has induced enormous, and I think justified, concern about the overexpansion of the antitrust laws and their increasing use to retard rather than promote competition."[21] Other critics contend that the treble-damage

Table 7.1 Private Antitrust Cases Commenced, 1960–84

Year	Cases	Year	Cases
1960	228	1973	1,125
61	378	74	1,230
62	2,005	75	1,375
63	380	76	1,504
64	363	77	1,611
65	472	78	1,435
66	722	79	1,234
67	543	1980	1,457
68	659	81	1,292
69	740	82	1,037
1970	877	83	1,192
71	1,445	84	1,100
72	1,299		

Source: Steven C. Salop and Lawrence J. White, "Economic Analysis of Private Antitrust Litigation," *Georgetown Law Journal* 74 (April 1986), p. 1001.

remedy promotes protracted litigation, encourages nuisance suits designed to extort large monetary settlements, and creates perverse incentives that magnify rather than mitigate the social cost of monopoly in the economy.[22] Indeed, two researchers have recently suggested that treble damages "provide a direct incentive for protectionist activity," that is, for using the antitrust laws in ways that subvert the competitive process.[23] And, if this were not enough, the direct costs of private antitrust litigation can be staggering. One study estimates litigation costs of $200,000–$250,000 per case, which translates into an estimate of $250 million per year for all private suits filed in recent years.[24] Another observer has calculated that $2.1 billion in private antitrust legal costs were incurred in 1979 alone.[25]

The private antitrust bar obviously benefits immensely from an actively enforced antitrust policy. As the number of antitrust complaints—both public and private—rises, its members have more clients to counsel, more settlements to negotiate, and more cases to litigate. Such activities are quite remunerative: The ratio of legal fees to plaintiffs' recoveries is in the range of 10 to 20 percent for private antitrust suits in which the court awards damages, and even higher for cases in which an out-of-court settlement is reached.[26] Thus, the private interests of the attorneys who represent clients in antitrust proceedings run strongly in the direction of zealous law enforcement on all fronts and, as we shall argue, these private interests, along with vague enforcement standards and the treble-damage remedy, help facilitate transfer seeking though antitrust processes.

THE INCENTIVE TO SUE AND THE INCENTIVE TO SETTLE

There is a long-standing debate about the purpose of private antitrust enforcement. One side sees its main objective as being that of enabling parties harmed by anticompetitive acts or practices to receive *compensation* for injuries sustained, that is, to be made whole by recovering in full the monetary value of whatever damages have been suffered.

Although quite complicated in practice, the calculation of compensatory damages in antitrust cases is conceptually straightforward. Consider the situation depicted in Figure 7.1, which shows a monopolized industry facing known linear demand and marginal revenue schedules, D and MR, and constant marginal production costs, MC. The sole supplier of the good or service in question maximizes its profits by producing Q_m units of output per time period and charging price p_m per unit sold. By contrast, had this same good or service been supplied by a perfectly competitive industry confronting the same demand and cost conditions, output would have been larger (Q_c) and price lower (p_c).

Comparing the two situations, we see that the injury sustained by the monopolist's customers has two distinct components. One part consists of the overcharge on the units the monopolist produces and sells. This overcharge is equal to p_m minus p_c dollars per unit times Q_m, or the area of the rectangle p_mABp_c. The rectangle so defined is simply the value of the pure economic profits earned by the monopolist. In addition, however, because the monopolist restricts output below the competitive level, its customers suffer a deadweight loss equal to the area of the triangle ABC. This injury is not an out-of-pocket expense as in the case of the monopoly overcharge, but is instead in the form of lost consumer surplus, which arises because the value customers place on units of output between Q_m and Q_c exceeds the value of the resources that could be used to produce those units. In other words, consumer welfare would rise if output were expanded from Q_m to Q_c, and the value of the additional surplus that consumers would enjoy but for the output restriction must be counted as a cost of monopoly. In total, then, the damages sustained by the monopolist's customers equal the overcharge, p_mABp_c, plus the deadweight loss, ABC, or the area of the trapezoid p_mACp_c.

It is easy to show that with linear demand and constant costs, the area of the deadweight loss triangle is one-half the area of the monopoly overcharge.[27] This result implies that the penalty that just compensates customers for the injury they suffer would be equal to 1.5 times the monopoly overcharge.[28] Of course, things will never be this simple in practice. The optimal damage multiple will vary depending upon

Figure 7.1 The Optimal Antitrust Penalty

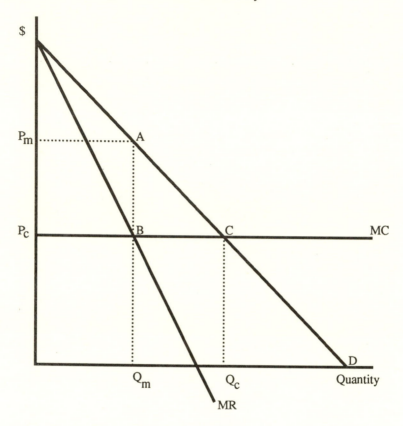

the specific functional forms of demand and marginal cost,[29] and so setting the fine at the appropriate level requires very detailed information about these functions that will normally not be available to any outside observer, including the law enforcement authorities. But, assessing compensatory damages is at least possible in principle.

The second purpose attributed to private antitrust enforcement is *deterrence*, that is, preventing law violations from occurring in the first place. If the penalty is large enough to deter violations, then there is no need to worry about compensating victims for injuries they might have sustained in connection with illegal acts or practices.

It should be obvious that the decision to commit any crime, including a violation of the antitrust laws, can be described as a solution to a capital-budgeting problem in which the prospective criminal compares the expected gain from illegal activity with the expected cost, where "cost" is the penalty assessed if the violation is detected and punished.[30] As such, obedience to the law can be taken for granted only if the rate of return to crime is nonpositive.[31] Now, in the simple case we have been discussing, the monopolist's expected gain is the overcharge, $p_m ABp_c$ (see Figure 7.1). As long as the expected penalty is at least this great, that is, if the damage multiple is just one times the monopoly overcharge, then no violation will occur because the net expected return to the violator is zero. Generally speaking, the penalty required to deter a law violation is less than the penalty necessary to compensate victims should the violation in fact occur. Under the conditions assumed, an overcharge multiple greater than one might be said to result in "overdeterrence."

Setting the penalty for antitrust law violations equal to the expected gain will have a deterrent effect only if the prospective violator is certain to be detected and punished. If, on the other hand, the law enforcement process works only imperfectly, that is, the probability of detection is less than one and, moreover, punishment is uncertain even when a violation is uncovered, then the penalty must be increased to maintain a given level of deterrence. For example, let M represent the gain from violating the law, p the probability that the violator will be detected *and* found guilty,[32] and F the amount of the fine assessed. All violations will then be deterred if

$$M - pF = 0,$$

which implies that the optimal fine is

$$F^* = M/p.$$

That is, if p = 0.5, then the penalty necessary to assure compliance is 2M; if p = 0.25, $F^* = 4M$; and so on.

Of course, given that law enforcement activities are themselves costly, it will not pay to deter all violations. Society's *net* return from investing resources in the process of detecting and punishing antitrust law violators, which such investments presumably tend to increase p in the above example, is equal to the value of the monopoly overcharges not imposed on consumers by reason of the law's deterrent effect minus the cost of the resources consumed in enforcement activities. As such, it is worth investing in law enforcement only up to the point where the last dollar spent just deters a dollar's worth of injury. Thus, efficient law enforcement does not imply complete deterrence of all antitrust violations.[33] It is nevertheless true that for whatever level of deterrence society selects, larger penalties tend to compensate for less effective enforcement.

Overcharge multiples greater than unity can also be justified under the assumption that law violators are risk averse.[34] In this case it is easy to show that a given increase in the amount of the fine has a greater deterrent effect than a proportionate increase in the probability of detection. Although the expected penalty increases by the same amount in both cases, violating the law becomes more of a gamble when the fine is raised in the sense that the cost, if caught, is larger. Risk averters would therefore be more deterred by this prospect than they would be by a proportionate increase in the probability of detection, holding the amount of the fine constant.[35]

Rational individuals will violate the law if the expected gain exceeds the expected cost. Only in those instances where the prospective violator anticipates that the illegal acts or practices will be detected, that an injured party will sue, that the suit will be successful, and that the damages assessed will be at least as great as the monetary payoff from the illegal activity will law violations be deterred. Because the outcome at each of these stages is uncertain, even detected violations will go unpunished. Injured parties themselves face a decision problem involving a comparison of the expected damage award and the cost of suit. Under what conditions will parties harmed by antitrust violations sue to recover damages, and what factors determine whether the adversaries will litigate their dispute or settle out of court?

There is a large literature that investigates the disposition of claims through the legal system.[36] These models stress that decisions concerning whether to sue, to litigate or settle, and the size of the settlement depend upon the maximum amount the defendant is willing to offer, which, in turn, depends on the expected award at verdict plus litigation costs, relative to the minimum amount asked by the plaintiff (expected award minus litigation costs). The theory also emphasizes the important role played by uncertainty and, more precisely, differences in the adversaries' perceptions of the plaintiff's probability of success should litigation occur, in influencing the method of dispute resolution.

Consider the following simplified model. Let J represent the size of the judgment the plaintiff will win in a successful lawsuit, and let P_p be the plaintiff's estimate of the probability that by incurring C_p dollars in litigation costs the judgment will be won. In general, then, the plaintiff will sue if

$$P_p J - C_p > 0,$$

which implies that the plaintiff's estimate of the probability of winning must be greater than the ratio of legal costs to the size of the judgment, that is, $P_p > C_p / J$. This result suggests that the plaintiff will be more likely to sue when litigation costs are lower and when the judgment awarded is larger. Lower litigation costs and larger judgments reduce the minimum probability of winning necessary for the suit to have a positive expected value.[37]

Similarly, let P_D represent the defendant's estimate of the plaintiff's probability of winning judgment J. Further assume that should litigation occur, the defendant expects to incur legal costs amounting to C_D dollars. Under these conditions, the suit is likely to be litigated only if

$$P_p J - C_p > P_D J + C_D,$$

that is, if the expected value of the suit as estimated by the plaintiff (the plaintiff's minimum asking price) exceeds the defendant's expected financial exposure in trial. The latter is the sum of the expected judgment in the defendant's eyes and the cost of defense, and represents the maximum amount the defendant would be willing to pay to avoid litigation.

The above inequality can be usefully rewritten as

$$(P_p - P_D) J > C_p + C_D,$$

which suggests that the suit will be litigated if the sum of the adversaries' litigation costs is less than the disparity between their separate estimates of the likely outcome. Thus, litigation will be more likely the more optimistic the plaintiff is of winning, the lower the defendant's estimate of the plaintiff's probability of success, the larger is the judgment at stake, and the lower are either party's legal costs. Note also that if both parties form the same estimate of the plaintiff's probability of winning, no matter how high or low the estimate may be, the left-hand side of the inequality will vanish, and the suit will be settled out of court because settlement avoids the cost of litigation. Litigation is only rational when the extent of disagreement about the expected outcome exceeds the cost of trial.

These relationships are summarized in Figure 7.2. In the upper panel, the expected value of the suit to the plaintiff is greater than the defendant's estimate of financial exposure should litigation occur. No settlement between the parties is possible in this case, and they will choose to litigate. By contrast, in the lower panel the maximum amount the defendant is willing to pay to avoid trial is greater than the maximum amount the plaintiff will accept to settle the claim. The adversaries can therefore strike a bargain on a dollar figure somewhere between the defendant's maximum offer and the plaintiff's

Figure 7.2   The Decision to Settle or Litigate

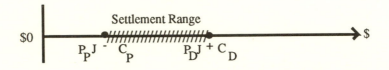

Source: William F. Baxter, "The Political Economy of Antitrust,"
in Robert D. Tollison, ed., *The Political Economy of
Antitrust: Principal Paper by William Baxter*
(Lexington, Mass.: D.C. Heath, 1980), p.12.

minimum ask that will resolve the suit to their mutual satisfaction, thereby avoiding the cost of litigation. Where in the range shown the actual settlement will lie is mostly a matter of the relative bargaining strengths of the two parties.

The model just presented is very simple. It assumes that the adversaries are both risk neutral, that the amount of the judgment at stake is fixed and certain, and that the resources invested in litigation by either party have no impact on the plaintiff's probability of winning. The model would be more realistic, but substantially more complicated, if we were to assume that larger stakes make it worthwhile for the parties to spend more in their own behalf (to seek more and better legal and economic advice, to gather more evidence, to prepare longer briefs, and so on), that these investments affect both the size of the judgment and the plaintiff's chances of success, and that the probability that the plaintiff will prevail varies as events related to the suit unfold. Despite these simplifications, the model does illustrate the principal factors involved in decisions to sue, settle, or litigate. In particular, the model shows that it is disparity between the parties' estimates of the plaintiff's probability of winning that leads to litigation, and that it is increased financial exposure for the defendant at trial that leads to settlement.

The data with respect to private antitrust suits consistently show that a large proportion of these disputes are settled rather than litigated. William Baxter, for example, found that nearly 82 percent of the 671 private antitrust cases disposed of between 1964 and 1970 were resolved by settlement between the two parties.[38] Similarly, in a recently completed project that involved the collection of detailed information from a sample consisting of over 2350 private antitrust cases filed between 1973 and 1983, 73 percent of the suits were settled before reaching trial.[39] What is even more remarkable about these figures is that plaintiffs appear to have a low success rate in those cases that actually proceed to a final court judgment. One estimate suggests that plaintiffs win final judgments only 15 percent of the time;[40] another places the proportion of plaintiffs' wins at 28 percent.[41]

In terms of our model of settlement versus litigation, the remarkable tendency for private antitrust suits to be resolved through settlement implies that the defendants in these matters typically view their financial exposure at trial to be unacceptably high. This could be due either to the expense of litigation, which the defendant will of course bear regardless of the verdict,[42] or to concern about the size of the expected judgment, or both. Indeed, the data suggest a disparity between the expected value of litigated antitrust suits to private plaintiffs and the corresponding financial exposure of defendants that makes settlement rational.

In the 28 percent of the private antitrust suits that proceeded to a final judgment in the plaintiff's favor between 1973 and 1983, the average award was $456,000 (in 1984 dollars), excluding one case in which the award was very large.[43] On average, then, the plaintiff had a 28-percent chance of winning $456,000. If we assume that the plaintiff's legal costs represented 20 percent of this figure (or $91,200), which expenses would be borne by the plaintiff 72 percent of the time, then the average plaintiff's net expected value was $(.28)(\$456,000) - (.72)(\$91,200) = \$62,000$. That is, $62,000 was the expected benefit to the average plaintiff of litigating an antitrust suit. On the other hand, the defendant in these cases faced a 28-percent probability of having to pay damages of $456,000 plus the plaintiff's legal costs. If we assume that the defendant would also incur legal expenses of $91,200, the defendant's expected financial exposure at trial was $(.28)(\$456,000 + \$91,200) + \$91,200 = \$244,400$.[44] Under such conditions, both parties would have an incentive to settle out of court at a figure somewhere between $62,000 and $244,400.

Initiating a private antitrust suit thus appears to be a profitable strategy for the average plaintiff. Whether this is because uncertain legal standards in antitrust cases cause defendants to form relatively high estimates of plaintiffs' probabilities of success, because the treble-damage remedy raises the stakes to an unacceptable level, or simply because litigation is costly, the possibility exists that the divergence in expected values between plaintiff and defendant will be exploited in the form of "nuisance" suits by plaintiffs or, even worse, attempts to extort large settlements from profitable enterprises.

EXTORTION BY LITIGATION

Private antitrust cases tend overwhelmingly to fall into two basic categories. One category consists of firms bringing charges of unlawful conduct against their competitors; the other is suits filed by downstream business entities—dealers, business customers, franchisees, and licensees—against their suppliers. As shown in Table 7.2, downstream firms as a group composed the largest category of private antitrust plaintiffs. These complainants tended to charge their suppliers with vertical price fixing, refusals to deal, and unlawful terminations of their business relationship. Competitors most often complained of conspiracy, predatory pricing, and other horizontal restraints of trade on the part of rival firms. They were also the private parties most likely to challenge mergers and joint ventures.[45]

An optimist could take the view that a competitor or a firm party to a contractual relationship with another is in the best position to spot conduct in violation of the antitrust laws because of its specialized business knowledge. But, another possibility is that firms employ the antitrust laws as a weapon to handicap their successful rivals or as a method of resolving contractual disputes. This possibility arises because even if a defendant thinks that the plaintiff's suit is likely to fail at trial, it still might be rational to settle out of court for some amount less than the expected costs of litigation. Settlement becomes even more worthwhile if the defendant is concerned that a final judgment in favor of the plaintiff will invite follow-on suits or have adverse consequences for other cases, or if the plaintiff's suit seeks injunctive relief in addition to monetary damages, thereby raising the defendant's financial exposure at trial.[46]

The possibility that private antitrust litigation is driven by extortion motives is a serious matter. Although the dimensions of the problem are far from clear, some limited evidence suggests that a large number

Table 7.2 Plaintiffs' Relationships to Defendants in Private Antitrust Cases

Relationship		Frequency
Competitor		36.5%
Downstream business entity		51.4
Dealer	27.3%	
Customer company	12.5	
Franchisee	1.6	
Licensee	1.3	
Final customer or end user	8.7	
Supplier		5.6
Employee or former employee		3.5
State or local government		1.4
Other		12.7
No information		13.8

Source: Steven C. Salop and Lawrence J. White, "Economic Analysis of Private Antitrust Litigation," *Georgetown Law Journal* 74 (April 1986), p. 1007.

Note: Percentages total more than 100% because a complaint may involve more than one business relationship.

of private suits cannot be explained in terms of benign objectives of compensating victims of unlawful conduct or deterring antitrust law violations. For example, one recent study of a large sample of antitrust cases that charged the defendant with the illegal use of resale price maintenance (RPM), included data on 130 private suits.[47] The vast majority (87 percent) of these private RPM suits were initiated by dealers against their upstream suppliers, and most of these by dealers that for various reasons had been terminated as a manufacturer's authorized distributor. (Consistent with the evidence drawn from private antitrust litigation in other areas of the law, approximately 70 percent of the cases were settled out of court; plaintiffs won only about 28 percent of the matters that actually went to a final judgment, however.)[48] The author of the study concluded that fewer than 15 percent of the private suits could be explained by anticompetitive theories of vertical price fixing: "In fact, based on a reading of the substance of the disputes, many of the private RPM cases appear to be essentially contract disputes recast as antitrust cases and embellished with a variety of antitrust charges."[49]

A recent attempt to document anticompetitive uses of the antitrust law produced 117 examples of "sham" litigation between 1972 and 1986.[50] The cases so identified involved defendants in private antitrust suits who countersued the plaintiff charging that the original complaint was baseless, frivolous, or undertaken solely with anticompetitive intent. The prototypical sham case arose during the attempt by Pepsico, Inc. to acquire the assets of Seven-Up in 1986. Shortly after Pepsico made its intentions public, and during the time that the Hart-Scott-Rodino premerger notification waiting period was in effect, Coca-Cola announced an agreement to purchase Dr. Pepper. In granting a preliminary injunction against the Coca-Cola/Dr. Pepper merger, a federal district court judge subsequently held that Coca-Cola's merger announcement had only been a ruse designed to plant in the minds of the Federal Trade Commission the idea that if it did not oppose the Pepsico/Seven-Up acquisition, it would be faced with a "merger wave" in the soft drink industry.

Hence, even on a very narrow definition—considering the possibility of sham only when the defendant countersues to that effect—extortion motives may be prevalent in private antitrust litigation. Such a conclusion is reinforced by evidence that a significant proportion of private suits are initiated either by competitors or by firms having an existing or prior business relationship with the defendant, and by the high settlement rates that characterize these actions. The evidence is far from definitive, however. Perhaps the frequency of settlement merely indicates that private antitrust enforcement is a well functioning system in which law violations are deterred and victims of illegal conduct receive compensation while economizing on costly litigation to the adversaries' mutual benefit. But, "once the possibility of extortion is added to the analysis . . . a high settlement rate could indicate that antitrust is a blackmailer's paradise."[51]

NOTES

1. The language first appeared in Sherman Act Section 7, which was superseded by Section 4 of the Clayton, 15 U.S.C. Section 15.

2. *Chattanooga Foundry & Pipe Works v. City of Atlanta*, 203 U.S. 390 (1906).

3. *Georgia v. Evans*, 316 U.S. 159 (1942).

4. *Pfizer, Inc. v. Government of India*, 434 U.S. 308 (1978).

5. *U.S. v. Cooper Corp.*, 312 U.S. 600 (1941). Section 4A of the Clayton Act, added to the statute in 1955, permits the federal government to recover actual damages and the cost of suit for injuries sustained by reason of antitrust violations. Section 4B, adopted at the same time, imposed a four-year statute of limitations on all damage claims.

6. *Hanover Shoe v. United Shoe Machinery Corp.*, 392 U.S. 481 (1968) (holding that the plaintiff was not injured by reason of having passed United Shoe's overcharges on to indirect purchasers), and *Illinois Brick Co. v. Illinois*, 431 U.S. 720 (1977) (holding that indirect purchaser plaintiffs could not recover damages from overcharges passed on to them by direct purchasers).

7. *Illinois Brick* did allow an exception for overcharges passed on according to a preexisting cost-plus contract.

8. *Mid-West Paper Products Co. v. Continental Group, Inc.*, 596 F.2d 573 (3rd Cir. 1979).

9. *Brunswick Corp. v. Pueblo Bowl-O-Mat, Inc.*, 429 U.S. 477 (1977).

10. *Hawaii v. Standard Oil of California*, 405 U.S. 251 (1972).

11. Richard A. Posner, "A Statistical Study of Antitrust Enforcement," *Journal of Law and Economics* 13 (October 1970), pp. 370–71.

12. Ibid., p. 371.

13. Roger D. Blair and David L. Kaserman, *Antitrust Economics* (Homewood, IL: Richard D. Irwin, 1985), p. 70.

14. Posner, "Statistical Study of Antitrust Enforcement," p. 371 and Blair and Kaserman, *Antitrust Economics*, p. 70.

15. Federal Rules of Criminal Procedure, Sections 23(a) and 23(b), amended in 1966.

16. Several scholars have pointed to *Bigelow v. RKO Radio Pictures, Inc.*, 327 U.S. 251 (1946), which greatly simplified the standards for proving damages in private antitrust suits. The decision did coincide roughly with the point in time when the annual number of private cases began to outpace the Antitrust Division's own enforcement efforts, but preceded by a decade and a half the explosion in private litigation.

17. Final Judgment, *U.S. v. General Electric Co., et al.*, Civil No. 28288 (October 1, 1962).

18. Posner, "Statistical Study of Antitrust Enforcement," p. 371.

19. Ibid., p. 372.

20. Ibid.

21. Richard A. Posner, *Antitrust Law: An Economic Perspective* (Chicago, IL: University of Chicago Press, 1976), p. 35. Concern about private antitrust litigation is not unanimous, of course. Phillip Areeda, for instance, thinks that the result of the treble-damage action "is that public enforcement, which is inevitably selective and least likely to concern itself with local, episodic, or less than flagrant violations, is supplemented by private enforcement, which increases the likelihood that a violator will be found out, greatly enlarges his penalties, and thereby helps discourage illegal conduct." See Phillip Areeda, *Antitrust Analysis: Problems, Text, Cases*, 3rd ed. (Boston, MA: Little, Brown, 1981), p. 75. Also see A.D. Neale and D. G. Goyder, *The Antitrust Laws of the U.S.A.: A Study of Competition Enforced by Law*, 3rd ed. (Cambridge, UK: Cambridge University Press, 1980), p. 418, arguing that "[t]he fear of treble-damage actions is one of the most potent influences in securing compliance with antitrust."

22. See Kenneth G. Elzinga and William Breit, *The Antitrust Penalties: A Study in Law and Economics* (New Haven, CT: Yale University Press, 1976); William Breit and Kenneth G. Elzinga, "Private Antitrust Enforcement: The New Learning," *Journal of Law and Economics* 28 (May 1985), pp. 405–43; and Frank H. Easterbrook, "Detrebling Antitrust Damages," *Journal of Law and Economics* 28 (May 1985), pp. 445–67.

23. William J. Baumol and Janusz A. Ordover, "Use of Antitrust to Subvert Competition," *Journal of Law and Economics* 28 (May 1985), p. 253.

24. Steven C. Salop and Lawrence J. White, "Economic Analysis of Private Antitrust Litigation," *Georgetown Law Journal* 74 (April 1986), p. 1016.

25. Robert B. Reich, "The Antitrust Industry," *Georgetown Law Journal* 68 (April 1980), p. 1068. Reich's estimate includes private legal costs incurred in defense against government antitrust complaints.

26. Salop and White, "Private Antitrust Litigation," p. 1003.

27. The area of the deadweight loss triangle is one-half the base times its height, or $\overline{BC} \times \overline{AB}/2$. The area of the profit rectangle is $\overline{p_cB} \times \overline{p_mp_c}$. But, $\overline{p_cB} = \overline{BC}$ and $\overline{p_mp_c} = \overline{AB}$, and so $\overline{p_cB} \times \overline{p_mp_c} = \overline{BC} \times \overline{AB}$.

28. William M. Landes, "Optimal Sanctions for Antitrust Violations," *University of Chicago Law Review* 50 (1983), p. 656. Also see Easterbrook, "Detrebling Antitrust Damages," pp. 454–56.

29. For example, if marginal cost is linear but rising, the optimal multiple will be less than 1.5.

30. Gary S. Becker, "Crime and Punishment: An Economic Approach," *Journal of Political Economy* 76 (March/April 1968), pp. 169–217.

31. More correctly, the law will be obeyed only if the rate of return to crime is less than the return available on at least one alternative, legal investment.

32. This is a conditional probability which depends jointly on the probabilities of detection and conviction. That is, if the probability that any violation will be discovered is 0.5 and the probability of being convicted when caught is 0.5, then $p = (0.5)(0.5) = 0.25$.

33. Becker, "Crime and Punishment."

34. Suppose that an individual is confronted with a lottery over two possible outcomes, A_1 and A_2. The expected value of this game is $E(L) = PA_1 + (1 - P)A_2$, where P is the probability of outcome A_1. Attitudes toward risk can be define by comparing the utility associated with the lottery's expected value, $U[E(L)]$, with the expected utility of the lottery, $E[U(L)] = PU(A_1) + (1 - P)U(A_2)$, where $U(A_i)$ is the utility associated with the individual prizes. Specifically, an individual is said to be *risk neutral* if $U[E(L)] = E[U(L)]$. Such a person is interested only in expected values and is otherwise oblivious to risk. For example, a risk neutral individual would be indifferent between receiving $10 with certainty and participating in a lottery offering a 50 percent chance of winning $20 and an equal probability of receiving nothing. By contrast, an individual is said to be *risk averse* if $U[E(L)] > E[U(L)]$. A risk averter will not take a fair gamble, that is, the prospect of receiving a sum with certainty is strictly preferred to participating in a lottery having the same expected value. Risk averters are willing to pay to avoid risk.

35. The answer is worked out formally by David de Meza and Michael Osborne, *Problems in Price Theory* (Chicago, IL: University of Chicago Press, 1980), p. 69.

36. William M. Landes, "An Economic Analysis of the Courts," *Journal of Law and Economics* 14 (April 1971), pp. 61–107; John P. Gould, "The Economics of Legal Conflicts," *Journal of Legal Studies* 2 (June 1973), pp. 279–300; and Richard A. Posner, "An Economic Approach to Legal Procedure and Judicial Administration," *Journal of Legal Studies* 2 (June 1973), pp. 399–458. More recent contributors include Patricia M. Danzon and Lee A. Lillard, "Settlement Out of Court: The Disposition of Medical Malpractice Claims," *Journal of Legal Studies* 12 (June

1983), pp. 345–77; Harold W. Elder, "Trials and Settlements in the Criminal Courts: An Empirical Analysis of Dispositions and Sentencing," *Journal of Legal Studies* 18 (January 1989), pp. 191–208; John C. Hause, "Indemnity, Settlement, and Litigation, or I'll Be Suing You," *Journal of Legal Studies* 18 (January 1989), pp. 157–79; George L. Priest and Benjamin Klein, "The Selection of Disputes for Litigation," *Journal of Legal Studies* 13 (January 1984), pp. 1–55; and Steven Shavell, "Suit, Settlement, and Trial: A Theoretical Analysis under Alternative Methods for the Allocation of Legal Costs," *Journal of Legal Studies* 11 (January 1982), pp. 55–82. The basic model is applied to antitrust disputes by William Baxter, "The Political Economy of Antitrust," in Robert D. Tollison, ed., *The Political Economy of Antitrust: Principal Paper by William Baxter* (Lexington, MA: D.C. Heath, 1980), pp. 3–49.

37. The stakes are somewhat different in antitrust disputes. If the plaintiff is successful, the cost of litigation for both sides will be borne by the defendant. Thus, with probability P_p the plaintiff will receive $J + C_p$; if the suit fails, which it will with probability $(1 - P_p)$ in the plaintiff's estimation, the plaintiff incurs costs of C_p. Thus, the expected value of the plaintiff's suit is

$$P_p \left(J + C_p \right) + (1 - P_p)(-C_p).$$

The plaintiff will sue if this expected value is positive, or if $P_p > C_p / \left(J + 2C_p \right)$. Because the ratio on the right-hand side of this inequality is smaller than C_p / J, the award of attorney's fees to successful plaintiffs makes suits more likely, everything else being the same. That is, the minimum probability of winning necessary for suits to have a positive expected value is smaller than when the plaintiff bears its own litigation costs regardless of the verdict.

38. Baxter, "Political Economy of Antitrust," p. 17.

39. Salop and White, "Private Antitrust Litigation," p. 1010.

40. Baxter, "Political Economy of Antitrust," p. 17.

41. Salop and White, "Private Antitrust Litigation," p. 1010.

42. In this regard it is worth noting that private antitrust cases that go to trial last almost twice as long as other types of cases in the federal courts. Specifically, litigated private antitrust matters have a median length of 16.6 months, compared to a median length of about nine months for other cases. See Salop and White, "Private Antitrust Litigation," p. 1009.

43. Ibid., p. 1019. In *Litton Systems, Inc. v. American Telephone and Telegraph Co.*, 568 F. Supp. 507 (S.D.N.Y. 1983), plaintiff Litton was awarded damages of $276 million.

44. Ibid.

45. Ibid., pp. 1005–6.

46. The cost of settlement is further reduced by the fact that antitrust damages are generally treated as a deductible business expense for federal income tax purposes. However, a deduction for only one-third the amount paid by an antitrust defendant is permitted when the defendant has previously been convicted or has pleaded guilty or nolo contendere in a related criminal action. See Areeda, *Antitrust Analysis*, p. 75.

47. Pauline M. Ippolito, *Resale Price Maintenance: Evidence from Litigation* (Washington, DC: Federal Trade Commission, 1988).

48. Ibid., p. 88.

49. Ibid., p. 89.

50. Christopher C. Klein, *Economics of Sham Litigation: Theory, Cases and Policy* (Washington, DC: Federal Trade Commission, 1989).

51. Salop and White, "Private Antitrust Litigation," p. 1030.

Part III

The Political Economy of
Antitrust

8

Using Antitrust to Subvert Competition

There is a specter that haunts our antitrust institutions. Its threat is that, far from serving as the bulwark of competition, these institutions will become the most powerful instrument in the hands of those who wish to subvert it. More than that, it threatens to draw great quantities of resources into the struggle to prevent effective competition, thereby more than offsetting the contributions to economic efficiency promised by antitrust activities. This is a specter that may well dwarf any other concern about the antitrust processes. We ignore it at our peril and would do well to take steps to exorcise it.[1]

The case for characterizing antitrust as a mechanism for wealth redistribution, or what Robert Bork calls predation through governmental processes,[2] derives from three distinct, but related, contributions to the literature on public policies toward business. One component of this literature consists of studies attempting—and failing—to find evidence in support of the hypothesis that antitrust cases are selected on the basis of their potential net benefit to society.[3] The second is comprised of research showing political influences on the enforcement process.[4] And the third element is represented by the normative literature on antitrust, which is highly critical of enforcement efforts in a large number of specific cases.

More fundamentally, however, the emerging appreciation of the incentives of firms to use the apparatus of antitrust policy for the purpose of subverting competition is grounded in the theories of economic regulation and rent seeking. The first of these theoretical contributions explains the level and pattern of traditional economic regulation of price and entry, as well as newer forms of "social" regulation (health, safety, and environmental policies, for example), in interest-group terms.[5] That is, certain groups, whose stake in regulation is sufficiently concentrated and whose costs of mobilizing political influence are sufficiently low, have an incentive to lobby for regulatory favors that increase their own wealth at the expense of other groups whose interests are more diffuse and that face relatively high costs of mobilizing to oppose regulation. The regulators, in turn, serve as brokers of these wealth transfers, clearing the market for regulation by pairing demanders of redistribution with suppliers. Their motivation for doing so has a self-interest basis grounded in the maximization of political support.

The rent-seeking model suggests that whenever returns over and above the minimum amount necessary to call forth the services of a factor of production exist, resources will be spent to gain access to them.[6] Under conditions of what might be called perfectly competitive rent seeking, where entry into rent-seeking activities is free, "bids" are nonrefundable, and rent seekers exhibit risk neutrality, the value of the resources devoted to efforts to capture a rent (or to prevent an existing rent from being taken away) will just equal the present value of the stream of excess returns in contention.[7]

Supracompetitive (monopoly) profits are one example of a rent. If $1 worth of excess returns is at stake, it will be worth spending up to $1 for the right to control the rent. The theory of rent seeking simply suggests that decisions concerning the strategic use of governmental processes to secure or protect such rents is a capital-budgeting problem not unlike most other investment choices the firm must make. That is, along with conventional methods of price and nonprice competition, the investment strategies available to the firm include lobbying for favorable legislation, attempting to influence a bureaucratic ruling, and so on. Instigating an antitrust law suit is just one other option in this regard. From an analytical viewpoint, all of these possible courses of action are equivalent and serve one and the same purpose, namely to gain a competitive advantage over rivals vying for access to a rent. The particular strategy chosen in any given circumstance will simply be the one that offers the highest expected rate of return.

As mentioned previously, the strategic use of antitrust processes to subvert competition offers at least two advantages over conventional forms of rivalry. If government is induced to sue a competitor, the costs of litigation can be shifted to the general taxpayer. More importantly, the police power of the state is brought to bear on the tasks of adjusting and monitoring the behavior of rivals. An antitrust decree enforced by public prosecutors and the courts affords a unique opportunity for securing protection from effective competition.

While antitrust may be equivalent to conventional forms of rivalry from the point of view of firms choosing among alternative competitive strategies, the options are not equivalent from the point of view of society. Cutting price or investing resources in some method of nonprice competition (advertising and research and development activities, for example) generates consumer surplus. Instigating a lawsuit imposes deadweight costs on the economy. There are both direct and indirect social costs involved when antitrust is used to subvert competition. Litigation expenditures comprise the bulk of the direct social costs of rent seeking through antitrust processes. These outlays can be astonishingly high. Alan Fisher and Robert Lande, for example, have estimated that du Pont, Seagram, and Mobil collectively spent $13.5 million in private legal fees to acquire Conoco, an effort in which du Pont ultimately prevailed.[8] In addition, they reckoned the cost of an average antitrust merger case to range somewhere between $700,000 and $1.4 million.[9] To these costs must be added the expenses incurred by the public antitrust enforcement agencies. Similarly, from 184 usable responses to a survey questionnaire sent to the parties involved in private antitrust suits filed in five federal court districts between 1973 and 1983, Steven Salop and Lawrence White estimated the average total legal costs per case (for both sides combined) to be in the range of $200,000–$250,000.[10]

The direct costs of litigation are only the tip of the iceberg, however. When antitrust proceedings are initiated, the energies of the firm's managers will be deflected from efforts to increase productivity or improve product quality toward issues related to the pending litigation. The attention of the firm's internal legal counsel will be focused on taking depositions, preparing witnesses, supervising responses to subpoenas, writing legal briefs, and so on, rather than drawing up contracts with suppliers or customers. On a deeper level, executives and lawyers will be hired for their adeptness in dealing with the antitrust agencies rather for their business acumen. Moreover, the priorities of the firm respecting conventional methods of rivalry will be altered in socially costly ways. Managers will hesitate to engage in the types of competitive behavior ("predatory" price cutting, external growth through merger, for instance) that risk the possibility of an antitrust lawsuit. While no estimate of the magnitude of the indirect costs of this sort is available, suffice to say that they are easily several multiples of the direct litigation costs.

The value of the resources consumed both directly and indirectly as a result of rent seeking through antitrust processes are wasted from society's point of view. This is because such costs are incurred in pursuit of wealth redistribution rather than in income-increasing activities. It is certainly true that lodging an antitrust complaint against a competitor may generate private benefits for the plaintiff if the rival is subsequently ordered to cease cutting price, prevented from consummating a merger that would reduce costs, or barred from using some other "unfair" method of competition, but nothing of value is thereby created for consumers. As such, the use of antitrust to subvert competition raises the social costs of allocative inefficiency in the economy above the amount indicated by the simple deadweight loss triangle (see Chapter 7). In the limit, the total welfare costs of such activities may be equal to the value of the deadweight loss triangle plus the present discounted value of the stream of excess returns secured when antitrust processes successfully insulate a firm from the forces of effective competition.

It has not yet been shown systematically whether the bulk of antitrust cases is pro- or anticompetitive. The indications are, however, that the strategic use of antitrust to subvert competition is potentially widespread. For example, anticompetitive theories could account for the behavior of the defendants in no more than 15 percent of the suits alleging illegal resale price maintenance filed by the government and private parties between 1976 and 1982.[11] This suggests that 85 percent or more of these vertical price restraint cases were aimed at deterring efficiency-enhancing distribution arrangements. Similarly, over 36 percent of the private antitrust lawsuits filed between 1973 and 1983 were brought by the defendant's competitors.[12] Another 30 percent of these matters were initiated by dealers, franchisees, or licensees of the defendant,[13] suggesting that antitrust is a weapon employed to resolve contractual disputes as well as to gain competitive advantages.

A few specific examples are sufficient to illustrate the power of antitrust to subvert competition. In 1983, General Motors Corporation proposed to enter into a joint venture with Toyota for the purpose of producing a new subcompact automobile in the United States.[14] The plan involved combining GM production facilities in Fremont, California, with Japanese-supplied engines and Toyota's designs and managerial expertise to produce a U.S. version of the Toyota Corolla. GM claimed that the venture would generate substantial economic benefits insofar as it would thereby learn from Toyota the secrets that made Japanese automobile manufacturers more efficient than their U.S. counterparts. GM would presumably then be able to apply those secrets in its other plants.[15]

Soon after the agreement was announced, both Chrysler and Ford, the horizontal competitors of GM and Toyota, petitioned the Federal Trade Commission to halt the joint venture. They argued that the combination of two of the world's largest automobile companies would substantially lessen competition in two ways. First, because GM and Toyota proposed to set the price of the new vehicle by reference to the average price of specified other subcompact car models they produced, the exchange of information between the two firms would facilitate collusion. Secondly, Chrysler and Ford alleged that the joint venture would increase GM's market power in the market for larger-sized automobiles. This argument was based upon a peculiarity in the behavior of car buyers. In particular, Chrysler and Ford presented results from marketing studies showing that consumers exhibit a high degree of brand loyalty in the sense that as the incomes of first-time car buyers increase over their lifetimes, they tend to "trade up" to a more expensive model produced by the same manufacturer. For this reason, automakers were said to adopt a strategy of selling subcompact cars at prices below cost with the idea that the associated losses would subsequently be made up on sales of larger vehicles carrying higher profit margins. As such, Chrysler and Ford claimed that sales of the joint venture vehicle, which was to be distributed through GM's franchised dealers, would allow the firm to "lock in" additional customers to its product line, allowing GM eventually to capture a larger share of the market for larger automobiles.

The opposition of Chrysler and Ford to the joint venture is a clear illustration of antitrust's potential to subvert competition. Indeed, the case illustrates what may be a general principle of antitrust analysis, namely that opposition by horizontal competitors is prima facie evidence that the challenged practice is procompetitive. If, as claimed by Chrysler and Ford, the GM-Toyota agreement would have facilitated collusion or increased GM's monopoly power in any segment of the domestic automobile market, then silent acquiescence from rivals would have been expected. This is because any attempt on the part of the joint venturers to charge supracompetitive prices would present its horizontal competitors with two profitable options. One alternative would be to raise their prices as well; the other option would be to maintain their prices at existing levels and thereby gain sales at the expense of the colluders. On the other hand, complaints by rivals are predictable if the joint venture is likely to result in lower costs or improved product quality. In that event, market forces place rivals at a competitive disadvantage; they must "run correspondingly faster in order to stand still."[16]

The GM-Toyota joint venture was ultimately approved by the FTC. In doing so, however, the commission provided Chrysler and Ford with an important victory. It ordered the joint venturers to limit their production of the new vehicle to no more than 250,000 units per year. This output restriction, which is hardly consistent with antitrust's stated goal of promoting consumer welfare, prevents GM and Toyota from taking full advantage of prospective scale economies, resulting in higher average production costs than might otherwise have been realized. Such an outcome is, however, consistent with a prediction of the interest-group theory of government, namely that no one interest group will get all that it wants from regulation, in other words, regulation will work to "share the gain, share the pain."[17]

A second example of the strategic use of antitrust comes from the telecommunications industry.[18] As a result of technological advancements in microwave transmission, MCI Communications Corporation and other firms began in the late 1960s and early 1970s to enter the long-distance telephone business in direct competition with the resident regulated monopolist, AT&T. Such "cream skimming" entry was profitable because of the Federal Communications Commission's policy of requiring AT&T to set prices on the basis of average cost nationwide. The firm's relative prices on different routes therefore bore little resemblance to relative costs and, hence, AT&T's profit margins tended to be much higher on heavy traffic, long-distance routes than on its local service routes. MCI and the other entrants understandably took advantage of this disparity by first specializing in serving the most profitable segment of AT&T's network.

As new entry proceeded, AT&T responded by adjusting its rate structure to correspond more closely with costs. MCI sued, charging that AT&T's price cuts on long-distance service were anticompetitive.[19] Furthermore, AT&T's rate reductions on routes where competition had not yet appeared were characterized by MCI as "preemptive strikes" against the threat of entry.[20]

At the end of the ten years of litigation that ensued, the appeals court decided in AT&T's favor on most counts. That MCI was ultimately unsuccessful in using antitrust processes to subvert competition does not detract from the law's potential for facilitating transfer seeking. The interest of competitors in restraining the ability of rivals to respond to entry in ways that economic theory predicts is clear. MCI's entry would have been substantially more profitable had it been able to obtain a court decree requiring AT&T to hold its prices at preentry levels.[21] In fact, although the appeals court refused to find AT&T's pricing policies to have been unlawful, it did confer a not inconsequential benefit on the new entrants by ordering AT&T to grant MCI and others access to its local telephone switching equipment on terms more favorable than AT&T had demanded previously.

A third example of predation through antitrust is provided by the *Utah Pie* case,[22] which involved allegations of primary-line injury under the Robinson-Patman Act. The Utah Pie Company was a moderately sized family-owned and operated business that by the late 1950s had been baking and selling fresh pies in the Salt Lake City area for 30 years. In 1957, the firm began selling frozen dessert pies locally, a product that until then had only been supplied by leading national companies like Pet, Carnation, and Continental, all of whom shipped their pies to Salt Lake City from plants located in California. Because Utah Pie adopted a strategy of setting price below those charged by the majors, its entry was an immediate success. By 1958, Utah Pie accounted for two-thirds of the frozen pies sold in Salt Lake City and had built a new plant to meet the rapidly growing demand for its product.

Table 8.1 Prices and Market Shares of Frozen Pie Sales in Salt Lake City

Prices per Dozen (Frozen Apple Pie)			
	Early 1958	**1961**	
Utah Pie	$4.15	$2.75 (August)	
Pet	4.92	3.46 (April)	
Carnation	4.82	3.46 (August)	
		3.30 (lowest)	
Continental	5.00+	2.85 (lowest)	
Market Shares (Percent)			
	1958	**1959**	**1960**	**1961**
Utah Pie	67	34	46	45
Pet	16	36	28	29
Carnation	10	9	12	9
Continental	1	3	2	8
Others	6	19	13	8

Source: *Utah Pie Co. v. Continental Baking Co. et al.*, 386 U.S. 685 (1967), pp. 690-92.

The national companies countered Utah Pie's expansion by lowering their own prices in Salt Lake City with the result that in many instances they were selling frozen pies there at prices below those charged in locations nearer their California plants. Utah Pie sued its three major competitors, charging them with conspiracy under Sections 1 and 2 of the Sherman Act and with illegal price discrimination under Section 2(a) of the Clayton Act.[23]

The evidence before the Supreme Court was superficially consistent with price discrimination in the sense that, given the cost of transport, one would not expect the prices of the majors to be lower in Salt Lake City than elsewhere. But this cost-determines-price argument conflicts sharply with other evidence pointing to vigorous and healthy competition between Utah Pie and its principal rivals. First, as shown in Table 8.1, the prices charged by Utah Pie were consistently lower than the prices of its competitors throughout the price discrimination episode. Second, Table 8.1 also shows that while the price reductions of the majors cost Utah Pie a portion of its market, at the end of the price discrimination period the Salt Lake City firm still accounted for 45 percent of the frozen pies sold in the area. Finally, Utah Pie consistently increased its sales volume and continued to make a profit during the time it was allegedly a victim of price discrimination (see Table 8.2).

Despite the fact that the frozen pie market in Salt Lake City was by all measures more competitive in 1961 than it had been in 1958 (the

Table 8.2 Selected Performance Measures for Utah Pie Company

	1958	1959	1960	1961
Sales (thousands of dozens)	38	38	84	103
Sales ($000's)	353	430	504	589
Profits ($000's)	7	12	8	9
Net Worth ($000's)	32			69

Source: *Utah Pie Co. v. Continental Baking Co. et al.*, 386 U.S. 685 (1967), pp. 689 and 691-92.

Herfindahl-Hirschman index of market concentration declined from 4882 to 3075), the Supreme Court held that the defendants' pricing policies constituted illegal discrimination within the meaning of Section 2(a) of the Clayton Act. Writing for the majority, Mr. Justice White placed heavy emphasis on the "drastically declining price structure," which he thought could rationally be attributed to below-cost pricing and predatory intent to injure Utah Pie. The Court, in essence, equated falling prices with a lessening of competition in the Salt Lake City area.

Interestingly, however, Utah Pie's success in using the courts to insulate itself from market forces was short-lived. The company went bankrupt in 1972 because of mismanagement. In addition, Carnation ceased production of frozen dessert pies in 1967, and by 1975 Pet's share of frozen pie sales nationally had declined to 3 percent.[24] Not all of these events can be attributed directly to the *Utah Pie* decision, but they do illustrate that not even the coercive powers of government can forever stem the tide of competition.

Although there is some dispute about the extent to which private antitrust suits by competitors are used to defeat horizontal mergers,[25] examples of this sort certainly do exist. One recent case along these lines involved a complaint filed by the Tasty Baking Company against an acquisition by one of its major rivals.[26] Until early 1986, Borden, Inc., had marketed snack cakes and pies under the Drake brand name through a wholly owned subsidiary. In May of that year, however, Borden entered into an agreement to sell the Drake division to Continental Baking Company, a subsidiary of Ralston Purina, Inc. The sale was reported to the Federal Trade Commission and the Department of Justice under the provisions of the Hart-Scott-Rodino Premerger Notification Act, and these agencies expressing no objection, the transaction was consummated immediately upon expiration of the required waiting period.

Tastykake then sued Ralston, claiming that its purchase of the Drake division constituted a violation of Section 7 of the Clayton Act. Tastykake's suit sought an order requiring that Ralston hold separate the assets acquired from Borden until such time as a trial could take place on the merits. After finding that "snack cakes and pies" constituted a relevant antitrust market for purposes of analyzing the competitive effects of the acquisition and, moreover, that within the market so defined the market shares involved were sufficiently high to provide prima facie evidence of a Section 7 violation, the district court found in Tastykake's favor. Thus, private antitrust litigation may be a feasible strategy for rivals even in matters where the public enforcement agencies see no reason for suspecting that a law violation has occurred.

The rule laid down in *Albrecht*,[27] which established that the practice of specifying a maximum resale price is illegal per se, rightfully stands condemned as interfering with an efficient method of product distribution. The case involved a suit brought by Albrecht, one of the 172 authorized distributors of *The Herald* newspaper in the St. Louis area. Albrecht's exclusive distributorship had been terminated by *The Herald* after he had refused to stop charging his customers more than the newspaper's suggested retail price. The court held that *The Herald's* pricing practices constituted an unlawful restraint of trade in violation of Section 1 of the Sherman Act, citing with approval an earlier decision's conclusion that agreements to fix maximum prices "no less than those to fix minimum prices, cripple the freedom of traders and thereby restrain their ability to sell in accordance with their own judgment."[28]

Now, it should be fairly obvious why a manufacturer has an interest in the price at which his or her product is sold to consumers. Because the retail price ultimately determines the quantity sold, the manufacturer will want the retail price set at the level where customers' purchases per unit time equal the manufacturer's profit-maximizing output rate. If the retail price is "too high," inventories of finished goods will pile up in the distribution system and eventually the manufacturer will be forced to cut back production. In the short run, this adjustment will raise unit production costs and reduce the manufacturer's profits. On the other hand, if the retail price is "too low," shortages will occur, sales will be lost when items are out of stock, and unit production costs will again rise as the manufacturer increases output to keep pace with demand. In short, the manufacturer has a strong interest in having sales at retail dovetail with its production and inventory plans.

Of course, one possible method of insurance in this regard is for the manufacturer to integrate vertically forward into distribution and retailing, and thereby exercise direct control over retail price. But, such integration requires that the manufacturer acquire specialized information and expertise in local marketing that may be relatively unfamiliar. The daily operations of many retail outlets in various locations will entail difficult problems of coordination. As Friedrich Hayek has so well observed, knowledge is dispersed and often contradictory.[29] In retailing particularly, knowledge of people, of local conditions, and of special circumstances are valuable assets that can best be acquired and put to most profitable use by the "man on the spot." Something will inevitably be lost in attempting to communicate relevant information of this sort up the hierarchy of the integrated company. Moreover, integration will often require learning about the peculiarities of marketing the products of other manufacturers that pass through the same distribution system. As a result of these and other factors, the total costs of combining manufacturing and retailing operations may well be greater than the sum of the costs of the two stages working under separate ownership. Under these conditions, resale price maintenance offers an economical contractual alternative to ownership integration in cases where the interests of manufacturers and retailers diverge with respect to price policy.

While it is true that minimum resale prices can have ambiguous welfare effects,[30] *maximum* resale prices always improve social welfare.[31] This conclusion follows from the fact that if retailers have local market power, as they would, for instance, when the manufacturer assigns exclusive territories to dealers, the retailer's profit-maximizing price will always exceed the price that maximizes the manufacturer's profits. Fixing a maximum resale price prevents the retailer from restricting sales below the level consistent with profit maximization upstream and, indeed, restores the price and quantity that would exist if the manufacturer integrated forward into retailing. Implementation of such a policy requires that the manufacturer have market power of its own; it will therefore be able to force compliance with the maximum resale price by threatening to withdraw business from retailers whose price exceeds the maximum, but consumers obviously benefit from this development. Price is lower and quantity is larger at retail when the manufacturer sets a maximum resale price. *Albrecht*, however, made a vertical price restraint of this sort illegal without exception.

Of course, not all examples of the use of the antitrust laws to subvert the competitive process necessarily arise in private litigation. The public antitrust agencies themselves often intervene in ways that appear inconsistent with the goal of enhancing consumer welfare. On March 7, 1961, for instance, the Federal Trade Commission issued a complaint against the Bakers of Washington, a trade association composed of bakers located in the western half of Washington State. The complaint charged that beginning in 1955 the trade association's members had unlawfully fixed prices on bakery product sales at both the wholesale and retail levels. After lengthy legal proceedings, the commission found the defendants guilty, and a final judgment was entered in December 1964 ordering the defendants to cease their illegal activities.[32]

A subsequent study of the case by the FTC in fact claimed that during the conspiracy period (1955–64), retail bread prices in Seattle were approximately 15 percent above the national average, but had fallen to the national average by late 1966 or early 1967.[33] The evidence therefore seems to suggest that antitrust intervention forced Seattle's bakers to cut price, with corresponding benefits for local bakery product consumers. A recent careful study by Craig Newmark, however, finds no basis for this conclusion.[34] First, Newmark's data show that retail bread prices in Seattle during the conspiracy period were fairly typical of those in most West Coast cities. Prices in San Francisco and Los Angeles were higher than those in Seattle, and the Portland price was nearly as high.[35] He attributes the generally higher West Coast prices to higher retail markups, higher labor costs, and a higher normal rate of return. Thus, the Seattle price was apparently the competitive price; the "conspiracy," if any, was wholly ineffective.

Moreover, Newmark suggests that the decline in average bread prices which followed the FTC's final order in 1964 actually resulted from the entry of new brands into the Seattle market. These new brands, the first of which was sold by a firm that imported bread from Canada, were able to undercut the incumbent bakers' prices by virtue of using a more efficient distribution system. The Seattle bakers' responses to these competitive inroads, and not the breakup of a price-fixing conspiracy, was responsible for the fall in bread prices that benefited Seattle's consumers.[36] In short, beyond imposing what were in all likelihood substantial legal costs on the members of the bakery trade association, it is not at all clear what the FTC accomplished by bringing this case. Perhaps the best characterization of the matter is given in the title to another scholar's commentary, "Rooting Out 'Low' Prices in the Bread Industry."[37]

It is by now widely accepted that the integration of successive stages of production under common ownership does not "foreclose" competitive opportunities in any meaningful sense. Vertical integration, in and of itself, can neither create horizontal market power nor increase or extend existing monopoly power. Horizontal market power *is* horizontal market power and if necessary, can always be attacked as such. Yet, conventional wisdom dies hard. So it is that with respect to contractual substitutes for ownership integration, superficially appealing explanations maintain their currency. Perhaps this is natural in light of the fact that buyer-seller relationships are complex; it is far easier to think that "nonstandard" contractual terms are imposed by the big and powerful on the small and weak, that the terms facilitate anticompetitive behavior, or that the contracts merely reflect differences in the parties' attitudes toward risk. Propositions such as these do, however, tend to impede research along potentially more fruitful lines.[38]

Consider the issues raised in the Federal Trade Commission's complaint against the major domestic producers of lead-based antiknock compounds.[39] The complaint alleged that four companies, Ethyl Corporation, E.I. du Pont de Nemours and Company, PPG Industries, and Nalco Chemical Company, which together accounted for 100 percent of domestic sales, had adopted certain contractual arrangements with their customers that effectively eliminated price competition in the market for antiknock compounds.[40] In particular, the challenged contractual terms included the practice of quoting list prices only on the basis of delivered price (inclusive of transportation charges), providing customers with a 30-day advance notice of price changes, and utilizing a "most favored nation" clause in their standard form sales contracts.[41] This last practice provides a particularly good illustration of the complex nature of buyer-seller relationships. Are such provisions an example of efficient contracting or do they represent a symptom of monopoly power?

A "most favored nation" (MFN) clause promises the buyer that during the time the contract is in force, he or she will be charged the lowest price at which the same product is sold to any other customer. Ethyl's MFN clause, for example, stated that

> If Ethyl sells a compound of equal quantity and quality at a price lower than that provided for herein to any oil company in the United States, BUYER shall pay such lower price on all shipments of such compounds made hereunder while such lower price is in effect.[42]

Similarly, du Pont guaranteed that

> If the seller should, during the term of this contract, offer or sell goods of equal quality and quantity to any consumer in the United States for use in motor fuels, other than the United States Government or department of agency thereof, at a price lower than provided herein, the BUYER shall receive the benefit of such lower price on all shipments made hereunder while such lower price is effective.[43]

Although it does not fit the facts of this particular case, one hypothesis about contractual guarantees of this sort is that they facilitate collusion among suppliers by raising the cost to any seller of cutting price.[44] Specifically, because a MFN clause requires that a price discount offered to one customer must be offered to all, a seller's incentive to reduce price is diminished. This effect, it has been alleged, helps stabilize a collusive agreement, keeping price above the competitive level.[45]

Of course, the main problem confronting any cartel is that of detecting and punishing *secret* price cutting.[46] MFN protection, by itself, does nothing to solve this problem. The fact remains that a chiseler can gain only if information about selective discounting is prevented from reaching other market participants, including some of the cheater's own established customers. Because the MFN clause will not be triggered by secret price cutting, its presence in contracts will not deter cheating. In recognition of this point, the anticompetitive theories about MFN typically assume that it is used in conjunction with a "meet or release" (MOR) provision whereby the seller also guarantees to meet a lower price offered by a rival supplier or release the customer from the sales contract.[47] On the one hand, it is suggested that MOR protection helps in the detection of cheating by encouraging customers to report any discounts offered to them in the hope of having them matched by their current supplier. On the other hand, MFN might discourage such matching because if the seller meets the selective price cut to one customer, the same offer must be made to all buyers having MFN status.[48] It is also worth pointing out, however, that customers will realize that if a sellers' cartel is in fact operating, reporting the offer of a secret discount will help police it.

Some limited experimental evidence seems to support the hypothesis that contractual price guarantees may enable firms to coordinate price increases and to resist the temptation to offer discounts. In a laboratory setting replicating the basic features of the *Ethyl* case, David Grether and Charles Plott studied transactions with advance notification of price changes and MFN protection for all buyers.[49] They found the prices in the experiments to be above the competitive benchmark, but below the level one would expect if the sellers were behaving according to Cournot conjectures. When both contractual provisions were removed, prices fell very close to competitive levels. However, because all of the experimental transactions were required to take place at announced "list" prices—no cheating was allowed—the basic issue concerning whether or not MFN deters secret price cutting remains unresolved.

What tends to get lost in the anticompetitive theories of best-price policies are the benefits of the contractual guarantees to buyers.[50] Put another way, why would buyers freely enter into contracts that some commentators suggest work so strongly against their own self interests? (In *Ethyl*, the buyers were the major domestic oil companies who, we can safely assume, were not pressured into accepting the terms out of weakness or ignorance.) One possibility is that the price premium identified by Grether and Plott represents the insurance value to buyers of avoiding the costs of switching suppliers.[51] These costs are not confined solely to the costs associated with going to the market to discover what the relevant prices are. As we have repeatedly emphasized, competition takes place along a variety of margins, and so buyers must search across the various combinations of price, quality, and service offered by rival sellers. Once such investments have been made and a supplier has been selected, certain transactions also require buyers to make special arrangements for credit and billing, delivery, storage, and so on. Under these circumstances, MFN protects the value of the buyer's pre- and postcontractual investments by assuring him or her of receiving the benefit of any price concessions secured by other purchasers from that same supplier during the time the contract is in force. Without such a guarantee, the buyer would be placed at a cost disadvantage relative to rival purchasers who subsequently negotiate a lower price. There would then be an incentive to breach the contract, an action that would both diminish the value of the buyer's prior investments in search and raise the prospect of costly litigation. In the limit, and depending on the frequency and magnitude of price reductions, long-term contracting, which tends to reduce supply uncertainty and the cost of transacting for both parties, would no longer be economical.

Another way of saying many of these same things is that a MFN price guarantee allows each purchaser to free ride on the search activities of its rivals. A customer whose contract has expired is in essence the representative searcher of all buyers remaining under contract. The customer who negotiates a lower price from any supplier confers an external benefit on all of that supplier's customers having MFN status. In short, examining both sides of a transaction often gives an entirely different meaning to specific contractual terms than is apparent when one focuses exclusively on the seller.

The evidence against the possible anticompetitive effects of MFN protection approached a definitive level in the *Ethyl* case.[52] Indeed, one is hard-pressed to explain why such guarantees were made at all given that both Ethyl and du Pont, the two defendants actually charged with the unlawful use of MFN, sold about half of their total output on a spotmarket basis. Moreover, all buyers typically had contracts with at least two suppliers simultaneously, and often terminated those contracts prior to their expiration date without penalty. Most importantly, five of the largest U.S. oil refiners jointly owned a Canadian firm, Octel, that produced lead-based antiknock compounds. It can therefore be assumed that these refiners had fairly accurate information about basic manufacturing costs and they would have switched their purchases of lead additives to Octel had they found the prices charged by the defendants in the case to be unreasonably burdensome.[53] The FTC nevertheless found the respondents guilty of unlawfully restraining trade and, among other things, ordered them to cease the practices of including MFN clauses in their contracts and of giving advance notice of price changes.

There are many other examples in the case law of predation through antitrust processes. To the management of a firm targeted by a hostile tender offer, for example, merger enforcement can operate very much like statutory antitakeover provisions, which have themselves been shown to reduce the number of successful takeovers in the economy, thereby reducing the wealth of the owners of targeted companies significantly.[54] In particular, incumbent management can repel a hostile tender offer by instigating an antitrust suit charging that the proposed merger would violate Clayton Act Section 7. At a minimum, such a strategy increases the cost of the merger to the acquiring company; the challenge may, in fact, be successful in defeating the attempted takeover altogether. Used in this way, the antitrust laws serve to insulate incompetent management from the forces of competition in the market for corporate control, benefiting themselves at the expense of stockholders and consumers.[55]

In short, opportunities for the strategic use of antitrust processes abound. The important point in all of this is not that these strategic activities represent "abuses" of the law in any meaningful sense, but rather that attempts by firms to secure protection from effective competition are rational, self-interest–seeking responses to given constraints. In this sense, decisions to invest resources in the prospective competitive advantages offered by the antitrust statutes are no different from any other capital-budgeting problem that firms confront. Moreover, the responses of the antitrust bureaucracy to the demand of firms for protection from competitive market forces also derive from rational, self-interest–seeking motives. Decisions to supply antitrust protection are no different from any other political-support–maximizing problem that policymakers confront in a representative democracy. Thus, to say that antitrust policy operates much like regulatory policy in general is neither to condemn the statutes themselves nor to question the competence or motives of the individuals charged with responsibility for enforcing the law. No normative criticisms are implied. Instead, the characterization of antitrust as an interest-group bargain represents a positive statement about how public policies toward business actually work, based upon the insights of the economic theory of governmental processes and the results contained in an emerging body of empirical research. Still, the literature on the strategic use of antitrust is relatively new and its basic propositions might yet be refuted. The implications of the positive theory for the debate about reforming public policy are nevertheless of obvious importance; they are ignored at peril by both the supporters and critics of antitrust.

There are two competing theories about the purposes and effects of public policies toward business. One is the public-interest theory; the other is the interest-group theory. The former theory is that antitrust and regulatory policies are the product of well-intentioned, but fallible, politicians and public servants. Whether correct or not in the economic theory or the situational facts they rely upon in any particular instance, the intention of the relevant laws, regulations, and enforcement personnel is to do what is believed to be in the best interests of consumers. Thus, while mistakes are certainly possible, public policy generally works to correct sources of allocative inefficiency in the economy. Output, according to the public-interest theory, rises (and prices fall) in the long run as a result of government intervention.

The interest-group theory looks behind the stated intentions of intervention's proponents to see if there is a hidden agenda of wealth redistribution. The main thrust of the interest-group theory shows how the enforcement of public policy toward business has, in fact, tended to protect competitors at the sacrifice of competition and economic efficiency. That is, the interest-group theory explains many (if not all) enforcement decisions as rational, political responses to the demands of inefficient, yet politically strong, producers. These demanders of protectionism offer political support (votes, campaign contributions, and the like) in return for having Congress, the antitrust and regulatory authorities, and the courts declare unlawful certain business practices or contracts that make their rivals more efficient. According to the interest-group theory, output declines (and prices rise) in the long run as a result of government intervention in the economy.

Strong a priori beliefs support the public interest theory of governmental process; the weight of the empirical evidence is increasingly consistent with the predictions of the interest-group theory. While no list of examples can conclusively establish the case for characterizing antitrust as an interest-group bargain, appreciation of the many instances in which both public and private law enforcement activities tend to subvert the competitive process rather than enhance it puts the burden of proof on those who would defend the public interest view.

NOTES

1. William J. Baumol and Janusz A. Ordover, "Use of Antitrust to Subvert Competition," *Journal of Law and Economics* 28 (May 1985), p. 247.

2. Robert H. Bork, *The Antitrust Paradox: A Policy at War with Itself* (New York: Basic Books, 1978), pp. 347–64.

3. See, for example, William F. Long, Richard Schramm, and Robert D. Tollison, "The Economic Determinants of Antitrust Policy," *Journal of Law and Economics* 16 (October 1973), pp. 351–64.

4. Roger L. Faith, Donald R. Leavens, and Robert D. Tollison, "Antitrust Pork Barrel," *Journal of Law and Economics* 25 (October 1982), pp. 329–42.

5. George J. Stigler, "The Theory of Economic Regulation," *Bell Journal of Economics* 2 (Spring 1971), pp. 3–21 and Sam Peltzman, "Toward a More General Theory of Regulation," *Journal of Law and Economics* 19 (August 1976), pp. 211–40.

6. Gordon Tullock, "The Welfare Costs of Tariffs, Monopolies, and Theft," *Western Journal of Economics* 5 (June 1967), pp. 224–32.

7. Richard S. Higgins, William F. Shughart II, and Robert D. Tollison, "Free Entry and Efficient Rent Seeking," *Public Choice* 46 (1985), pp. 247–58.

8. Alan A. Fisher and Robert H. Lande, "Efficiency Considerations in Merger Enforcement," *California Law Review* 71 (1983), p. 1673.

9. Ibid.

10. Steven C. Salop and Lawrence J. White, "Economic Analysis of Private Antitrust Litigation," *Georgetown Law Journal* 74 (April 1986), pp. 1014–15.

11. Pauline M. Ippolito, *Resale Price Maintenance: Economic Evidence from Litigation* (Washington, DC: Federal Trade Commission, 1988).

12. Salop and White, "Economic Analysis of Private Antitrust Litigation," p. 1007.

13. Ibid.

14. See Baumol and Ordover, "Use of Antitrust to Subvert Competition," pp. 256–57, and Franklin M. Fisher, "Horizontal Mergers: Triage and Treatment," *Journal of Economic Perspectives* 1 (Fall 1987), pp. 36–37.

15. *General Motors Corp. et al., Federal Register* 48 (1983), p. 57246. Note that the joint venture was in large part driven by existing "voluntary export restraints" (VERs) which limited the number of automobiles Japanese companies could export to the United States on an annual basis. An important benefit of the joint venture to Toyota was that automobiles produced under the agreement were not subject to the VER requirements.

16. Baumol and Ordover, "Use of Antitrust to Subvert Competition," pp. 256–57.

17. Jack Hirshleifer, "Comment," *Journal of Law and Economics* 19 (August 1976), p. 243.

18. Baumol and Ordover, "Use of Antitrust to Subvert Competition," pp. 257–58.

19. *MCI Communications Corp. v. AT&T*, 369 F. Supp.1004 (E.D. Pa. 1973), vacated and remanded, 496 F.2d 214 (3d Cir. 1974); *MCI Communications Corp. v. AT&T*, 462 F. Supp. 1072 (N.D. Ill. 1978), reversed, 708 F.2d 1081 (7th Cir. 1983).

20. Baumol and Ordover, "Use of Antitrust to Subvert Competition," p. 258.

21. Indeed, MCI was already so confident of the profitability of entry that it was willing to spend $10 million on capital up front and wait seven years for FCC approval before beginning operations. See B.L. Copeland, Jr. and Alan Severn, "Price Theory and Telecommunications Regulation: A Dissenting View," *Yale Journal on Regulation* 3 (Fall 1985), pp. 53–85, who argue that these facts suggest that telecommunications is a natural monopoly requiring regulation, not competition.

22. *Utah Pie Co. v. Continental Baking Co. et al.*, 386 U.S. 685 (1967).

23. Continental countersued, charging Utah Pie with price discrimination violations of its own. The trial court found in favor of Continental, but nevertheless granted a judgment on Utah Pie's behalf. On appeal, the lower court's decision in favor of Utah Pie was reversed, but because a new trial was ordered on Continental's claim, the issues raised by the countersuit were not addressed by the Supreme Court.

24. Kenneth G. Elizinga and Thomas F. Hogarty, "Utah Pie and the Consequences of Robinson-Patman," *Journal of Law and Economics* 21 (October 1978), pp. 427–34.

25. James Miller reports data from a study conducted by National Economic Research Associates suggesting that such suits accounted for only 3 percent of the total antitrust cases filed in the Southern District of New York between 1973 and 1978. See James C. Miller III, "Comments on Baumol and Ordover," *Journal of Law and Economics* 28 (May 1985), pp. 267–68.

26. *Tasty Baking Co. and Tastykake, Inc. v. Ralston Purina, Inc. and Continental Baking Co.*, 653 F.Supp. 1250 (E.D. Penn. 1987).

27. *Albrecht v. Herald Co.*, 390 U.S. 145 (1968).

28. *Kiefer-Stewart Co. v. Joseph E. Seagram & Sons*, 340 U.S. 211 (1951).

29. Friedrich A. Hayek, "The Use of Knowledge in Society," *American Economic Review* 35 (September 1945), pp. 519–30.

30. For an exhaustive analysis of RPM, see Thomas R. Overstreet, *Resale Price Maintenance: Economic Theories and Empirical Evidence* (Washington, DC: Federal Trade Commission, 1983).

31. Roger D. Blair and James M. Fesmire, "Maximum Price Fixing and the Goals of Antitrust," *Syracuse Law Review* 37 (1986), pp. 43–77.

32. *In the Matter of Bakers of Washington, Inc., et al.*, 64 F.T.C. 1079 (1964).

33. U.S. Federal Trade Commission, *Economic Report on the Baking Industry* (Washington, DC: FTC, 1967).

34. Craig M. Newmark, "Does Horizontal Price Fixing Raise Price?: A Look at the Bakers of Washington Case," *Journal of Law and Economics* 31 (October 1988), pp. 469–84.

35. Ibid., pp. 473–74.

36. Ibid., p. 484.

37. Mayo J. Thompson, "The FTC Strikes Again: Rooting Out 'Low' Prices in the Bread Industry," *Antitrust Law and Economics Review* 7 (1974), pp. 85–95.

38. Victor P. Goldberg and John R. Erickson, "Quantity and Price Adjustment in Long-Term Contracts: A Case Study of Petroleum Coke," *Journal of Law and Economics* 30 (October 1987), p. 371.

39. *Ethyl Corp. v. FTC*, 729 F.2d 128 (2d Cir. 1984); and *E.I. du Pont de Nemours & Co. v. FTC*, 729 F. 2d 128 (2d Cir. 1984).

40. These compounds are added to gasoline to improve the fuel's octane rating. Following passage of the Clean Air Act of 1970, the Environmental Protection Agency promulgated a series of regulations, such as requiring that automobile manufacturers install catalytic converters on all new cars built, that gradually phased the antiknock compound industry out of existence. For a detailed analysis of the *Ethyl* case, see Samson M. Kimenyi, *Antitrust Policy and the Use of Non-Standard Contracts and Practices: The Case of Best-Price Policies*, unpublished Ph.D. dissertation, George Mason University, Spring 1986.

41. Only Ethyl and du Pont were actually charged with the use of most favored nation clauses. The two other respondents had at times included such clauses in their contracts, but not as a standard practice.

42. Kimenyi, *Antitrust Policy*, p. 37. Emphasis in original.

43. Ibid. Emphasis in original.

44. The collusion theory does not fit the facts of *Ethyl* because of our previous observation that two of the four defendants rarely used MFN clauses. (PPG had MFN clauses in only two contracts written between 1974 and 1979; Nalco used MFN with seven customers between 1967 and 1974.) Because the collusion was alleged to be in effect between 1974 and 1979, perhaps we could say that MFN helped facilitate a "50 percent cartel."

45. See, generally, George A. Hay, "Oligopoly, Shared Monopoly, and Antitrust Law," *Cornell Law Review* 67 (1982), pp. 439–81; Thomas E. Cooper, "Most-Favored-Customer Pricing and Tacit Collusion," *Rand Journal of Economics* 17 (Autumn 1986), pp. 377–88; Steven C. Salop, "Practices That (Credibly) Facilitate Oligopoly Coordination," in Joseph E. Stiglitz and G.F. Mathewson, eds., *New Developments in the Analysis of Market Structure* (Cambridge, MA: MIT Press, 1986), pp. 265–90; and Charles A. Holt and David T. Scheffman, "Facilitating Practices: The Effects of Advance Notice and Best-Price Policies," *Rand Journal of Economics* 18 (Summer 1987), pp. 187–97.

46. George J. Stigler, "A Theory of Oligopoly," *Journal of Political Economy* 72 (February 1964), pp. 44–61.

47. MFN and MOR provisions together have sometimes been referred to as either "best price" or "price protection" policies.

48. Holt and Scheffman, "Facilitating Practices," pp. 193–94.

49. David M. Grether and Charles R. Plott, "The Effects of Market Practices in Oligopolistic Markets: An Experimental Examination of the Ethyl Case," *Economic Inquiry* 22 (July 1984), pp. 479–528.

50. This point is not lost on everyone. See Vernon L. Smith, "Theory, Experiment, and Antitrust Policy," in Steven C. Salop, ed., *Strategy, Predation, and Antitrust Analysis* (Washington, DC: Federal Trade Commission, 1981), pp. 579–606. One explanation offered by Smith is that because a MFN clause is essentially a promise by a seller not to engage in price discrimination, such guarantees are designed to avoid antitrust liability under the Robinson-Patman Act.

51. Kimenyi, *Antitrust Policy*.

52. Ibid.

53. For additional examples of the efficiency aspects of hard-to-explain contractual terms, see Goldberg and Erickson, "Quantity and Price Adjustments in Long-Term Contracts" and William J. Lynk and Michael A. Morrisey, "The Economic Basis of *Hyde*: Are Market Power and Hospital Exclusive Contracts Related?," *Journal of Law and Economics* 30 (October 1987), pp. 399–421.

54. Gregg A. Jarrell and Michael Bradley, "The Economic Effects of Federal and State Regulations of Cash Tender Offers," *Journal of Law and Economics* 23 (October 1980), pp. 371–407.

55. Two recent cases in which private antitrust suits filed by takeover targets against the acquiring firm helped defeat the attempted acquisition are *Gruman Corp. v. LTV Corp.*, 665 F.2d 10 (2d Cir. 1981) and *Marathon Oil Co. v. Mobil Corp.*, 669 F.2d 378 (6th Cir. 1982).

9

Reform in the Realm of Interest-Group Politics

Early in 1986, word began to leak out that the Reagan administration was developing a proposal to modify the language of the Clayton Act, one of the three legislative pillars of U.S. antitrust policy. Accounts published in February of that year suggested that the plan contained several major provisions.[1] One was to change the litmus test of Section 7, which declares mergers to be unlawful where the effect "may be to substantially lessen competition or tend to create a monopoly." The new standard would have called for challenging mergers having a "significant probability" of an anticompetitive effect. Other provisions would have required the antitrust agencies to analyze proposed mergers within the framework of the Department of Justice's Merger Guidelines, exempted import-injured industries from the antimerger law for a period of five years, placed restrictions on treble-damage awards in private antitrust suits, and relaxed somewhat Section 8's prohibitions against interlocking directorates. Reports appearing at the time touted the plan as a significant departure from the "big-is-bad" philosophy that has guided antitrust law enforcement policy throughout much of its history. Supporters hailed the proposal as an important step toward the objective of bringing the antitrust laws up to date, making them more compatible with the realities of the modern global marketplace in which U.S. firms must compete. The then assistant attorney general for antitrust, for example, stated that "it is not an immodest goal to try to bring the antitrust laws into the 1980s before they're over."[2]

Although the administration's plan died a quiet political death, it represented the latest in a long series of proposals for reforming U.S. antitrust policy. These proposals, which range from suggestions for modest changes in the provisions of the existing laws to recommendations for repealing entirely one or more of the statutes themselves, continue to have currency because antitrust enforcement has changed remarkably little in substance over the past one hundred years. That is, while the emphasis has certainly varied over time depending on the preferences for antitrust intervention of the administration in office, the policy "failures" of the past continue to be perpetuated. To take just one recent example, the Robinson-Patman Act apparently remains alive and well, despite its condemnation as anticonsumer by virtually every economist and legal scholar. In December 1988, the Federal Trade Commission issued a complaint against six major book publishers, charging them with offering discriminatory discounts to several major retail bookstore chains.[3]

Antitrust is not unique in this regard. Government policies of all sorts survive against overwhelming evidence that their social costs exceed any conceivable estimate of the private benefits they confer. Minimum wage legislation, trade protectionism, and agricultural price support programs are just a few examples of public policies that fail such a benefit-cost test. Where antitrust differs from these other forms of government regulation of the private economy is that its underlying purposes still remain almost universally beyond dispute. The conventional wisdom takes the primary goal of antitrust to be the maximization of consumer welfare, an objective pursued by public-spirited officials who (costlessly) intervene to (perfectly) correct perceived market failures. As a result of this preconception, defects in antitrust policy are attributed to correctable errors. All that is necessary is for the "right" people to be in a position to enforce the "right" laws.

By and large, then, the basic assumption of proposals for reforming the antitrust laws is that by rewriting the statutes, the actual effects of antitrust policy can be made to match more closely the intended effects. As we have argued, however, evidence is accumulating to suggest that the actual effects of antitrust *are* the intended effects. That is, antitrust may be just another example of a public policy apparatus designed purposely to facilitate the strategic use of governmental processes to disadvantage consumers and rivals. In other words, antitrust may afford some firms with an alternative mechanism—a mechanism of particular value in sectors of the economy where the political process has not yet acted to impose industry-specific regulatory or legislative constraints—for seeking governmental protection from the rigors of effective competition. Instigating an antitrust law suit, like efforts to influence legislation or to affect a ruling by a regulatory body, provides an opportunity for firms to win in the courts what they are unable to win in the private marketplace. Antitrust can be employed to restrict the entry of rivals, to limit price or nonprice competition, to impose costs on certain members of an industry differentially, to restrict the production of substitute goods and services, to shore up cartels, and so on. Used strategically in this way, antitrust has several unique advantages. In the case of public enforcement, the costs of litigation can be shifted to the general taxpayer. Rulings by the courts bring the police power of the state to bear on the tasks of adjusting and monitoring the behavior of rivals. Moreover, even unsuccessful law suits can impose a capital loss on the owners of a firm targeted by an antitrust complaint.[4]

In contrast to the conventional wisdom, the emerging conception of antitrust as an interest-group bargain is not a normative view about how public policies toward business *should* work. Instead, it is a positive statement about how antitrust *does* work, based upon the results of nearly a decade of hard-nosed empirical research. Still, the literature on the strategic use of antitrust is relatively new, and its lessons are only just beginning to reach the level of the debate on reforming antitrust policy. The positive literature has obvious implications for that debate, however. For one, the interest-group theory of antitrust suggests that reform will not simply be a matter of writing "better" laws and appointing "better" enforcement personnel, but rather a matter of changing the incentives of the relevant actors—the firms subject to the law, the private antitrust bar, the public enforcement agencies, and the courts. Changing incentives involves complex questions about efficient assignments of the right to sue, optimal payoffs from such suits, and so on. Secondly, the positive literature suggests that the process of reform is not simply a matter of articulating efficient antitrust rules. Reform does not take place in a political vacuum. The same incentives and constraints that operate in the enforcement of existing policies will influence decision making about the design of new policies.[5] Most importantly, the positive literature suggests that as long as government holds a monopoly of antitrust policy, there will be strategic use of that policy by private interest groups having a stake in its exercise. Thus, while the "unintended" consequences of antitrust might in principle be mitigated by efforts at reform, they cannot be wholly eliminated even by the best intentioned of reformers.

PROPOSALS FOR REFORMING THE ANTITRUST LAWS

When errors in antitrust policy are uncovered, as they are quite often in the normative literature, the common recommendation is for closer adherence to economic principles in the future. But, some commentators have gone so far as to call for wholesale changes in the antitrust statutes themselves. Such proposals range from suggestions for minor revisions that would clarify statutory language to advocating the repeal of entire sections of the law. Before discussing the specific recommendations, however, we first consider an important general principle that underlies the debate.

Rules versus Discretion

There is a long-standing controversy among antitrust scholars about the relative merits of rules versus discretion in the enforcement of antitrust policy. "Rules," such as those laid down by a Supreme Court decision to declare a specific business practice subject to a standard of per se illegality, the Department of Justice's promulgation of market share and market concentration criteria for analyzing the effects of proposed mergers, or a legislative mandate declaring a particular industry or activity beyond the reach of the antitrust laws, are favored by some "for the sake of business certainty and litigation efficiency."[6] Discretion, on the other hand, which can arise from broad and, hence, vague statutory language or from the adoption of a rule of reason standard for judging a particular business practice, is valued by others for its flexibility, allowing the enforcement agencies and the courts to consider each case on its merits, weighing the social benefits and costs of the practice at issue in passing on its legality.

Indeed, the pros and cons of rules versus discretion were important issues in the turn-of-the-century reform movement that grew out of widespread dissatisfaction with early enforcement efforts under the Sherman Act. In the U.S. House of Representatives, the favored course of action for correcting the defects perceived in existing law was to declare specific business practices as illegal per se and make those practices criminal offenses. By contrast, the Senate favored the creation of an expert law enforcement body with a broad mandate to attack "unfair methods of competition." Proponents of discretion argued that because lawmakers in 1914 could not be expected to foresee all of the possible anticompetitive business practices that would be utilized by imaginative law violators in the future, Congress should avoid enumerating and declaring illegal specific restraints of trade.[7] From this point of view, the "unfair" standard of the FTC Act would provide the flexibility needed by law enforcement officials to deal with antitrust problems arising in an ever-changing market economy. To the critics of this approach, who argued that flexibility encourages vague enforcement standards, the supporters responded that because the courts would ultimately interpret the meaning of "unfair methods of competition," any aberrations resulting from the discretion conferred on the proposed Federal Trade Commission would never attain the status of enforceable precedent.

The conflict between these two opposing points of view was resolved by adopting both approaches. The specific provisions of the Clayton Act were retained, but violators were not made subject to criminal penalties. Qualifying phrases, declaring the enumerated practices to be illegal only where the effect "may be to substantially lessen competition or tend to create a monopoly," were inserted to provide the FTC with flexibility in enforcing the law. As we shall soon see, however, the compromise reached in 1914 did not resolve the debate. These same issues are an important point of contention underlying modern proposals for reforming antitrust policy.

The reason for the enduring debate about rules versus discretion is that both approaches entail costs and benefits. To illustrate, suppose that the courts apply a standard of per se illegality to a particular business practice. Such a rule has several advantages. First, firms in the economy face no uncertainty about the legality of the practice. They are aware that its use will subject them to antitrust liability if discovered. Secondly, the rule conserves on litigation costs. The government or a private plaintiff is not required to invest resources in determining whether or not consumers or competitors have suffered adverse consequences; it is only necessary to show that the illegal practice has in fact been employed. For this reason, defendants have an incentive to resolve the complaint through a consent order or a private out-of-court settlement before the matter ever goes to trial. In short, a per se rule promotes economy in the enforcement of the law.

On the other hand, by making all uses of a specific business practice illegal, a per se rule runs the risk of impairing economic efficiency by deterring procompetitive conduct. This would be the case if the practice at issue has ambiguous welfare implications. For example, economic theory suggests that vertical price restraints can either facilitate collusion between manufacturers or they can mitigate free rider problems at the retail level. As such, the benefits of a per se rule in terms of deterring collusion and conserving enforcement resources are offset by the injury caused to consumers by preventing firms from adopting a practice that in some instances enhances economic efficiency.

Suppose, instead, that a rule of reason standard is applied to resale price maintenance. Allowing discretion in the enforcement of the law confronts firms in the economy with uncertainty about whether use of the practice is legal in their particular circumstances. If challenged, the firm may have a greater propensity to defend itself in court,[8] and both plaintiff and defendant will be required to invest resources to resolve the question of liability. But, discretion entails benefits in the sense that fewer procompetitive uses of resale price maintenance will be deterred. At the same time, however, the possibility exists that some anticompetitive uses of the practice will either fail to be prosecuted or, if tried, fail to be held illegal under a rule of reason standard.

Put in these terms, and ignoring for the moment differences in the degree of business uncertainty and the costs of litigation, the decision to select rules or discretion basically involves a tradeoff between the differing weights attached to two types of error. An error of the first kind (a Type I or "false positive" error) in this context occurs whenever an anticompetitive business practice escapes condemnation. By contrast, a Type II ("false negative") error occurs whenever a procompetitive business practice is held to be illegal. A per se rule obviously reduces the probability of a Type I error to zero, but because the two types of error are inversely related, such a standard also maximizes the occurrence of errors of the second kind. All procompetitive uses of the practice are deterred. On the other hand, discretion reduces the probability of Type II error. Of necessity, however, fewer Type II errors come at the expense of an increased probability of errors of the first kind.

The foregoing considerations suggest that efficient enforcement of the antitrust laws would entail applying per se rules only to those practices whose purposes and effects are uniformly anticompetitive, or where the incidence of procompetitive uses is sufficiently small that the social cost of deterring them is low. By contrast, efficiency considerations dictate that the discretion permitted by a rule of reason standard ought to apply when the procompetitive uses of a practice are frequent and the social cost of a Type II error is large. In such cases, the optimal amount of discretion occurs where the social marginal cost of committing an error of the first kind (failing to condemn an anticompetitive use of the practice) is just equal to the value of the marginal benefit to society of *not* committing an error of the second kind (condemning a procompetitive use of the practice).

The relevance of this discussion to the debate about reforming antitrust policy should be transparent. The normative critics of public policies toward business who advocate less government intervention into the private economy in essence argue that the cost of Type II error is "too large" under current enforcement standards. Individuals on this side of the debate typically want to push reform in the direction of increased discretion by, for example, applying a rule of reason standard to the analysis of all vertical restraints of trade; relaxing, if not doing away completely with rigid market share rules for evaluating mergers and acquisitions; expanding the number of antitrust law exemptions (joint ventures for research and development purposes or for increasing international competitiveness are two recently popular proposals in this vein); and so on. The antitrust critics who advocate stricter enforcement efforts, particularly as they apply to horizontal mergers and to vertical price restraints, in essence take the position that the cost of Type II error is currently "too small." Such reformers typically want closer adherence to existing rules. In the recent past, they pressed for additional rules to condemn "shared monopoly," to attack "the problem of continued dominance of an industry by a single firm which has obtained its position by lawful means,"[9] and to limit more effectively "undue market power."[10] What is somewhat ironic in all of this is that individuals who otherwise seem to place great faith in government's ability to use its discretionary powers to correct "failures" perceived in market outcomes respecting a wide range of socioeconomic issues advocate constraints on policy discretion in the area of antitrust. On the other hand, individuals who generally favor constraining government's discretionary powers in the areas of social and economic regulation tend to argue for fewer rules and more discretion in the case of antitrust policy.

In what follows, we discuss some specific proposals for reforming U.S. antitrust policy. To a greater or lesser degree, they all derive from the basic premise that the defects perceived in enforcement can be corrected if only policymakers would "rethink antitrust with the aid of economics."[11] The positive approach to antitrust policy, by contrast, suggests that the basic premise of reform is mistaken. If the intended effects of antitrust can be deduced from its actual effects, the antitrust laws were not designed to maximize consumer welfare in the first place. Instead, antitrust was intended to facilitate wealth redistributions in favor of firms willing to offer political support in return for protection from the rigors of competition. As such, proposals for reform that seek to improve antitrust policy in some normative sense are irrelevant because social benefits and costs do not appear as arguments in the objective function being maximized by the relevant policymakers.

Specific Reform Proposals

Generally speaking, the critics of U.S. antitrust policy have directed most of their attention to the Federal Trade Commission. For this reason, much of the debate about reform is difficult to separate from condemnation of the FTC's case selection record, failures in which have been variously attributed to the commission's organizational structure, its broad enforcement authority, and its overlapping jurisdiction with the Department of Justice's Antitrust Division. As early as 1925, just a decade after the FTC began operation, the National Industrial Conference Board complained that the commission's vigorous program of resale price maintenance prosecutions had encroached on an area of antitrust law enforcement activity that

Congress had not intended to be within its purview. The board went on to recommend that

> in order to bring about a more logical and efficacious distribution of functions, and thereby contribute to the expedition of Federal Trade Commission procedure in its proper sphere, [it seems necessary] to provide by law that whenever the Commission secures evidence pointing to a violation of the Sherman Act it shall transmit the same to the Department of Justice, with such recommendations as it may deem suitable.[12]

Over the next half-century, the FTC's performance was appraised by special committees of Congress and other outside observers on at least seven separate occasions.[13] Virtually all of these studies concluded that the commission had not lived up to its promise, and most made recommendations for reform. None of these studies were as influential as the report published in 1969 by the American Bar Association (ABA),[14] however, which had been initiated at President Richard Nixon's request following a highly critical attack on the FTC by Ralph Nader.[15]

The ABA's overall evaluation of the commission was unfavorable to say the least.[16] Comments like "failure," "disappointing," and "less than satisfactory" are strewn throughout the report.[17] The bar association reserved its strongest criticism for the FTC's apparent unwillingness to take advantage of its unique resources and broad discretionary authority, however. As the ABA put it,

> the idea of creating an administrative agency to operate in the antitrust field arose out of a concern that federal district judges, unequipped with a staff of fact finders, evaluators, and economists, would not be able to apply the antitrust laws effectively to halt the growth of anticompetitive practices and at the same time not unduly interfere with vigorous economic growth.[18]

But the commission's organizational virtues, along with its wide powers to investigate and require submission of reports, its opportunity to decide antitrust questions through industrywide rule-making activities rather than on a case-by-case basis, and its "power to issue studies and reports to the President, Congress, and the public" so as to "illuminate antitrust issues and evaluate the need for additional legislation" remained largely unexploited in the ABA's judgment.[19] In particular, "if the measure of quality of FTC performance in the antitrust area is whether the agency has broken new ground and made new law by resort to its unique administrative resources, it seems clear that the record is largely one of missed opportunities."[20] The dominant view of the ABA was that the commission had devoted a disproportionate share of its resources to Robinson-Patman prosecutions, to the exclusion of cases that would have had beneficial effects on competition.[21]

The ABA attributed the commission's poor performance to its failure to establish goals and priorities;[22] an inability to manage its enforcement activities "in an efficient and expeditious manner,"[23] using "passive" case selection methods rather than weighing the anticipated returns from enforcement initiatives against their cost;[24] and resort to an "informal" or "voluntary compliance" approach that had "gone too far," damaging the agency's enforcement credibility.[25] To correct these perceived defects, the ABA recommended a series of administrative reforms to streamline the FTC's internal procedures. The bar association particularly wanted to see the commission promptly "embark on a program to establish goals, priorities, and effective planning controls."[26] The report proposed three specific changes in the FTC's antitrust priorities. First, the ABA recommended that the commission devote more of its enforcement resources to vertical restraints of trade, a "complicated and economically significant" area of antitrust in which the agency had previously "foregone opportunities to participate in the constructive development of law that might contribute to the attainment of antitrust objectives." Second, the ABA proposed that the commission "initiate a study and appraisal of the compatibility of the Robinson-Patman Act and its current interpretations to the attainment of antitrust objectives" and, while this study was underway, enforce the act only in "instances in which injury to competition is clear." Finally, the commission was urged to expand its merger enforcement efforts.[27]

Indeed, merger enforcement was the one area of the commission's record that the ABA found commendable:

[T]he FTC did lead the way in implementation and interpretation of Section 7 of the Clayton Act. Moreover, that program has been carried out not simply by the institution of formal proceedings, but by the publication of economic reports and the promulgation of guides, i.e., by use of the full panoply of administrative resources available to the FTC.[28]

It was the hope that the agency would be able to duplicate its merger enforcement successes in other program areas that led the ABA to endorse a continued antitrust role for the FTC. The bar association commission suggested, however, that this role be confined to matters

"where issues of anticompetitive effects turn essentially on complicated economic analysis, and where decided cases have not yet succeeded in fashioning a clear line marking the boundary between legal
and illegal conduct. . . . " Cases of per se illegality (price fixing, market
allocation, boycotts designed to facilitate collusion, and so on) and
criminal matters should be left to the Department of Justice.[29]

But, noting the similarity of its recommendations to the reforms
proposed in earlier studies of the agency, the ABA Commission flatly
stated that if the FTC did not soon take steps to correct its many
deficiencies, it should be abolished. The report concluded that

> this Commission believes that it should be the last of the long
> series of committees and groups which have earnestly insisted
> that drastic changes were essential to recreate the FTC in its
> intended image. The case for change is plain. What is required is
> that the changes now be made, and in depth. Further temporizing
> is indefensible. Notwithstanding the great potential of the FTC in
> the field of antitrust and consumer protection, if change does not
> occur, there will be no substantial purpose to be served by its
> continued existence; the essential work to be done must then be
> carried on by other government institutions.[30]

How well the FTC may have responded to the ABA's recommendations is a matter of debate. Robinson-Patman enforcement activity
certainly declined markedly beginning in 1970 (see Table 4.4). Increased activism on a number of fronts became evident. The commission initiated industrywide rule-making proceedings in the areas of
television advertising aimed at children, used car sales, insurance, and
self-regulating professional organizations, and issued its "shared
monopoly" complaints against the leading U.S. oil companies and the
manufacturers of ready-to-eat cereals.[31] Perhaps the most enduring
legacy of the ABA's report, however, was an increase in the degree of
congressional interest in—and extent of the legislature's influence
over—the commission's antitrust activities, an impact that has been
noted by a number of scholars.[32] There clearly has been no decrease in
the number of attacks on the FTC's performance since 1969—indeed,
just the opposite might be true.[33]

In sum, major questions about the efficacy of the commission's role
in the enforcement of antitrust policy remain unresolved, as they have
almost since the beginning. The most important of these questions
include the potential conflict of interest arising from the FTC's dual
function as both prosecutor and judge,[34] constitutional issues of due
process and self-incrimination,[35] the quality of the commission's case
selection record,[36] and the vagueness of Section 5.[37] More generally,

however, the FTC's modern critics increasingly view the agency as a creature of Congress whose primary function is that of redistributing wealth, not maximizing consumer welfare:

[T]he FTC can be understood only as a political institution. As such it offers no reason to expect its actions to make sense from the standpoint of market analysis—and they do not. Congress needs the commission as an institution to which to refer complaints from its constituents about all the tedious ills of life that can, plausibly or not, be blamed on the business community. It is not to be supposed that Congress expects the FTC to respond to these complaints in any way that seriously interferes with the operation of the market. The commission's real function is (or at least was intended to be) to relieve the Congressman of blame when no satisfaction is produced for the constituent—as, in the vast majority of cases, it cannot be.[38]

For these reasons, most concrete proposals for reforming U.S. antitrust policy call for repeal of the FTC Act. Richard Posner, for example, has made this recommendation; he, in fact, "would like to see the antitrust laws other than section 1 of the Sherman Act repealed."[39] Posner argues that the major provisions of the Clayton and FTC Acts are "almost entirely superfluous. . . . Section 1 of the Sherman Act, which forbids contracts, combinations, and conspiracies in restraint of trade, is sufficiently broad to encompass any anticompetitive practice worth worrying about. . . . "[40] Moreover, the reasoning of the courts, which over time have interpreted the Clayton and FTC Acts to forbid more than Section 1, has been both unhistorical and unrealistic, ignoring completely the circumstances in which those two statutes were enacted.[41] Posner, in fact, charges that the interpretive errors he attributes to the Clayton and FTC Acts are directly responsible for two of antitrust's four major problem areas. One of these problems is the inability of the courts "to formulate consistent, sensible, and workable standards of illegality for mergers either between competitors or between potential competitors." The other is that "the category of exclusionary practices has been permitted uncritically to expand, embracing many practices that actually reduce the social costs of monopoly."[42] Section 5 of the FTC Act, which was "directed primarily against exclusionary practices, although it was later held to forbid virtually anything forbidden by any other antitrust provision, and then some,"[43] deserves blame in Posner's judgment for much of this second major problem. Thus, Posner's suggestion for reform is to remove redundancy from the antitrust statutes. Perhaps drawing upon his own contributions to the literature on the political economy of antitrust enforcement,[44] however, Posner characterized his recommendations as both "academic and impractical."[45]

Similarly, little room exists for the FTC in the reform proposals advanced by Robert Bork.[46] Although he did not address changes to specific statutes, Bork's prescription is for antitrust law to attack only horizontal restraints of trade and "deliberate predation." In particular, he would have antitrust policy strike at three types of behavior:

(a) The suppression of competition by horizontal agreement, such as the nonancillary agreements of rivals or potential rivals to fix prices or divide markets.
(b) Horizontal mergers creating very large market shares (those that leave fewer than three significant rivals in any market).
(c) Deliberate predation engaged in to drive rivals from a market, prevent or delay the entry of rivals, or discipline existing rivals. . . . [C]are must be taken not to confuse hard competition with predation.[47]

In addition, Bork makes some general recommendations and advances one specific proposal for reforming the process of antitrust enforcement. First, "the only goal that should guide interpretation of the antitrust laws is the welfare of consumers." Second, "in judging consumer welfare, productive efficiency, the single most important factor contributing to that welfare, must be given due weight along with allocative efficiency."[48] Third, "the law should permit agreements on prices, territories, refusals to deal, and other suppressions of rivalry that are ancillary . . . to an integration of productive economic activity."[49] This last general proposal would have antitrust ignore all vertical and conglomerate mergers; all contractual substitutes for such ownership integration, including tying arrangements, vertical price restraints, and market division; price discrimination; and increases in firm size due to internal growth. Finally, Bork suggests a reallocation of enforcement resources within the Antitrust Division for the purpose of increasing the number of price-fixing prosecutions and to increase the attention paid by the antitrust authorities to the misuse of the courts and federal, state, and local administrative agencies and regulatory bodies to engage in anticompetitive behavior with government's blessing. Both of these objectives could be met by creating "more Antitrust Division field offices by dispersing the personnel now concentrated in Washington."[50]

In short, Bork recommends a major reformulation of public policy toward business so as to strike only at horizontal antitrust problems. It appears that Sections 1 and 2 of the Sherman Act would be sufficient for this purpose, but Clayton Act Section 7 would perhaps serve a supplementary role in Bork's concept of horizontal merger policy. Although Bork's recommendations certainly did not lead to any statutory reforms, it is noteworthy that during the 1980s the Antitrust Division did shift its enforcement activities in the direction of price-fixing matters, and both the division and the FTC initiated "competition advocacy" programs to comment upon the anticompetitive effects of government regulation at the federal, state, and local levels. The two agencies also brought antitrust policy to bear on the restrictive practices of self-regulating professional organizations and trade associations.[51]

In contrast to the foregoing proposals, few recommendations for more stringent antitrust enforcement have recently been advanced. Those commentators who do take such a position typically focus on a specific type of business behavior rather than advocating broad policy initiatives.[52] Others call for more careful analysis,[53] or express cautious optimism.[54] This situation is quite remarkable in light of the fact that within the past two decades, structural relief for dominant firms was being urged,[55] and legislative proposals were advanced making market shares in excess of 12 percent,[56] or after tax rates of return over 15 percent,[57] prima facie evidence of monopoly power against which antitrust proceedings leading to asset divestiture would be initiated.

That such recommendations were never implemented is testimony to the impact of the "new learning" in industrial organization that began appearing in the wake of the deconcentration proposals.[58] To paraphrase Ronald Coase, this literature brought an end to an era; the study of market concentration and its effects was thereafter in shambles.[59] Yet, all of the antitrust policy reforms that ensued, such as the modest relaxation of the Justice Department's Merger Guidelines and the reallocation of enforcement resources away from structural matters, price discrimination violations, and attacks on vertical ownership integration, were accomplished administratively rather than through statutory change. Perhaps the failure to amend antitrust policy legislatively so as to make its enforcement more consistent with the intended goal of promoting consumer welfare reflects faith in the ability of the lawyers and economists employed by the Antitrust Division and the FTC "to sort real from contrived claims of efficiency and thus permit the . . . statutes to be enforced with net social gains."[60] On the other hand, the persistence of the legislative status quo may be definitive evidence that the actual effects of antitrust *are* the intended effects.

My own view is that the FTC should be abolished, that the Clayton Act should be repealed, and that the Antitrust Division should confine its attention solely to cases involving either hard evidence of horizontal price fixing or monopoly created through the merger of horizontal competitors. In the latter regard, the Justice Department's Merger Guidelines should be rewritten in such a way that all but the most overwhelmingly large mergers are allowed to proceed without government interference. The antitrust authorities could then observe the actual as opposed to the predicted effects of business combinations, and take action to dissolve anticompetitive mergers when appropriate. More efficiency-enhancing mergers would take place in the economy and antitrust law could be invoked ex post on the basis of observed price and output data rather than ex ante on the basis of "significant probabilities" of anticompetitive effects and the complaints of competitors.

The theory propounded in this book suggests, however, that all proposals for reforming antitrust processes, including my own, are likely to fall on deaf ears. Neither the Congress nor the antitrust authorities can be said to be ignorant of the substantial evidence that now exists concerning the injury caused by antitrust policy to consumer welfare. If reform was simply a matter of dispelling misconceptions about the actual effects of antitrust policy, reform would have taken place long ago. It is not uncorrected errors that explain the persistence of a policy that has failed to live up to its promise of protecting the interests of consumers, but rather that "consumer welfare" does not appear in the objective function being maximized by antitrust.

Some commentators have pointed to changes in law enforcement philosophy evident during the administration of President Ronald Reagan as support for the proposition that new ideas and new personnel can in fact influence the direction taken by antitrust policy. But, all of the antitrust "reforms" instituted during the Reagan years were carried out administratively rather than through more permanent legislative action. No constraints were imposed to prevent a return to older enforcement philosophies. For this reason, the 1980s will, I think, come to be viewed as merely a temporary aberration in the long march of activist antitrust policy.[61]

CONCLUDING REMARKS

The year 1990 marks the centennial anniversary of the Sherman Act, the centerpiece of U.S. antitrust policy. Many undoubtedly consider this event as a cause for celebration. There is a strongly held belief that the Sherman Act stands as the "Magna Carta of free enterprise," which broke the backs of the "robber barons" in the late nineteenth century and today continues to serve as the principal guarantor of a freely functioning competitive economy. At the same time, however, nearly universal support for the ideals of antitrust policy has from the beginning been plagued by disappointment with its execution. Critics from all points of the political compass have identified a large number of cases in which antitrust has failed to live up to its promise. Although the critics may disagree as to whether the errors have been on the side of too little or too much enforcement and may differ on how to go about remedying past mistakes, it is virtually an article of faith among them that the failures can be corrected. Changes in statutory language, changes in enforcement personnel, and a greater role for economic analysis in the policy process have all been recommended as ways of improving the execution of what is basically viewed as a well-intentioned program designed to keep the private, profit-seeking interests of the business community in line with the public interest.

This book has argued that such a conception of the purposes of the laws and institutions of antitrust policy is disingenuous in the extreme. Antitrust is not a unique area of government activity where the incentives and constraints of ordinary politics are held in suspense while policymakers and enforcement personnel go about maximizing social welfare. Instead, antitrust policy operates much like government policy in general. Special interests and not the public interest dominate the formulation and execution of antitrust policy as they do in all other areas where government holds a policy monopoly.

The conventional wisdom on antitrust insists that Congress, the law enforcement agencies, the antitrust bar, and the courts act with the intention of helping that most diverse and unorganized of all political interest groups—consumers. Greater appreciation of the roles played by self-interests and ordinary politics in the antitrust policy process should help dispel this naive point of view.

In taking stock of the first one hundred years of antitrust policy in the United States, duly noting the countless failures that never seem to be corrected, one might be tempted to conclude that economics has been singularly unhelpful in its advice to antitrust policymakers. To quote George Stigler, "economists may have their glories, but I do not believe that the body of American antitrust law is one of them."[62] This is not the point, however, and, indeed, taking the position that antitrust policy is well meaning but deformed in its execution by fallible human beings misdirects our attention toward unfruitful lines of research and consumes our time in unproductive preaching. The point is not that economics is unhelpful in informing those who formulate and execute antitrust policy of the errors of their ways, but, on the contrary, that economics is extraordinarily helpful in understanding the policy process itself.[63]

NOTES

1. Nadine Cohodas, "Reagan Seeks Relaxation of Antitrust Laws," *Congressional Quarterly Weekly Report* 44 (February 1, 1986), pp. 187–92. Also see William F. Shughart II, "Don't Revise the Clayton Act, Scrap It!," *Cato Journal* 6 (Winter 1987), pp. 925–32.

2. Cohodas, "Reagan Seeks Relaxation of Antitrust Laws," p. 188.

3. The commission charged that the publishers treat orders placed by bookstore chains as a single order, even if books are separately packed, invoiced, and shipped to individual chain outlets. As a result, the chains are able to pay lower prices than independent bookstores "that receive shipments as large as or larger than the shipments to individual chain outlets." See Monica Langley, "FTC Charges Six Publishers with Price Bias," *Wall Street Journal*, December 23, 1988, p.B4.

4. For example, see Thomas W. Ross, "Winners and Losers under the Robinson-Patman Act," *Journal of Law and Economics* 27 (October 1984), pp. 243–71 (reporting evidence that firms that win their contested cases fare as poorly in the capital market as those that lose).

5. Some of the practical difficulties blocking the adoption of more efficient antitrust rules are: "(a) public ignorance about many of the issues, an ignorance pandered to shamelessly by demagogues (the popular press discussion of resale price maintenance is but one example); (b) strongly vested interests (for example, any modernizing of Robinson-Patman language would incur extraordinary political opposition from the small business community—a sector of the economy that suffers proportionately more Robinson-Patman [enforcement] abuses, but considers the benefits of the act an article of faith); and (c) a widespread demand for 'fairness' in business relations (for example, a Jeffersonian preference for small entrepreneurial units over large). From my own experience, antitrust officials typically appreciate the need to articulate clearer and more efficient rules but face significant restraints in bringing the effort off."

See James C. Miller III, "Comments on Baumol and Ordover," *Journal of Law and Economics* 28 (May 1985), p. 269.

6. *Arizona v. Maricopa County Medical Society*, 457 U.S. 332 (1982), p. 344.

7. American Bar Association, *Report of the American Bar Association Commission to Study the Federal Trade Commission* ("*ABA Report*") (Chicago, IL: American Bar Association, 1969), p. 436.

8. In terms of the model developed in Chapter 7, uncertainty about the legality of a particular practice may cause the defendant to revise downward the estimate of the plaintiff's probability of winning.

9. Oliver E. Williamson, *Markets and Hierarchies: Analysis and Antitrust Implications* (New York: The Free Press, 1975), p. 209.

10. Carl Kaysen and Donald F. Turner, *Antitrust Policy* (Cambridge, MA: Harvard University Press, 1959), pp. 44–49.

11. Richard A. Posner, *Antitrust Law: An Economic Perspective* (Chicago, IL: University of Chicago Press, 1976), p. 236.

12. Quoted by Gilbert H. Montague, "The Commission's Jurisdiction over Practices in Restraint of Trade: A Large-Scale Method of Mass Enforcement of

the Antitrust Laws," *George Washington Law Review* 8 (January/February 1940), pp. 385–86.

13. Gerard C. Henderson, *The Federal Trade Commission: A Study in Administrative Law and Procedure* (New Haven, CT: Yale University Press, 1924); Thomas C. Blaisdell, *The Federal Trade Commission: An Experiment in the Control of Business* (New York: Columbia University Press, 1932); Commission on Organization of the Executive Branch of the Government ("Hoover Commission"), *Task Force Report on Regulatory Commissions, Appendix N* (Washington, DC: USGPO, 1949); U.S. Bureau of the Budget, *Federal Trade Commission Study 4* (No. CF-60–124) (Washington, DC: USGPO, 1960); U.S. Congress, Senate Committee on the Judiciary, *Report on Regulatory Agencies to the President-Elect* (Report prepared by James M. Landis), 86th Cong., 2d sess., 1960; Carl A. Auerbach, "The Federal Trade Commission: Internal Organization and Procedure," *Minnesota Law Review* 48 (1964), pp. 383–522; and Louis M. Kohlmeier, Jr., *The Regulators* (New York: Harper & Row, 1969).

14. *ABA Report*.

15. Edward F. Cox, Robert C. Fellmeth, and John E. Schultz, *The Nader Report on the Federal Trade Commission* (New York: Richard W. Baron, 1969).

16. For details, see William E. Kovacic, "The Federal Trade Commission and Congressional Oversight of Antitrust Enforcement: A Historical Perspective," in Robert J. Mackay, James C. Miller III, and Bruce Yandle, eds., *Public Choice and Regulation: A View from Inside the Federal Trade Commission* (Stanford, CA: Hoover Institution Press, 1987), pp. 65–81.

17. *ABA Report*, pp. 35 and 64.

18. Ibid., pp. 406–7.

19. Ibid.

20. Ibid., p. 407.

21. This conclusion was echoed in still another report on the FTC issued in 1969. See "President's Task Force Report on Productivity and Competition," Appendix to U.S. Congress, House Committee on Interstate and Foreign Commerce, *Hearings Before the Special Subcommittee on Small Business and the Robinson-Patman Act*, 91st Cong., 1st sess., October 1969.

22. *ABA Report*, p. 77.

23. Ibid., p. 1.

24. Ibid., p. 80.

25. Ibid., pp. 8–9 and 25–26.

26. Ibid., p. 3.

27. Ibid., pp. 67–69.

28. Ibid., p. 65.

29. Ibid., p. 66.

30. Ibid., p. 3.

31. This increased activism became a liability for the commission in 1979 when new members of congressional oversight committees blasted the FTC as an agency run amok. See Chapter 5.

32. Kovacic, "Federal Trade Commission and Congressional Oversight" and Roger L. Faith, Donald R. Leavens, and Robert D. Tollison, "Antitrust Pork Barrel," *Journal of Law and Economics* 15 (October 1982), pp. 329–42.

33. See, for example, Ernest Gellhorn, "Two's a Crowd: The FTC's Redundant Antitrust Powers," *Regulation* 5 (November/December 1981), pp. 32–42; "Debate: The Federal Trade Commission Under Attack: Should the Commission's Role Be Changed?," *Antitrust Law Journal* 49 (1982), pp. 1481–97; Murray Weidenbaum, et al., "On Saving the Kingdom—Advice for the President-Elect from Eight Regulatory Experts," *Regulation* 4 (November/December 1980), pp. 14–35; "Proposed Budget Cuts Fuel Debate Over FTC's Role," *Legal Times of Washington* 3 (February 3, 1981), p. 1; Milton Handler, "Reforming the Antitrust Laws—Dual Enforcement, FTC's Mission," *New York Law Journal* 188 (April 12, 1982), p. 4; E.E. Vaill, "The Federal Trade Commission: Should It Continue as Both Prosecutor and Judge in Antitrust Proceedings?," *Southwestern University Law Review* 10 (1978), pp. 763–94; Thomas E. Kauper, "Competition Policy and the Institutions of Antitrust," *South Dakota Law Review* 23 (Winter 1978), pp. 1–30; Wesley J. Liebeler, "The Role of the Federal Trade Commission, Proceedings of the Symposium: Changing Perspectives in Antitrust Litigation," *Southwestern University Law Review* 12 (1980–81), pp. 166–229; D.L. Roll, "Dual Enforcement of the Antitrust Laws by the Department of Justice and the FTC: The Liaison Procedure," *The Business Lawyer* 31 (July 1975), pp. 2075–85; J.B. Sloan, "Antitrust: Shared Information Between the FTC and the Department of Justice," *Brigham Young University Law Review* 4 (1979), pp. 883–912; T.J. McGrew, "Antitrust Enforcement Has More Staff Than Policy," *Legal Times of Washington* 4 (October 12, 1981), p. 11; Robert A. Katzmann, *Regulatory Bureaucracy: The Federal Trade Commission and Antitrust Policy* (Cambridge, MA: MIT Press, 1980); Kenneth W. Clarkson and Timothy J. Muris, *The Federal Trade Commission Since 1970: Economic Regulation and Bureaucratic Behavior* (Cambridge, UK: Cambridge University Press, 1981); and the papers collected in Mackay, Miller, and Yandle, eds., *Public Choice and Regulation.*

34. See Chapter 6.

35. Vaill, "Federal Trade Commission," pp. 793–94. Vaill sees no place for a law enforcement system in which if an alleged violator "happens to draw the Justice Department, he will be accorded a federal court trial and due process, but if he draws the FTC, he will be relegated to a quasi-judicial procedure, where his rights are not so great." Also see Sloan, "Antitrust: Shared Information," p. 883 (the exchange of information about prospective defendants taking place within the liaison process for allocating cases between the Antitrust Division and FTC "raises substantial constitutional questions, including issues of due process and self-incrimination").

36. B. Espen Eckbo and Peggy Wier, "Antimerger Policy Under the Hart-Scott-Rodino Act: A Reexamination of the Market Power Hypothesis," *Journal of Law and Economics* 28 (April 1985), pp. 119–49 ("the additional enforcement powers granted under the HSR Act apparently have not led the agencies to pick cases better").

37. Handler, "Reforming the Antitrust Laws," p. 4 (Section 5's vagueness allows the FTC to "roam at large, extending at will the frontiers of antitrust").

38. Liebeler, "Role of the Federal Trade Commission," p. 229.

39. Posner, *Antitrust Law,* p. 212.

40. Ibid.

41. Ibid., p. 213.

42. Ibid., p. 31. Two additional major problem areas identified by Posner are the ineffectiveness of the Sherman Act "in dealing with forms of collusive pricing that do not generate detectable acts of agreement or communication" and the inclusion within the rule forbidding price fixing many practices (resale price maintenance, for example) which are often procompetitive rather than anticompetitive.

43. Ibid., p. 30.

44. Richard A. Posner, "The Federal Trade Commission," *University of Chicago Law Review* 37 (1969), pp. 47–89.

45. Posner, *Antitrust Law*, p. 212.

46. Robert H. Bork, *The Antitrust Paradox: A Policy at War with Itself* (New York: Basic Books, 1978), pp. 405–7.

47. Ibid., p. 406.

48. Ibid., p. 405.

49. Ibid., p. 406.

50. Ibid., pp. 406–7.

51. See Fred S. McChesney, "Law's Honor Lost: The Plight of Antitrust," *Antitrust Bulletin* 31 (Summer 1986), pp. 359–82; Robert D. Tollison, "Antitrust in the Reagan Administration: A Report from the Belly of the Beast," *International Journal of Industrial Organization* 1 (1983), pp. 211–21; and William F. Shughart II, "Antitrust Policy in the Reagan Administration: Pyrrhic Victories?," in Roger E. Meiners and Bruce Yandle, eds., *Regulation and the Reagan Era* (New York: Holmes & Meier, 1989), pp. 89–103.

52. See, for example, Robert Pitofsky, "In Defense of Discounters: The No-Frills Case for a Per Se Rule Against Vertical Price Fixing," *Georgetown Law Review* 71 (1983), p. 1491 (the procompetitive uses of resale price maintenance are only "occasional" and it "almost always generates anticompetitive horizontal effects") and Richard Schmalensee, "Horizontal Merger Policy: Problems and Changes," *Journal of Economic Perspectives* 1 (Fall 1987), p. 54 ("current enforcement policy toward horizontal mergers, while certainly capable of substantial improvement, is not fundamentally flawed. I oppose major legislative changes . . . ").

53. Franklin M. Fisher, "Diagnosing Monopoly," *Quarterly Review of Economics and Business* 19 (Summer 1979), p. 33.

54. Oliver E. Williamson, *The Economic Institutions of Capitalism: Firms, Markets, Relational Contracting* (New York: Free Press, 1985), p. 370.

55. Williamson, *Markets and Hierarchies*, pp. 260–61.

56. P.C. Neal et al., "White House Task Force on Antitrust Policy," *Antitrust and Trade Regulation Report*, no.411, Special Supplement, part II, May 27, 1969.

57. "The Industrial Reorganization Act of 1972" (S.1167), introduced by Senator Philip Hart (D-Mich.), 92nd Cong., 2d sess., July 24, 1972.

58. For specific criticisms of the "Neal Report," see Yale Brozen, "The Antitrust Task Force Deconcentration Recommendation," *Journal of Law and Economics* 13 (October 1970), pp. 279–92.

59. Ronald H. Coase, "Industrial Organization: A Proposal for Research," in Victor R. Fuchs, ed., *Policy Issues and Research Opportunities in Industrial Organization* (Cambridge, MA: National Bureau of Economic Research, 1972), p. 69.

60. Williamson, *Economic Institutions of Capitalism*, p. 370.

61. See Shughart, "Antitrust Policy During the Reagan Administration."

62. George J. Stigler, "The Economists and the Problem of Monopoly," *American Economic Review Papers and Proceedings* 72 (May 1982), p. 7.

63. George J. Stigler, *The Citizen and the State: Essays on Regulation* (Chicago, IL: University of Chicago Press, 1975), p. xi.

Select Bibliography

BOOKS

American Bar Association. *Report of the American Bar Association Commission to Study the Federal Trade Commission*. Chicago: American Bar Association, 1969.

Armentano, Dominick T. *Antitrust and Monopoly: Anatomy of a Policy Failure*. New York: John Wiley & Sons, 1982.

Arnold, R. Douglas. *Congress and the Bureaucracy: A Theory of Influence*. New Haven, CT: Yale University Press, 1979.

Bork, Robert H. *The Antitrust Paradox: A Policy at War with Itself*. New York: Basic Books, 1978.

Clarkson, Kenneth W. and Timothy J. Muris. *The Federal Trade Commission Since 1970: Economic Regulation and Bureaucratic Behavior*. Cambridge: Cambridge University Press, 1981.

Coase, Ronald H. *The Firm, the Market, and the Law*. Chicago: University of Chicago Press, 1988.

Cox, Edward F., Robert C. Fellmeth, and John E. Schultz. *The Nader Report on the Federal Trade Commission*. New York: Richard W. Baron, 1969.

Crain, W. Mark and Robert D. Tollison (eds.). *Predicting Politics: Essays in Empirical Political Economy*. Ann Arbor: University of Michigan Press, 1990.

Elzinga, Kenneth G. and William Breit. *The Antitrust Penalties: A Study in Law and Economics*. New Haven: Yale University Press, 1976.

Hawley, Ellis W. *The New Deal and the Problem of Monopoly*. Princeton: Princeton University Press, 1966.

Ippolito, Pauline. *Resale Price Maintenance: Economic Evidence from Litigation*. Washington, DC: Federal Trade Commission, 1988.

Katzmann, Robert A. *Regulatory Bureaucracy: The Federal Trade Commission and Antitrust Policy*. Cambridge: MIT Press, 1980.

Mackay, Robert J., James C. Miller III, and Bruce Yandle (eds.). *Public Choice and Regulation: A View from Inside the Federal Trade Commission*. Stanford: Hoover Institution Press, 1987.

McCormick, Robert E. and Robert D. Tollison. *Politicians, Legislation, and the Economy: An Inquiry into the Interest-Group Theory of Government*. Boston: Martinus Nijhoff, 1981.

Meiners, Roger E. and Bruce Yandle (eds.). *Regulation and the Reagan Era*. New

York: Holmes & Meier, forthcoming.

Neale, A.D. and D.G. Goyder. *The Antitrust Laws of the U.S.A.: A Study of Competition Enforced by Law*. 3rd ed. Cambridge: Cambridge University Press, 1980.

Olson, Mancur. *The Logic of Collective Action: Public Goods and the Theory of Groups*. Cambridge: Harvard University Press, 1971.

Phillips, Almarin. *Market Structure, Organization and Performance*. Cambridge: Harvard University Press, 1962.

Posner, Richard A. *Antitrust Law: An Economic Perspective*. Chicago: University of Chicago Press, 1976.

———. *Economic Analysis of Law*. 3rd ed. Boston: Little, Brown, 1986.

———. *The Robinson-Patman Act: Federal Regulation of Price Differences*. Washington, DC: American Enterprise Institute, 1976.

Shughart, William F. II. *The Organization of Industry*. Homewood, IL: Richard D. Irwin, 1990.

Stigler, George J. *The Citizen and the State: Essays on Regulation*. Chicago: University of Chicago Press, 1975.

Tollison, Robert D. (ed.). *The Political Economy of Antitrust: Principal Paper by William Baxter*. Lexington, MA: Lexington Books, 1980.

Weaver, Suzanne. *The Decision to Prosecute: Organization and Public Policy in the Antitrust Division*. Cambridge: MIT Press, 1977.

Wilcox, Clair. *Public Policies Toward Business*. 3rd ed. Homewood, IL: Richard D. Irwin, 1966.

Williamson, Oliver E. *The Economic Institutions of Capitalism: Firms, Markets, Relational Contracting*. New York: The Free Press, 1985.

———. *Markets and Hierarchies: Analysis and Antitrust Implications*. New York: The Free Press, 1975.

JOURNAL ARTICLES

Altrogge, Phyllis and William F. Shughart II. "The Regressive Nature of Civil Penalties." *International Review of Law and Economics* 4 (1984), pp. 55–66.

Amacher, Ryan C., Richard S. Higgins, William F. Shughart II, and Robert D. Tollison. "The Behavior of Regulatory Activity over the Business Cycle: An Empirical Test." *Economic Inquiry* 23 (January 1985), pp. 7–20.

Anderson, Gary M., William F. Shughart II, and Robert D. Tollison. "The Incentives of Judges to Enforce Legislative Wealth Transfers." *Journal of Law and Economics* 32 (April 1989), pp. 215–28.

Asch, Peter. "The Determinants and Effects of Antitrust Policy." *Journal of Law and Economics* 18 (October 1975), pp. 575–81.

Asch, Peter, and Joseph J. Seneca. "Is Collusion Profitable?" *Review of Economics and Statistics* 58 (February 1976), pp. 1–12.

Baumol, William J., and Janusz A. Ordover. "Use of Antitrust to Subvert Competition." *Journal of Law and Economics* 28 (May 1985), pp. 247–65.

Becker, Gary S. "Crime and Punishment: An Economic Approach." *Journal of Political Economy* 76 (March/April 1968), pp.169–217.

Bittlingmayer, George. "Decreasing Average Cost and Competition: A New Look at the Addyston Pipe Case." *Journal of Law and Economics* 25 (October 1982), pp. 201–30.

Bork, Robert H. "Legislative Intent and the Policy of the Sherman Act." *Journal of Law and Economics* 9 (April 1966), pp. 7–48.

DiLorenzo, Thomas J. and Jack C. High. "Antitrust and Competition, Historically Considered." *Economic Inquiry* 26 (July 1988), pp. 423–35.

Easterbrook, Frank H. "Detrebling Antitrust Damages." *Journal of Law and Economics* 28 (May 1985), pp. 445–67.

Eckbo, B. Espen. "Horizontal Mergers, Collusion, and Stockholder Wealth." *Journal of Financial Economics* 11 (1983), pp. 241–73.

Eckbo, B. Espen, and Peggy Wier. "Antitrust Policy under the Hart-Scott-Rodino Act: A Reexamination of the Market Power Hypothesis." *Journal of Law and Economics* 28 (April 1985), pp. 119–49.

Elzinga, Kenneth G. "The Antimerger Law: Pyrrhic Victories." *Journal of Law and Economics* 12 (April 1969), pp. 43–78.

Elzinga, Kenneth G. and William Breit. "Private Antitrust Enforcement: The New Learning." *Journal of Law and Economics* 28 (May 1985), pp. 405–43.

Faith, Roger L., Donald R. Leavens, and Robert D. Tollison. "Antitrust Pork Barrel." *Journal of Law and Economics* 15 (October 1982), pp. 329–42.

Gallo, Joseph C., Joseph L. Craycraft, and Steven C. Bush. "Guess Who Came to Dinner: An Empirical Study of Federal Antitrust Enforcement for the Period 1963–1984." *Review of Industrial Organization* 2 (1985), pp. 106–30.

Gould, John P. "The Economics of Legal Conflicts." *Journal of Legal Studies* 2 (June 1973), pp. 279–300.

Hay, George A. and Daniel Kelley. An Empirical Study of Price-Fixing Conspiracies." *Journal of Law and Economics* 17 (April 1974), pp. 13–38.

Higgins, Richard S. and Fred S. McChesney. "Truth and Consequences: The Federal Trade Commission's Ad Substantiation Program." *International Review of Law and Economics* 6 (1986), pp. 151–68.

Higgins, Richard S. and Paul H. Rubin. "Judicial Discretion." *Journal of Legal Studies* 9 (January 1980), pp. 129–38.

Higgins, Richard S., William F. Shughart II, and Robert D. Tollison. "Free Entry and Efficient Rent Seeking." *Public Choice* 46 (1985), pp. 247–58.

Jarrell, Gregg A. "The Wealth Effects of Litigation by Targets: Do Interests Diverge in a Merge?" *Journal of Law and Economics* 27 (April 1985), pp. 151–77.

Klein, Benjamin, Robert G. Crawford, and Armen A. Alchian. "Vertical Integration, Appropriable Rents, and the Competitive Contracting Process." *Journal of Law and Economics* 21 (October 1978), pp. 297–326.

Lande, Robert H. "Wealth Transfers as the Original and Primary Concern of Antitrust: The Efficiency Interpretation Challenged." *Hastings Law Journal* 34 (September 1985), pp. 65–151.

Landes, William M. "An Economic Analysis of the Courts." *Journal of Law and Economics* 14 (April 1971), pp. 61–107.

Landes, William M. and Richard A. Posner. "The Independent Judiciary in an Interest-Group Perspective." *Journal of Law and Economics* 18 (December

1975), pp. 875–901.

Lindsay, Cotton M. "A Theory of Government Enterprise." *Journal of Political Economy* 84 (October 1976), pp. 1061–76.

Long, William F., Richard Schramm, and Robert D. Tollison. "The Economic Determinants of Antitrust Activity." *Journal of Law and Economics* 16 (October 1973), pp. 351–64.

McGee, John S. "Predatory Price Cutting: The Standard Oil (N.J.) Case." *Journal of Law and Economics* 1 (October 1958), pp. 137–69.

Peltzman, Sam. "The Effects of FTC Advertising Regulation." *Journal of Law and Economics* 24 (December 1981), pp. 403–48.

———. "Toward a More General Theory of Regulation." *Journal of Law and Economics* 19 (August 1976), pp. 211–48.

Peterman, John L. "The Brown Shoe Case." *Journal of Law and Economics* 18 (April 1975), pp. 81–146.

Posner, Richard A. "An Economic Approach to Legal Procedure and Judicial Administration." *Journal of Legal Studies* 2 (June 1973), pp. 399–458.

———. "The Federal Trade Commission." *University of Chicago Law Review* 37 (1969), pp. 47–89.

———. "A Statistical Study of Antitrust Enforcement." *Journal of Law and Economics* 13 (October 1970), pp. 365–419.

———. "Theories of Economic Regulation." *Bell Journal of Economics* 5 (Autumn 1974), pp. 335–58.

Priest, George L. and Benjamin Klein. "The Selection of Disputes for Litigation." *Journal of Legal Studies* 13 (January 1984), pp. 1–55.

Rogowsky, Robert A. "The Economic Effectiveness of Section 7 Relief." *Antitrust Bulletin* 31 (Spring 1986), pp. 187–233.

———. "The Justice Department's Merger Guidelines: A Study in the Application of the Rule." *Research in Law and Economics* 6 (1984), pp. 135–66.

Roll, David L. "Dual Enforcement of the Antitrust Laws by the Department of Justice and the FTC: The Liaison Procedure." *The Business Lawyer* 31 (July 1975), pp. 2075–85.

Ross, Thomas W. "Store Wars: The Chain Tax Movement." *Journal of Law and Economics* 29 (April 1986), pp. 125–37.

———. "Winners and Losers under the Robinson-Patman Act." *Journal of Law and Economics* 27 (October 1984), pp. 243–71.

Salop, Steven C. and Lawrence J. White. "Economic Analysis of Private Antitrust Litigation." *Georgetown Law Journal* 74 (April 1986), pp. 1001–64.

Shughart, William F. II. "Don't Revise the Clayton Act, Scrap It!" *Cato Journal* 6 (Winter 1987), pp. 925–32.

Shughart, William F. II, Brian L. Goff, and Robert D. Tollison. "Bureaucratic Structure and Congressional Control." *Southern Economic Journal* 52 (April 1986), pp. 962–72.

Shughart, William F. II and Robert D. Tollison. "The Positive Economics of Antitrust Policy: A Survey Article." *International Review of Law and Economics* 5 (1985), pp. 39–57.

Siegfried, John J. "The Determinants of Antitrust Activity." *Journal of Law and Economics* 18 (October 1975), pp. 559–74.

Stigler, George J. "The Economic Effects of the Antitrust Laws." *Journal of Law and Economics* 9 (October 1966), pp. 225–58.

———. "The Economists and the Problem of Monopoly." *American Economic Review Papers and Proceedings* 72 (May 1982), pp. 1–11.

———. "The Origin of the Sherman Act." *Journal of Legal Studies* 14 (January 1985), pp. 1–12.

———. "The Theory of Economic Regulation." *Bell Journal of Economics* 2 (Spring 1971), pp. 3–21.

Stillman, Robert. "Examining Anti-Trust Policy Towards Horizontal Mergers." *Journal of Financial Economics* 11 (1983), pp. 225–40.

Tollison, Robert D. "Antitrust in the Reagan Administration: A Report from the Belly of the Beast." *International Journal of Industrial Organization* 1 (1983), pp. 211–21.

Tullock, Gordon. "The Welfare Costs of Tariffs, Monopolies, and Theft." *Western Economic Journal* 5 (June 1967), pp. 224–32.

Weingast, Barry R. and Mark J. Moran. "Bureaucratic Discretion or Congressional Control? Regulatory Policymaking by the Federal Trade Commission." *Journal of Political Economy* 91 (October 1983), pp. 765–800.

Index

ABOUT THE AUTHOR

WILLIAM F. SHUGHART II is Professor of Economics and holder of the P.M.B. Self, William King Self, and Henry C. Self Free Enterprise Chair at the University of Mississippi. He was previously a Research Associate at the Center for Study of Public Choice at George Mason University, and has held an appointment on the economics faculty at Clemson University. During the early 1980s, the author served as Special Assistant to the Director of the Federal Trade Commission's Bureau of Economics. He has published over 60 articles and book chapters in the areas of antitrust policy, industrial organization, and public choice; his most recent book is *The Organization of Industry*.